THE OFFICIAL INSIDE STORY

Splendid
BOOKS

Steve Clark has been specialising in behind-the-scenes reports on television programmes for more than twenty years. He is author of *The Only Fools and Horses Story* (BBC Books, 1998), *The World of Jonathan Creek* (BBC Books, 1999), *On Set* (Blake Publishing, 1999), *Captain Corelli's Mandolin – The Illustrated Film Companion* (Headline, 2001) and *The British Television Location Guide* (Splendid Books, 2011). He lives in Hampshire with his wife and son. He doesn't drive a Robin Reliant... but he'd secretly quite like one.

THE OFFICIAL INSIDE STORY

STEVE CLARK

Series written and created by

JOHN SULLIVAN

Splendid
BOOKS

Only Fools and Horses – The Official Inside Story

First published in 2011

Only Fools and Horses format and television scripts
© John Sullivan / Shazam Productions

Text copyright © Steve Clark 2011

The right of Steve Clark to be identified as the Author of the work has been asserted by
him in accordance with the Copyright, Designs and Patents Act 1988.

Published by Splendid Books Limited, The Old Hambledon Racecourse Centre,
Sheardley Lane, Droxford, Hampshire SO32 3QY

www.splendidbooks.co.uk

ISBN: 978-0955891694

Designed by Design Image Ltd.

www.design-image.co.uk

Printed in the UK by CPI Group (UK) Ltd, Croydon, CR0 4YY

Every effort has been made to fulfil requirements with regard to reproducing copyright
material. The writer and publisher will be glad to rectify any omissions at the
earliest opportunity.

Contents

This book is dedicated to the memory of
John Sullivan
1946-2011

Introduction

Only Fools and Horses is a programme that was nearly never made. Turned down by BBC executives when it was first offered to them, the first series made little impact and there was no great enthusiasm at the Corporation for a second run.

Of course, it did get a second chance and soon after established itself as a firm favourite with viewers and, as time went by, it became a comedy phenomenon. So much so that the writer John Sullivan used to get letters from publicans complaining about a drop in trade on the nights when the show was screened.

Adored by everyone from real-life market traders to senior members of the Royal Family, it went on to achieve the highest ratings in British television history and lines from the show are heard every day, up and down the country.

As you might imagine, writing a book about *Only Fools and Horses* has been both a labour of love and a privilege. My aims with this book are to celebrate this unrivalled series and tell the story of how it came about and became the classic it is.

In the pages that follow you'll hear from the show's writer, producers and cast about how they made this truly exceptional series. So do read on...you know it makes sense...

Steve Clark

Acknowledgements

I am very grateful to everyone who has given up their time to talk to me about *Only Fools and Horses* over the years. These include: Paul Barber, Ronnie Barker, Jim Broadbent, Ray Butt, John Challis, Tony Dow, Phoebe De Gaye, Lynn Faulds Wood, Gareth Gwenlan, Roy Heather, David Hitchcock, Sue Holderness, Sir Anthony Hopkins, Carole James, Graham Jarvis, Sir David Jason, Sydney Lotterby, Roger Lloyd Pack, Nicholas Lyndhurst, Kenneth MacDonald, Buster Merryfield, Patrick Murray, Daniel Peacock, Tessa Peake-Jones, Tony Snoaden, Michael Fenton Stevens, Gwyneth Strong, John Sullivan, Deanne Turner and Donal Woods.

I am also very grateful to Theo Paphitis for sparing the time to write the foreword and to Al Murray for his generous contribution. Thanks for their help also to: Perry Aghajanoff, who runs The *Only Fools and Horses* Appreciation Society, Gail Evans, Adrian Pegg, Jim Sullivan, Jane Redmond and Richard Hamilton-Jones at BBC TV Locations and the staff of the BBC Archives at Caversham. Thanks also go to Jenny Bradley, Janet Bruton, Nicola Clark, designer Chris Fulcher, Kealey McVeagh, Adrian Notter, Michele Notter, Kathryn Perkins, Amber Ross, Annabel Silk and Shoba Vazirani.

Foreword by Theo Paphitis

I am honoured to have been asked to write this foreword because I love *Only Fools and Horses* and think it is a wonderful show. I started watching it pretty much from the start - in fact I can't remember being without it and I just couldn't wait for the next episode. And now, even though I've seen some episodes literally dozens of times, I still love it. Despite the fact that you know what's going to happen when you watch the falling chandelier episode or the one where Del falls down in the bar they still make me laugh.

It is classic and timeless and I'm still to meet somebody who doesn't like *Fools and Horses* or can't recount an episode or talk about it. It's very much part of our culture and it's in our psyche and forever will be. It's always been a big part of mine and my family's life. It really is one of those programmes that spans the generations.

One of the many strengths of *Only Fools* is its rich characters which is down to its creator John Sullivan, who had a great eye for observing people and creating very believable characters that you could relate to. Chief amongst them, of course, is Del Boy. He's a geezer, a real man's man and when he walked into a room it was always all about Del; it wouldn't have mattered if the Queen was there. I think we all know a Del Boy. Chris Tarrant once said to me: 'You're a bit of a Del Boy aren't you…' and I do think there is a bit of Del Boy in all of us. He might have bent the rules but Del's heart was in the right place. As an entrepreneur Del wasn't what you'd call the real deal. With Del it was always about making a quick buck and there were always going to be victims. Whatever he was doing, you knew someone was going to get tucked up with some bit of dodgy gear and lose out – and quite a lot of the time it was him. That's what was so funny. That said, Del never did a vicious thing in his life. He would always be there to help if someone asked, although they might have regretted it because he'd usually mess things up but his first instinct was to try. He always does his best, even though he's not very successful at what he does, and God loves a trier.

David Jason is a boyhood hero of mine and I met him a few years ago at Pinewood Studios. I was taken aback by his humility and just how different he was to his character. He wasn't as big as I imagined. How such a gentle, softly-spoken man like David was able produce such a cheeky, confident character like Del is, I guess, the mark of a great actor.

It was usually poor Rodney who found himself on the receiving end of one of Del's crazy schemes but as the years went by he began to get the measure of him to some degree. Grandad and then Uncle Albert, representing the older generation were both great - and had some wonderful one-liners. There was also a great line-up of supporting characters like Trigger, Boycie, Denzil, Marlene and even Mickey Pearce, who I liked despite all the grief he gave Rodney.

John Sullivan could make us laugh – but could also move us. There were sad moments, like Grandad's funeral and, much later, Uncle Albert's and moving moments like Damien's birth, which brought a tear to everybody's eye – but then it made us laugh because Damien terrified Rodney. John Sullivan had an amazing skill in writing brilliantly clever lines that you wouldn't have expected in a million years and they often made you cry with laughter. Those one-liners are legendary and so, of course, are Del's catchphrases. You do hear people saying Del's lines all the time and we've all said them. I have been known to say 'mange tout' from time to time and some people look at you as if to say: 'Are you a complete idiot?' And on more than one occasion I've wrapped up a serious business meeting where we've been discussing embarking on a new venture with: 'This time next year we'll be millionaires' before one of my colleagues points out that I already am one...

Trying to pick my favourite moments is a very tough job – there are just so many to choose from. I love the cringe-worthiness of what happens in the chandelier episode. I don't know how the actors managed to pull it off with such deadpan faces – it must have been very hard to do. It wasn't just the chandelier falling, it was their expressions as well. Of course the famous scene of Del falling over in the wine bar is quite brilliant. It wasn't just the fall, it was the whole way it was done so you didn't see it coming. Then, there was that superb episode *As One Door Closes* where Del, Rodney and Uncle Albert spend ages trying to catch a valuable butterfly and then just after they finally get it Denzil comes along on roller skates, gives Del high fives and crushes it. You just want to cry...

There's a great moment in *A Royal Flush* where Del turns up at a stately home clay pigeon shoot with a pump-action shotgun. Rodney's face is a picture and he asks Del where he got it from. "Iggy Iggins," says Del. "Iggy Iggins robs banks," says Rodney. "I know," says Del. "But it's Saturday!" - just brilliant. I also love that scene of them running through Peckham as Batman and Robin in *Heroes and Villains* and the hilarious moment when Del asks for directions from a bloke on an oil rig in *To Hull and Back*.

There was a great line in the first episode *Big Brother* - and also heard in *Time On Our Hands* - that I have heard so many times since. Grandad was talking about Del being a trier and then he says to Rodney: "Your dad always said that one day Del Boy would reach the top. Then again, he used to say that one day Millwall would win the cup..." During the 2003-2004 football season, while I was chairman, Millwall got to the FA Cup Final - against everyone's expectations. That line was heard everywhere - at the ground, in the press and on the radio. We lost to Manchester United so unfortunately Grandad was right. Another classic moment was, of course, in *Danger UXD,* the one with the exploding inflatable dolls. The bit where they popped up in the back of the van was priceless. And who can forget the scene in *A Losing Streak* when Boycie and Del have a game of cards and at the end Del says he knew Boycie had been cheating. Boycie says: "How?" and Del replies: "Because that wasn't the hand that I dealt you..." Just a great line...There was that brilliant moment when we discover that singing dustman Tony Angelino couldn't pronounce his Rs and sang *Cwying* - and who could forget Del bottling tap water and selling it as Peckham Spring. I could go on all day...

I would love to invest in Del Boy if he came on *Dragons' Den* despite everything I've just said about him - like his unpaid tax, stitching people up, leaving someone with shoddy goods and only doing what he does in the short term to make a quick buck – all of which goes against every ethos I've got in business. I believe you've got to be long-term and that everyone should leave the party with a balloon - that means everyone's a winner and you pay your taxes and do everything by the book and that way you sleep at night.

But wouldn't it be great to try to convert him? Del needs mentoring and he needs to think long-term. It can't be all about making the quick buck today. It's not like "this time next year bruv we'll be millionaires" it will be this time in five years' time or this time in ten years' time we'll be millionaires. I'd love to do it – and I'd really like to take him down to meet the taxman and hear him say: "Hello, my name is Del Boy Trotter. I'm sixty years old and I don't exist as far as you are concerned - I don't pay taxes, I've never worked" - explain that one away.

John Sullivan's passing earlier this year was very sad, but he's left behind a comedy legacy that will outlive us all. *Only Fools and Horses* is in our every day psyche and also our business psyche. Del Boy Trotter was everything the rules say you shouldn't be as an entrepreneur, but we love him.

Bonnet de douche

PART 1
In The Beginning

John Sullivan always remembered 1980 as the year his second television series was cancelled by the BBC. For the young writer with a family to support it was nothing short of a disaster. Three years previously he'd risen meteorically from his job as a scene shifter at BBC Television Centre in Wood Lane, London, working behind the scenes on programmes like *The Morecambe and Wise Show*, *Porridge*, *I, Claudius*, and *To The Manor Born*, to become a writer on a BBC contract with a hit series, *Citizen Smith*, to his name.

The show, which starred Robert Lindsay as Tooting revolutionary Wolfie Smith, had been a hit with viewers and Sullivan went on to write a further three series. However, during the filming of the fourth series it became apparent it would be the last. John had decided that he'd gone as far as he could with the character of Wolfie, and Robert Lindsay had indicated that he would like to move on and try his hand at something new.

John wasn't too worried as he had another idea up his sleeve, a sitcom called *Over The Moon* about a football manager running a down-at-heel club but with aspirations for glory that were never likely to be fulfilled. A pilot episode was recorded on November

30th at Television Centre starring Brian Wilde – best known as Foggy in *Last of the Summer Wine* – as Ron Wilson, the manager.

The show also starred George Baker as the club's chairman Major Gormley and Paula Tilbrook, who went on to star as Betty Eagleton in *Emmerdale*, as Wilson's landlady Mrs Allardyce.

"The BBC liked the pilot and commissioned a series and I went off and wrote a second and third episode," John recalled. "I had high hopes for the show and was confident it would work."

The man in charge of the series was to be a smart senior BBC producer and director called Ray Butt, who had already made the successful pilot episode of the show. He and John had met previously when Ray was called in to direct several episodes of the second series of *Citizen Smith* and sort out some problems to do with cast punctuality. "Ray was brought in to kick some backsides," said John.

The two men got on well and had gained a healthy respect for one another. Their similar working class backgrounds produced a natural rapport and they shared a mutual passion for the business they worked in. They became friends and began a fruitful working partnership that would last for many years.

"The first good thing was that we had similar accents," said Ray Butt, a genial and likeable man who joined the BBC in 1955 after National Service in the RAF, when a lot of vacancies were created at the Corporation following an exodus of employees to the newly formed ITV. "John is a south London boy and I'm an east London boy so we seemed to talk the same language."

Everything was looking good for *Over The Moon* and John Sullivan was busy writing the third episode when disaster struck. Ray Butt was called into a meeting at Television Centre and told that the show was to be cancelled. He rang John Sullivan and broke the bad news.

Sullivan remembered the moment well. "I was working on the fourth episode when Bill Cotton, who was the Controller of BBC1, came back from a trip to America and killed it. As you can imagine

I wasn't very happy. Ironically one of the reasons that they decided to shelve the idea was because they'd decided to make a new series about a boxer called *Seconds Out* starring Robert Lindsay. They didn't want two comedies with sporting themes, so I lost out."

For John it was terrible news. He was overdrawn and had been banking on *Over The Moon* to keep him and his family afloat. "I had no work in the pipeline," he recalled. "We'd just bought our first house in Sutton, Surrey, and frankly I was worried about being able to pay the mortgage because prior to that we'd only been renting somewhere. I was under contract for a year but after that the future looked very uncertain. Not only that but no show on the box means no repeat fees."

He and Ray arranged to meet for a lunchtime drink the following week at Ray's local, The Three Kings in North End Road. Over several pints the two friends talked of their disappointment and Sullivan looked for inspiration. Their conversation was wide-ranging and included talk of their childhoods and their families. Now and again John would bounce ideas off Ray and make suggestions about new characters.

John had one vague idea at the back of his mind that wouldn't go away about a wheeler-dealer street market trader who dealt only in cash and would sell anything to anyone. But he knew the BBC didn't like it because he'd already talked to the Corporation's Head of Light Entertainment, Jimmy Gilbert, a few years before and it had been given a very firm thumbs down.

"I'd written a one-page treatment thing explaining the idea," said John. "It was all about modern working-class London. I was sick to death of the kind of comedies I saw on telly which were almost always based in the forties or earlier with toffs and that sort of tugging the forelock 'Gor bless you guv' type of stuff which didn't exist. Now we had a modern, vibrant, multi-racial, new slang London where a lot of working class guys had suits and a bit of dosh in their pockets and that was a very different thing.

"That's what I wanted to write about. It would be a bit more aggressive and feature the pubs, clubs and tower blocks and even touch on the drug problem. Jimmy just looked at me for a while and then he went away. I got a message back some time later through someone else that the BBC didn't want to go along that road and that was that."

Ray Butt, however, thought it was a great idea. He recalled: "At the time the papers were full of all this stuff about the black economy and this fella John talked about was that sort of bloke. He'd only deal in cash. He was a guy who would do anything for readies and he didn't pay any tax. He didn't take anything from the state but wouldn't give anything to the state, either. He was a readies man, simple as that."

Both men liked the idea and both knew a fair bit about the world that the character lived in. Ray Butt's father Bill had come out of the RAF after the Second World War and, finding his pre-war job as a printer rather dull, pooled his money with a friend, bought an old NAAFI wagon and set up a business selling ice creams around markets. That was fine as a summer trade but to earn a living in winter Bill Butt had to diversify out of ice cream. So he set up a stall on the Roman Road market near his home selling everything from ladies' stockings to toffee apples. As a youngster Ray used to work the stall at weekends and during his school holidays.

The family also travelled to other markets in Ashford and Maidstone in Kent and Epsom, Surrey. Ray also spent time working for another street market trader who would later become a legend of the entertainment world – Tommy Cooper. "Tommy was a market grafter long before he was a comic," said Ray. "And I worked for him as a kid in the markets. He used to sell saccharin and elastic and stuff like that but he was wonderful. His selling routine was great as you might imagine.

"In the eighties people were talking about the black economy like it was something new but after the war it was all the rage," said Ray. "Market traders were all working for readies. They had this cash and there was no way they were going to declare all of it to the Inland Revenue. You had to declare something but basically the vast majority went straight into your bin and the tax man never saw it."

"Ray and I decided that the most interesting market characters were the fly pitchers," said John. "They were funny guys who'd turn up with their gear in a box or a suitcase. They'd never have a licence and they'd just flog their stuff to passers-by. You never knew their names and we wondered where they came from and where they went back to after a day selling their wares." A few pints on, the pair decided that there might be some merit in John's trader idea.

"This idea didn't come as some great blinding flash," said Ray Butt. "It was just one of a number of ideas John was bouncing off me. I just told him to go away and see what he came up with and that was pretty much that."

John Sullivan went home that afternoon full of renewed enthusiasm. "I took the archetypal fly pitcher with the gold watch and the battered suitcase and decided to give him a family and a home life," he said. "I made him a guy with a burning ambition to make it big – but who never quite managed it.

"Part of my inspiration for Del was a guy I knew called Chicky Stocker. He was a working class Londoner and a tough man but always dressed very neatly. He wasn't the sort of bloke that you'd go out of your way to annoy but nevertheless he was a very nice man. He was very genuine and I liked his attitude to life. He was very loyal to his family and I tried to instil that into Del. Other aspects of his character, like buying drinks for people down the pub even when he couldn't really afford to, came from people I knew in the car trade. They always wanted to keep face and even if they were doing badly, they'd borrow money to flash about to let everyone think they were doing well. Wearing lots of gold rings was also part of that."

John was also fascinated by the idea of writing about the age gap between his main character and a younger brother. He recalled in 1998: "That idea came from three different sources. Firstly, my sister Maureen is thirteen years older than me and because of that she was never really like a sister until I was twenty or so. It was weird. She wasn't like a mother but it was odd because of the age gap and it took a few years when I was older to catch up with that.

"Secondly, the brother of my oldest friend Colin was eleven or so years older than him and thirdly, another mate of mine also had a much younger brother. In both cases the older guy had some little business going and took the younger brother in so there was this continual big brother thing throughout their lives. That fascinated me.

"The character of Grandad gave the situation the voice of an old man who'd seen all of life. He'd witnessed the end of the First World War and lived through the Second and now couldn't really give a monkeys about the world. Del Boy was the man in the middle, with enough experience of life to know the pitfalls, but still young enough to have a dream and be ambitious. Rodney was the naïve young lad at the beginning of the road who was very, very green. With the three ages you had a balance."

The inspiration for Rodney was a little closer to home. "Rodney reminded me of myself when I was young," John said. "I was a dreamer and an idealist, just like Rodders. There was a kid in school with us who had two GCEs – and he went round acting like he was Einstein. Whenever there was an argument he'd behave like his two GCEs made him automatically right. I thought that was pathetic. I used that idea for Rodney, who was so proud of his two 'O' Levels. On one hand Del would use them to praise him because he was proud that someone in the family had passed exams and on the other hand he'd send him up because of them."

To bond the brothers even closer John brought in the idea that their father had deserted them and that their mother Joan had died when Rodney was just three, leaving Del to bring up his little brother. "In those cockney and Irish working class worlds the mother figure, particularly the late mother figure, was so incredibly important," said John.

"Over the years people would still be crying over the memory of a mother even though she'd passed away ten years ago – and then you'd hear from someone else that she was a really horrible person! That means there's warmth and love there but you could also paint the picture that she was nothing like how Del describes her. But we had all these suspicions about what she was really like. Rodney didn't really remember her and Del loved her so much and just couldn't see what she was really like."

A few weeks after John's initial conversation with Ray in the pub, he arrived at Ray's office at BBC Television Centre with a draft script for *Readies*, as he called the show at that time. Butt was impressed. "I read it, liked it and sent it to Head of Comedy, John Howard Davies," he recalled. "He read it and then sent me a memo back saying he quite liked the script but that he didn't think it was an opener, a first episode.

"I kept that memo on my wall until the day I left the BBC and I treasured it. He was totally and utterly wrong because we made that episode and it stayed as the first episode, *Big Brother*."

Despite his reluctance over the first episode, John Howard Davies did see potential in the series. With pressure from Ray Butt, Davies commissioned John Sullivan to write a full series, although there was no guarantee that it would ever actually go into production.

"It was a tremendous moment for me," John recalled. "I think they were a little bit shocked about how colourful it was, but they went with it."

Several factors worked in John's favour this time, compared with the first time he'd talked to the BBC about *Readies*. Firstly, the BBC had to pay him anyway, under the terms of his contract, so they knew they might as well get him to write something. Secondly, they had a gap in their transmission schedules left by *Over The Moon*.

Thirdly, *Minder* had begun on ITV and was proving to be a big ratings success. There was a realisation that there was an audience for shows about modern-day, rough, tough, London wheeler-dealers and the BBC wasn't yet tapping it.

"When *Minder* first came out I was choked because I thought that they'd done that modern London," said John. "They weren't doing markets or tower blocks but it was modern London and it was very good and I just thought: 'Shit. That's that idea gone.' But after *Over The Moon* was axed and I wrote *Readies* the BBC changed their minds. I've always given credit to *Minder* for opening that door for me, because without it I don't think that idea would have ever got used."

Within two weeks John Sullivan had written a second episode and the rest followed quickly. Senior executives liked them and the show – BBC project number 1149/0601 – was given the green light to go into production.

Ray Butt set about finding a cast for the series. This proved terribly simple on one side – and fiendishly tough on the other. Nicholas Lyndhurst, who'd begun his acting career as a child and gone on to find fame as Wendy Craig's screen son Adam in Carla Lane's BBC comedy series *Butterflies* was first to be cast in the role of Rodney Trotter.

John Sullivan recalled: "John Howard Davies came down to the production office and told us, sort of point blank, that Nick Lyndhurst was going to play Rodney. He thought Nick was right for the part and neither Ray nor I disagreed. The only thing I doubted, and it was only for a moment, was whether Nick could play working class convincingly.

"That was because I'd only seen him as middle class in *Butterflies* and as I really hate false accents I didn't want some middle class boy coming in trying to do his version of cockney. John told me about Nick having played Ronnie Barker's cockney son Raymond in *Going Straight*, the follow-up to *Porridge*, and convinced me about him – and of course once I'd seen him in action I was happy. There was no argument."

Lennard Pearce only landed the role of the Trotter boys' elderly Grandad by chance. Ray Butt rang an agent he knew and trusted, Carole James, and told her what he was looking for. "What I was really after was almost an old man Steptoe character but I didn't want to use Wilfrid Brambell because he was so well known from *Steptoe and Son*, but it was that sort of part," said Ray.

"Carole said she didn't have anyone who fitted the bill on her book but she knew of this actor called Lennard Pearce who was with another agent. So I rang the other agent and we got Lennard in to see us and I thought he was perfect."

John Sullivan recalled: "We saw two or three actors for the part and then Lennard came in and he read a bit for us and we just heard that lovely old growly voice of his. When he'd gone I said to Ray: 'That's him.'

"Ray said: 'Let's see the others' and I said: 'Well, we can see the others but that's him'. There was no doubt in my mind whatsoever that he was right as our Grandad. To me his voice was just like everyone's grandad."

Lennard was perfect for the part – except in one way, as John explained. "Being an old man I assumed he had some false teeth, so I wrote one episode, *It Never Rains*, where he didn't have his teeth in. Lennard read it and piped up: 'But I've got all my own teeth!'"

Casting Del proved to be the biggest headache. First choice was actor Enn Reitel. "I thought Enn was right for the original character of Del as written," said Ray Butt. "He was physically very different to David Jason though and much taller. I thought casting Enn would appease Jimmy Gilbert, the BBC's Head of Light Entertainment, because he looked more like Nick Lyndhurst."

Ray Butt approached Enn Reitel's agent only to find that he was away busy filming a series for Yorkshire Television called *Misfits* and would not be available. Enn went on to find fame in the BBC series *The Adventures of Lucky Jim* and the ITV series *Mog*, but his versatility with voices has been his fortune. He provided many of the voices for *Spitting Image* including Lester Piggott, Dustin Hoffman and Donald Sinden and is now one of Britain's top voice-over artists.

John Howard Davies then suggested to Ray Butt that he went to see another actor, Jim Broadbent, who was appearing in Mike Leigh's play *Goosepimples* at the Hampstead Theatre in north London. "He was very good and afterwards we had a drink and I offered him the part," recalled Ray Butt. "He turned it down because the play was transferring to the West End. He didn't think he could split his energies between opening in the West End and doing a new sitcom series. I understood his problem and thought it was very nice of him to be so upfront about it." Jim did appear in three episodes of *Only Fools and Horses* as dodgy detective Roy Slater, who viewers later found out had once been married to Del's long-time girlfriend, Raquel.

Two other names in the frame to play Del were Robin Nedwell and Billy Murray, who was starring in the play *Moving* in the West End with Roger Lloyd Pack and Penelope Keith. Ray didn't think Billy, who went on to star as Detective Sergeant Don Beech in *The Bill* and as Johnny Allen in *EastEnders*, would work, but the trip to the theatre wasn't a complete waste of time. Ray concluded that Roger Lloyd Pack would be perfect for the role of dozy roadsweeper Trigger who first appeared in episode one.

Ray Butt was getting nowhere fast in his search for Del. "I remember thinking: 'Christ, we start filming in a couple of weeks and we're still missing a main character.' Time was getting tighter and tighter and we were getting close to being up the creek without a paddle."

There was a real possibility of losing Nick Lyndhurst and Lennard Pearce, for he didn't have the budget to contract them to the show until it was due to go into production and therefore there was a chance they'd be signed up for other work in the meantime.

Sitting at home one Sunday evening, Ray switched on his television and happened to catch a repeat of *Open All Hours*, written by Roy Clarke, the hugely successful comedy series about stuttering northern corner shop keeper Arkwright, played by Ronnie Barker, and his delivery boy nephew Granville, played by David Jason.

One particular part of the episode caught Ray's attention. Granville was in the shop's store room and had a long solo scene. "The penny dropped," he recalled. "I thought: 'David could be just right for Del.'" The following morning Ray arrived at his office at BBC Television Centre and immediately telephoned John Sullivan to suggest David Jason for the lead role.

"John was a bit tepid to put it mildly," Ray recalled. "He wasn't that keen at all because his first impression was that David wasn't right for the role. He wasn't dead against him and was willing to listen but he wanted time to think about the idea."

"It wasn't that I was against the idea of David for the role as such," said John. "It was more that I couldn't actually see him in the part. I was terrified that he couldn't play that sharp edge that we needed for Del."

"John had it very fixed in his mind what sort of character Del Boy was," said David Jason. "And he didn't think I could play that."

Ray Butt had another ally in senior producer Syd Lotterby. He'd worked with David Jason on shows like *Open All Hours* and *Porridge* and had produced and directed a pilot show, written by Roy Clarke and starring David, called *It's Only Me – Whoever I Am*, which was never transmitted. "It turned out to be pretty disastrous," said David. "Unfortunately it just didn't work. It was loosely based on the character of Granville and we thought there might be something in it for me so we made a pilot. It was about a guy who lived with his mother in the north and wasn't allowed to grow up, basically."

Ray Butt had worked on that show as production manager

alongside Syd Lotterby. After filming he, Syd and David often played pool at the hotel where they were staying. David was fascinated by Ray's east London accent and often mimicked him.

"Ray had got a very strong East End accent," said David. "When we got back from filming, we'd be stuck in a hotel and there was nothing to do so we'd play pool or snooker. I'd mimic Ray, so we'd both be talking like east enders. It was: 'Alright mate, alright pal', that kind of thing. His accent just fascinated me so I was just copying it. Sydney Lotterby thought this was extremely amusing. Ray took it well, too. I mean it was meant well, we got on great.

"Some time later I was working with Sydney Lotterby on *Open All Hours*. We got in the lift to go down for lunch and Syd said to me: 'I've got something here that I want you to read – just tell me what you think of it. There's nothing in it – it's not an offer. It's a comedy and I'd just like your opinion of it.' I was really pleased that my opinion was being sought, if you like. So I took it home – I can't remember whether it was called *Only Fools and Horses* back then – but it was the script for the pilot.

"I came in the next day and Syd said: 'What did you think of that?' and I said: 'I think it's one of the funniest things I've ever read. It's brilliant. I couldn't wait to turn over to the next page.' He said: 'If there was a part going, what part would you like to play?' and I immediately said: 'Del Boy'.

"The reason he asked that was because I'd been playing old men in shows like *Porridge*. I was a character actor. I could – and was quite happy to – play anything. So he wasn't sure if I might have wanted to play Grandad, for example."

Or even Rodney? "Could have been, could have been, because, don't forget, at that time you could have cast it any way. It wasn't until later that we found out that Ray had already cast Nick Lyndhurst. Anyway, that was that. Syd Lotterby said: 'Thanks very much. Say no more.' I didn't know any more about this thing. I'd just been asked my opinion and I forgot about it."

David kept quiet about the lift conversation until a party at BBC Television Centre after the studio recording of the episode *Time On Our Hands*. "I'd kept Syd's confidence because he'd asked me to, but I decided to break my silence," said David. "So because the show was now all over I told the story to John Sullivan and Ray Butt. Ray didn't believe it."

Sydney Lotterby reminded Ray Butt of those mickey-taking pool games when Ray said he was going to get David Jason in to read the part of Del Boy. "It was obviously Syd Lotterby who reminded Ray of the time we were filming that programme and I was taking the piss out of Ray," David recalled. "It must have been Syd who said: 'You ought to think about David Jason.'" This only added to Butt's certainty that he'd found the right man for the part.

Real resistance to David Jason being cast came from Head of Light Entertainment, Jimmy Gilbert, and other senior executives. For one, they feared casting him in his own series could jeopardise their relationship with Ronnie Barker. At that stage Barker was Britain's number one TV star and a major asset to BBC Television. Both *Open All Hours* and *The Two Ronnies* were huge successes for the Corporation and the risk of offending Barker was deemed too great.

Yet Barker saw David Jason almost as his prodigy and it seems unlikely now that he would have been anything other than delighted that his friend and colleague should gain the recognition he was due by way of his own starring vehicle.

There was further reluctance to consider Jason on the basis that he didn't look at all like Nicholas Lyndhurst, a fact which was actually a key part of John Sullivan's Trotter mythology.

For as John Sullivan recalled: "The whole point is that Del and Rodney are actually the only ones who think they are brothers. Everyone else thinks they might well have different fathers. They had to be counterpoints to each other: one tall, one short; one blond; the other dark-haired. They had to look different to each other and at one point when we were casting there was even a suggestion that we had one of them mixed-race.

"The age difference between them was important too because Del is almost a father figure to Rodney and he is supposed to be about fifteen years older than him."

The more Ray Butt thought about David Jason as Del – not to mention the closer his filming deadline became – the more he convinced himself that he was the right man for the job. "I always knew that David was a fine actor and a particularly fine comedy actor," said Ray. "He's also capable of playing very heavy drama and has shown that time and time again."

A week after he'd been given a script by Sydney Lotterby, David Jason was sent a script by the BBC. "It was the same script," he recalled. "And they asked if I would come in and read for the character of Del Boy. I said: 'Of course.'"

Even in 1981 David Jason was established enough that he wouldn't normally be asked to audition for a part as producers and directors knew what he could do. "But this was so good and it was the sort of character that I'd never played before," said David.

"I'd played the hundred year-old gardener Dithers in *His Lordship Entertains* and old Blanco in *Porridge* and I'd also been playing a lot of hapless characters like Granville in *Open All Hours*, which I was still doing, and then there were the parts I'd played in *Lucky Fella* and *A Sharp Intake Of Breath*.

"For most of my career I'd been playing losers and then here was the part of Del – this sharp, bright, upfront bloke with all the bounce and balls. It was the sort of part that normally nobody would ever have dreamed of offering me. I went to that meeting desperately wanting the job. I thought it was one of the best things I'd ever read. It was just very funny, although there was no guarantee it would be successful. I suppose I just had a gut feeling that it would work out."

David, knowing it would be him who missed out if BBC bosses couldn't be convinced to let him and Nicholas Lyndhurst play brothers because they didn't look alike, had his own explanation prepared for their differences. "Just because they were brothers didn't mean they had to look alike and they might not genetically have the same father," he said. "One of them could actually be the milkman's! Of course we didn't know that at the time but later John quite rightly exploited the fact that they don't necessarily look like brothers. After all there's one three foot five and the other eight foot six!"

The following day David was asked to come back and read with Nicholas Lyndhurst and Lennard Pearce. This time John Sullivan was at the meeting and he was impressed. "He read with Nick and Lennard for about a quarter of an hour and that was it," said John. "Ray and I looked at each other and nodded. We had our Del and Rodney."

David Jason recalled: "Ray suddenly said: 'OK, thanks. We're going to go with you three.' As you can imagine I was delighted. Then we all shook hands and went off to have a drink." That was it. After all the discussions and disagreements, the cast was finally decided in fifteen minutes. Within weeks, the show went into production.

WHY ONLY FOOLS AND HORSES?

John Sullivan had to fight his corner over the title of the show. As far as he was concerned, *Readies* had simply been a working title. He recalled: "I always thought longer titles grab people's eyes and obviously I wanted to make viewers aware of us. I liked the idea of calling the show *Only Fools and Horses* from the old expression 'only fools and horses work', because Del's main aim in life is not to work and yet he scurries around till eleven at night working his socks off not to work.

"The man himself is a contradiction. So I wanted to call it that and Jimmy Gilbert said: 'What does it mean? Oh, it's a London saying'. In the end we found out it was an American saying from Vaudeville theatre days that came over here through music halls. One day we did a straw poll in the BBC bar and asked people what they thought the expression meant. The answers ranged from 'A quote from Shakespeare' to Lester Piggott's autobiography."

Other than *Readies* and *Only Fools and Horses* other names were considered for the show including *Big Brother.* That title was rejected because it was thought it might confuse viewers with George Orwell's book 1984, with the real year 1984 just over two years away. John was due to have a final meeting with Jimmy Gilbert and John Howard Davies over the show's name and spent a weekend trying to come up with an acceptable alternative. He couldn't.

Gareth Gwenlan, who was at that time an executive producer in the BBC comedy department, and later became the show's producer, had heard the saying, supported John Sullivan's argument and helped him win the day. "Gareth is a great politician," said John Sullivan. "He said: 'Go into the meeting and say you haven't got a clue what else to call it. Tell them it's up to them to come up with another title. They won't be able to and you'll get your title.'

"That was just what happened. They looked at each other and said: 'OK, you can have it.' After weeks of haggling, finally they decided to go with the name *Only Fools and Horses*."

DESIGNING THE FLAT

John Sullivan's original script for the first episode of *Only Fools and Horses* gave clear guidance on how the Trotters' flat should look. It read:

```
The room should reflect their styles of business.
Nothing is permanent. The settee and two armchairs
are from three separate suites. (The other pieces
being used as make-weights in various past swops).
There are three TV sets, one colour, one black
and white and the other has its back off awaiting
repair. There are a couple of stereo music centres
standing one on top of the other. Various video
games, talking chess game etc litter the room.
Their phone is one of the ornate 1920s types
with separate ear-piece (on an alabaster base).
The décor is clean but gaudy. Dozens of clashing
patterns. It should look like a bad trip.
```

That gave Designer Tony Snoaden a clear idea as to how he should turn Sullivan's brief into reality. For inspiration about the actual layout of the flat he visited two different blocks of council flats, one near Kew Bridge in south west London and another in north Acton in north west London. There, he measured up and drew up plans for the set that would become one of the most familiar flats in Britain.

Cheap wallpaper was chosen from books in the BBC Design Department's sample room as was poor quality carpet. Both were then ordered from the manufacturer. Tony then went out with props buyer Chris Ferriday and chose the props that would litter the flat. They scoured specialist firms that sell or hire bits and pieces for TV shows and came back with everything from Del's ice bucket to reproduction paintings and from a tacky wrought iron guitar to ornaments. They also looked round Del's fictional stomping ground like markets to pick up oddments.

"We were looking for the sort of things that people like the Trotters would have in their living room," said Tony Snoaden. "I had quite a lot of freedom to dot things around, like leaving an old tyre in a doorway, and that was because Del thought he could sell almost anything and therefore would have all sorts of stuff just hanging around."

Each episode would feature different boxes of junk and reflect Del's latest line, but some things like the old chairs, Del's cocktail bar and telephone would remain constant. "It had to have a constancy about it but we'd still add things each week depending on what Del was selling," said Tony. "Even in much more recent episodes I've spotted things that we had during my time on the show."

More than a decade on designing the sets for *Only Fools* fell to Donal Woods, whose first episode was the 1992 Christmas special *Mother Nature's Son*. He inherited the main sets – the flat, Rodney and Cassandra's pad and the Nag's Head interior from a string of different designers who had gone before him.

Each time a new series or special was filmed the set would be rebuilt from scratch because it's cheaper to do that than store old sets. "Each designer would keep detailed records of what they'd used in the way of props and wallpaper and carpets so we could follow on from that," explained Donal.

"The wallpaper might change each year depending on whether we could get it. In the end we had real trouble getting the same old cheap stuff we used because it had gone out of fashion, and Fads, the company we got it from, scoured the country and found us their last four rolls."

"Some of the props – things like the bar, the wall lights and the drapes have stayed the same for years - and then we'd add things for each episode. The stuff that Del was selling would be John Sullivan's ideas. He'd write something in and we'd have to find them or make them and get boxes specially printed with the details of the contents on the sides."

The most difficult prop that Donal had to find was a watch to play the Harrison timepiece for *Time On Our Hands*. "It needed to look right so it took a lot of research," he said. "In the end we made three of them to be used for different scenes. We had one that could open, one that could be thrown around, and a nice one that could be used in the auction scene at Sothebys. They were only shells made of brass but they cost a total of about £1,000."

The best thing about working on the show, said Donal, is that because it was so popular, people and companies were really keen to help. "Wherever you go people have heard of it. For instance when we filmed at Sothebys for *Time On Our Hands* they couldn't have been more helpful. They got in early a whole set of seriously valuable Old Master paintings to decorate their gallery for us, brought in their telephone dealers and got porters in for us. Then, of course, we put the Trotters' van outside. When you think about it – this is one of the major auction houses in the world and you want to put a three-wheeled Reliant van outside their building. If it was any other show they'd probably tell you to get lost. But they even took down scaffolding for us for a day so we could film it there. No one would normally do that."

DRESSING THE TROTTERS

Creating the look for the characters in *Only Fools and Horses* was a matter of evolution involving the cast, the writer, producers and various costume designers who worked on the show over the years. The woman responsible for the outfits used for the first series which then set the tone throughout the programme's history was costume designer Phoebe De Gaye.

"*Only Fools and Horses* was my design job at the BBC," recalled Phoebe, who has since gone on to design costumes for films like *Tom and Viv* and *Killing Me Softly* and television series such as *Lark Rise To Candleford* and *Agatha Christie's Marple*. "I was allocated to the show and went off to meet Ray Butt and then I met the actors."

Phoebe got her inspiration for Del's gear by going to car boot sales and looking at people not unlike Del Boy. "I remember one guy struck me," she recalled. "He was a real jack-the-lad type with a paunch and white shoes and pushed up hair. I thought Del ought to have had permed hair like footballer Charlie George but I couldn't persuade David to go for that!"

Once she had some ideas Phoebe made some rough sketches that she then presented to the production team. They approved them and with just a very small budget to spend she then set about gathering what she needed. Del's costumes needed a little more variety so she took David Jason shopping in London's Oxford Street to find the stuff for Del Boy to wear.

"I had this old mini at the time which I drove him in and when the engine got going all these fumes started drifting up through the floor – it was quite like the Trotter van in that respect!" she recalled. "We went to lots of different shops and I got David to try on all these horrible suits after looking around for a while and finally bought the suit in a really cheap and cheerful shop.

"I bought some horrible tight, brightly-coloured Gabicci shirts from their warehouse in Edgware. They were very fashionable at the time and were made of fine, silky material. One of the ones I got was a red one with a black suede pocket on it. It was disgusting! The sheepskin coat we ended up buying was memorable too because it was made of lots of pieces of sheepskin and had lots of horrible seams.

"Things would be bought at the sort of places that the Trotters themselves would have shopped at," said Phoebe. "And all Del's rings and his bracelet were fake gold and came from Chapel Street market as did his chain with his initial on, which I've still got somewhere in my kit, although I've absolutely no idea why!"

In the early days Rodney was rarely seen without his green camouflage combat jacket which came from BBC costume department stock and Phoebe added a Yasser Arafat-type headscarf which she bought at Shepherd's Bush market. "Rodney always had a grungy look well before grunge became fashionable!" she said. "I soon got rid of that scarf though," laughed Nick Lyndhurst. "Purely because it kept getting in the way."

Grandad's costume was very straightforward. "The idea with Grandad was that he never took his hat off even when he went in the bath," she said. "Nor did he ever really get dressed properly. He would almost always have part of his pyjamas on under anything else he might be wearing – and his clothes would never be very clean. To get that crusty effect I'd make it dirty with Vaseline, bit of make-up and even real food."

Robin Stubbs took over as costume designer on the show in 1986 and was responsible for getting Del's costume together for his new yuppy image in the sixth series. Del's new more upmarket suits were bought from Austin Reed in

London's Regent's Street and cost about £200 each.

Trying them on though was far from easy. "We always had to be discreet where we went for them," said Robin. "Because if David is recognised he gets mobbed."

After Del smartened up his act everything else came from High Street stores. His ties were bought in Tie-Rack, his raincoat came from Dickens and Jones in Regent Street and his shirts came from Austin Reed and Marks and Spencer. His jewellery was just as worthless as before though, even if it looks like it's worth hundreds of pounds. "We usually replaced it for each series because it's so cheap and the gold paint wears off," said Robin. "It's the sort of stuff Del would sell himself!" It came from cheap jewellery stores in London's Soho and "cost just a few pence". His rings with D on them cost just 50p each. Del's necklace with D on it is actually worth something! Robin had it specially made and it was worth around £70 – more than all the rest put together.

PART 2
The Writer – John Sullivan

When young John Sullivan failed his eleven-plus in 1957 no one would have predicted that he would one day become an acclaimed writer and creator of the most popular comedy series in British television history. Four years after failing the exam he left school without any qualifications and took the first of a long line of fill-in jobs to make ends meet.

John was born at 35 Zennor Road, Balham, south London on December 23rd 1946. His father, also John, was a plumber and his mother Hilda was a housewife who occasionally worked as a charlady. "My childhood was almost clichéd working class," he recalled. "Our house had three floors. We had the ground and first floors and another family lived at the top. There was a tin bath hanging out in the yard that would come into the scullery on a Friday and we'd heat water up on the stove for it. We didn't have an inside toilet until I was about five when my father, being a plumber, finally condescended to put a toilet into the house."

Ambition for John was not high and school was something to be tolerated until he could get out and begin earning a living. However, from the age of twelve one lesson began to hold his attention – English. And the British people owe a great debt of thanks to a certain Mr Trowers, a young English teacher with an eye patch who taught at Telferscot School. Jim Trowers, more than anyone else, inspired John to take an interest in English and that would eventually lead to him trying his hand at writing scripts.

"Up until Jim Trowers started teaching us, all we had done during English classes was be given a book and told to read it in silence," said John. "Afterwards we'd be asked questions about it and we never took it in. You'd rather go to sleep. Suddenly Mr Trowers came along and instead of just letting us read the books, he'd read them to us, acting it out and doing all the voices. He made it come alive.

"I remember being almost hypnotised by Charles Dickens' *David Copperfield*. I was enthralled by it and, for the first time in all my school days I was actually looking forward to something other than football. From that moment on I was very keen on English and I started to enjoy writing. I liked Dickens because he was the first author whose work had come alive for me and had colour in it. He was writing about areas that I knew about and the class system that was familiar to me. He became my favourite author."

However at fifteen John left school without any qualifications. "The middle class kids in their school uniforms would do 'O' Levels but us working class mob from the poor areas didn't," he said. "Their parents worked in offices and they knew they might be going somewhere. That didn't apply to the rest of us. We wanted to get out and earn some money to help the family out."

The same had applied with the eleven-plus. "I remember taking the exam but it never seemed to matter if we passed or not because we were all going to work in factories anyway," he said in an interview in 1987. He added later: "That's how it was and so we approached it with that attitude. Teachers would say how important the exam was and our attitude was: 'Yeah, right'. We knew we were going to be factory fodder so there seemed to be no point trying."

John's first job, at fifteen, was as a messenger with Reuters, then at sixteen he joined advertising agency Collett, Dickinson and

Pearce, again as a messenger, where he worked for, amongst others, David Puttnam and Alan Parker, who would later become famous filmmakers. "There was a café opposite where I was sent to get sandwiches for people and I read in a biography of Dickens years later that he'd lived above it," John said. "I hadn't known it at the time but I was within a few yards of where the man had lived."

A year later, fed up earning just £3.50 a week, he joined his best friend Colin Humphries cleaning cars for a second-hand motor trader and his wages shot up to a respectable £20 a week. "Suddenly I was earning more money than my father and I could afford to do up the family home a bit and have a phone line put in," he recalled. Later John and Colin would begin selling cars. "But I was not a very successful salesman," he said, laughing. "I used to do stupid things. One time, when I was asked to go out and test a car my boss was thinking of buying in, all I did was go out and test how good the radio was. I thought it was great driving this fast MG and didn't bother listening to the engine. I came back and said it was brilliant and he bought it on my word. He came in the following day furious. It turned out the engine was knackered but I hadn't heard it over the noise of the radio. In the end I decided that it wasn't the job for me."

His next job was at Watneys Brewery and it was there that he first decided to try his hand at scriptwriting. "I had a job stacking crates of beer and going out delivering to pubs," he said. "I worked with a guy called Paul Saunders who I knew from school. He was a very funny bloke with a very dry wit and we got on well. The job was so dull that we used humour to keep us from going mad. One day he read an article about Johnny Speight which said he earned £1,000 a script for *Till Death Us Do Part* and Paul said: 'We're pretty funny guys. We could do this.'

"I said: 'Yeah, anything for a laugh' and I went out and bought an old typewriter for about £2 and for the next two months we wrote this idea we had for a sitcom which we then sent off to the BBC. It was called *Gentleman* and it was about an old ex-soldier who ran an old-fashioned gents' toilet with brass pipes and a china trough. It was his pride and joy and he had his regular people who used to come in every morning. He suddenly started to lose his customers because the council opened a brand-new loo down the road with piped muzak and aftershave on tap and hot air hand-dryers. In the last episode we wrote he had father and son tramps come in full of blarney – almost Micawber and son – and pay their penny and go in a cubicle each and they wouldn't leave because it was freezing cold outside. There was then a legal battle between them and the caretaker over how long is a call of nature – because there is nothing prescribed in law for it – it could be a year! It became a battle for him to try to persuade them out, which finally he did. Then he realised they were the only company he'd had for a month and he should have left them. It sounds alright but it was so badly written. After three months we got a letter back saying: 'We are not looking for this kind of material' which was quite right because it was awful."

The rejection put Paul off the idea of writing but John was undaunted. "I'd enjoyed the process of writing and developing characters so much that I carried on on my own and wrote various scripts," he said. "One was about a family called the Leeches who lived off the state and knew every fiddle there was. Another was about a football team. I'd send the scripts off to the BBC and get nowhere, so I'd re-write them, change the names and send them in again, giving myself a different name. Everything I wrote about was based on people that I knew and places I was familiar with. That hasn't really changed much over the years."

It was John's working class roots that gave him most of his writing ideas. "My Dad was my greatest influence," he once said. "He was a prisoner of war, a bookies' runner, an illegal boxer and he had some great stories. He swore blind that he saw Hitler after the war.

"It was after the Americans had released Dad from his prisoner of war camp. He went scavenging for food and went into a barn and there was a tall German in a full-length leather coat who pulled a gun out. With him was Hitler wearing a suit and Eva Braun and they asked if my Dad could get clothes from anywhere. He said yes and he went off and never said a word to anyone at the time about seeing them – nor did he get them any clothes. I once asked him why and I think it was because he hated the British army so much because of the class system in the prisoner of war camp that by the end of the war I don't think he was too sure which side he was fighting on – he hated the Germans and the British! He was a great socialist and he hated the whole class thing in the army. Even in the prisoner of war camp the officers got the Red Cross parcels first.

"I remember my old man telling how the German guards had all left about a week before the Americans arrived. They had their civvie suits ready for them and they all went out wearing them.

"He used to tell horror stories about how the Germans treated the Russians and the Slavs. At roll call the Russians and Slavs used to bring their dead out and hold them up because the Germans did a head count and gave out bowls of gruel depending on the numbers so they brought their dead out to get extra bowls. He said the British were treated quite well and the Germans shared their food with them. One time the prisoners had been doing tree felling and the Germans had two great big shire horses to pull the lumber. The morning after the Germans left all that was left of the horses were their heads. The Russians and Slavs had had them overnight.

"He also used to tell a tale about how, when the Yanks arrived, they were all gung ho and said: 'Where are the Germans? Where are the Germans?' The former prisoners told them they were long gone. The Americans decided to search the forest and after half an hour the former prisoners heard all this firing. When the Americans came back it was revealed they'd shot fourteen of their own men. There were no Germans out there – they'd just got into one big gunfight and shot at anything that moved."

After his brewery job John went to work with his father as a plumber. "But I was an even worse plumber than I was a car salesman," he admitted. "I was terrible. The last guy I worked for said that I flooded more houses than Hurricane Hilda. I just didn't check things properly and then I'd switch the water on and would have forgotten to tighten something up somewhere and water would start pouring from some joint or start coming through a ceiling!"

At the same time as working John tried to learn more about some of the subjects that he'd missed out on at school. "Most weeks after I got paid I'd go and buy one of those yellow and blue Teach Yourself books. Teach Yourself English, Maths or anything. I was also keen on buying books like paperback Dickens – I even bought *Beowulf* once, because I'd heard about it and wanted to know about it – a waste of time that was! When I was a kid there were only two books in the house – the Bible and Littlewoods perm football pools book. My parents weren't big book readers and I was trying to make up for having little education."

In 1972 John met a pretty secretary called Sharon in The Drugstore pub in London's Kings Road. "I was working as a plumber at the time and I went out with her a few times before I told her about my ideas of becoming a writer," he said. "At the time she said: 'Oh, really?' but later she admitted she thought: 'Oh God, I've got a weirdo!' She thought I must be a bit of a dreamer." She was earning more than him at the time, but Sharon decided she could put up with his writing ambitions. Two years later they married and Sharon then had to put up with John bashing away at his typewriter on the kitchen table for the next few years.

As an aspiring writer John would make up stories and situations at random by picking bits out of newspapers. He'd decide to open a paper on a certain page and would make up a story about whatever was on the top of a certain column. "It could be anything from a big financial company crashing to a court report," he recalled. "I'd try to think of what I'd write about it if I was given it as subject matter. When would-be writers come to me for advice I now recommend the idea to them as a way of challenging themselves, giving themselves flexibility and encouraging them to be ready to change and adapt their scripts."

Every time he had a rejection letter from the BBC John redoubled his efforts. But he also had a theory about the staff of the Corporation's script reading department whose job it was to sift through the mountains of ideas from would-be writers, filter the ones they thought had potential for producers and send rejection slips to the writers of the rest. "I used to think that if these people were that good then why were they just reading scripts all day?" he said. "Surely if they were any good they'd be producing shows and doing things. I didn't have much faith in them."

One day he came up with an idea about a Tooting man who planned to start a revolution. It was based upon a man he knew from a south London pub who was always talking about doing the same thing. He called the show *Citizen Smith*. "I knew it was my best idea yet," he said. "I thought it had lots of potential and talk of revolution was topical in the seventies. I was almost frightened to send it in and have it rejected. It was like having an ace in a poker game; I didn't know when to throw it! I figured that if *Smith* didn't go I'd have to give up the idea of writing because I had nothing else."

He decided his best bet was to get a job at the BBC, any job, learn more about the business and then meet someone who might actually take some notice of his script. "I wrote a letter to them telling them what I wanted to do and the moment I posted it, I regretted it," he said. "I thought they'd think I was a maniac and I wouldn't get considered."

Fortunately they didn't. John went for an interview and was given a job at BBC Television in the props department on the understanding that he didn't annoy the stars. He soon switched jobs and became a scenery shifter because it was a studio job and brought him closer to actual filming. Among the sets he helped build was one for the famous Morecambe and Wise *Singing in the Rain* sketch.

John had been biding his time waiting to meet a producer to talk to about his idea for *Citizen Smith*, then one Sunday a colleague pointed out a dapper little man in a blazer and tie who he said was a producer called Dennis Main Wilson. John knew Main Wilson was a bit of a legend at the BBC and the producer of hit shows like *Till Death Us Do Part*. At last John had a face he could talk to who he actually knew had some creative influence. "But I was a bit intimidated by the fact he had a double-barrelled name and that he had a sort of ex-RAF officer air about him," John said.

"A few evenings later I found him in the small BBC bar which I thought was reserved for producers and directors but I was too nervous to approach him. Twice I started walking across to him and both times I bottled it. The third time he spotted me. Our eyes met and I had no choice but to actually go over and introduce myself. Everyone else in there was smartly dressed and I felt very conspicuous in my scruffy jeans and big boots. I thought: 'I'm going to get sacked for this.'

"I said: 'Dennis. I'm John Sullivan. I thought I'd introduce myself because we're going to be working together soon.' And he said: 'Oh, what on?' thinking I was going to be working on one of his shows and I said: 'On this new thing I've just written' and he just roared with laughter. He said: 'Buy me a drink' and I did – a large Bells Scotch and a half a pint of Ruddles real ale chaser – and we sat at the bar chatting and he gave me lots of advice and encouragement. I think he liked my cheek and I later found out he liked people who were upfront so I obviously picked the right guy to approach."

One of his main pieces of advice was that John should go off and write sketches for shows like *The Two Ronnies* and *The Dave Allen Show*. Breaking his promise not to bother the stars, while working on *Porridge* John asked its star, Ronnie Barker, for advice. He told Ronnie that he had some ideas for sketches and the star told him to bring them in. A week later he did and Barker took them home to read. The following Sunday Ronnie called John over and asked him if he could write any more. "He was terrific to me," said John. "He said he liked them and he put me on a contract. I was ecstatic."

Five weeks later John met Dennis again and the producer was impressed by the fact that John had been hired to write material for *The Two Ronnies*. He told John to go off and write *Citizen Smith* and the writer didn't wait around. He took two weeks' leave and went to Sharon's parents' home in Crystal Palace where he bashed out a pilot script for *Citizen Smith*, which he delivered to Dennis as soon as it was finished. He then promptly took another week off, which again he spent at his in-laws. That week he had no idea that Dennis Main Wilson was chasing all over London trying to track him down.

Main Wilson loved the script and so did his boss, Jimmy Gilbert, and they wanted to make it for a Comedy Playhouse series which tried out new ideas with a view to them becoming series. When he returned home a week later John phoned Main Wilson for his verdict. "'Where the hell have you been?' came the reply," John recalled. "'We've been looking for you everywhere.' I said: 'What's the matter?' and he said: 'We're doing it!' I couldn't believe it. After ten years of trying, something was finally happening. It was a great moment. It went into production and eight weeks later it was on the telly."

The show did well and a full series was commissioned. John Sullivan was on his way. After two years shifting scenery he quit his job and decided to throw himself into writing full time. The rest, to quote a well-known cliché, is history. There are plenty of comedy writers working in television who create popular shows that have good ratings and a wide appeal, but none seem to have quite matched John Sullivan's ability to capture such a wide-ranging audience and no comedy is likely to better the huge ratings he achieved with *Only Fools and Horses*.

"There are some great writers but John is the best," David Jason told me in 1998. "I saw the strengths in his work and what he was capable of very early on and would encourage him to be bolder and braver about the emotional side of his characters. A lot of people would dismiss things in a comedy and say: 'Hang on, this is a comedy – you're getting too serious here.' But I realised that that was his strength and the way he wrote. He made them more human and not just sitcom characters."

"John writes about real people," said Nicholas Lyndhurst, also in 1998. "He's so clever because he can lead you up one garden path with his writing and you can be convinced that you think you know where it is going and then suddenly something completely different happens."

Only Fools and Horses may be the show that everyone talks about, but John also had huge successes with the other shows he created. *Just Good Friends,* about two former lovers who meet in a pub five years after he jilted her, was a huge hit and *Dear John*, about a hapless divorcee played by Ralph Bates, was very popular and a Hollywood version became very successful in the United States. His 1992 sitcom *Sitting Pretty* about the life of a sixties good-time girl Annie Briggs wasn't a big hit but he bounced back with a two-part comedy drama set during the Second World War called *Over Here,* which starred Martin Clunes. *Roger, Roger*, based around a mini-cab firm and starring Robert Daws ran for three series and he also penned *Heartburn Hotel,* which starred Tim Healy as a Falklands vet who ran a downmarket hotel, and *Micawber*, which starred David Jason. He garnered a host of awards for his work and in 2004 was awarded an OBE by Her Majesty The Queen for services to drama.

John tragically died on Friday April 22nd 2011 following a short illness. He was just sixty-four. His death robbed Britain of its finest comedy writer, whose work had brought laughter and joy to the lives of millions. But much more than that though, it was a terrible personal loss for his wife Sharon and their three children Dan, Jim and Amy. He was also a devoted grandfather to Dan and his wife Kelly's two children, Joe and Mia.

Tributes to John were led by BBC Director General Mark Thompson who said: "John created some of the UK's most loved comedies, from *Only Fools and Horses* to his most recent work, *Rock & Chips*. He had a unique gift for turning everyday life and characters we all know into unforgettable comedy. His work will live on for years to come."

BBC Head of Comedy Mark Freeland said: "No one understood what made us laugh and cry better than John Sullivan. He was the Dickens of our generation. Simply the best, most natural, most heartfelt comedy writer of our time."

His close friend and colleague, producer Gareth Gwenlan said: "John was a writer of immense talent and he leaves behind him an extraordinary body of work which has entertained tens of millions of viewers and will continue to do so for many decades to come. I have had the privilege of working with John for over thirty years as a colleague and close friend. He was a writer at the peak of his creative powers with so much more to give."

"I heard about John's death whilst on holiday in Florida and so driving back through Miami brought back all the memories of *Miami Twice* and the fun we'd had over there," said Sir David Jason. "Then to get back to the UK and see so many wonderful tributes in the press, brought it home again to me what a great friend I had lost.

"Being at his funeral was like being in the wrong scene in the wrong script – it shouldn't have been happening. What a sad, sad day for his family, his friends, the entire cast and crew of *Only Fools*, not to mention the other shows he had so skilfully crafted. Thanks for all the laughs, John. You really made a difference to our lives."

Nicholas Lyndhurst told the BBC he was "shocked" and "deeply saddened" and described his friend as "without doubt" Britain's finest TV writer. He added: "He was a shy and self-effacing man, but had a huge passion for his work and was looking forward to writing more *Rock & Chips*."

Patrick Murray, who played Mickey Pearce in *Only Fools and Horses*, said: "I will always feel privileged to have known such a warm and considerate man and to have worked with a truly great writer. John wonderfully mastered the very many aspects of classic situation comedy writing. His comedies were often about love, family loyalty, friendship, forgiveness, moral integrity and ambition. And that is fitting as these important virtues are those that John Sullivan possessed in abundance."

At such times it is inevitable to think about what might have been. John Sullivan loved his work and had so much more that he wanted to do. He was working on an *Only Fools and Horses* West End musical which several producers were vying to make. He always planned to keep writing *Rock & Chips* up to the already known deaths of Joan Trotter and Freddie Robdal. Indeed, had the BBC commissioned a full series as he'd hoped in 2009, rather than the three hour long episodes it plumped for, then we may have already known what he'd planned for the characters. John had planned to write at least three and possibly six more episodes. He had a development deal with the BBC and had ideas for a new sitcom. He was also keen to help new writers develop their ideas, not least his son Jim, who had already written a number of episodes of *The Green Green Grass* and had been writing his own sitcom.

John also planned to write his autobiography, which would have been fascinating and although he might have been best known for his scripts, he was also a successful composer, having penned the theme music for *Citizen Smith*, *Over The Moon*, *Only Fools and Horses*, *Just Good Friends*, *Dear John* and *The Green Green Grass*. He had a real passion for music and wanted to write more. Of the many awards he won, he was most proud of the ASCAP (American Society of Composers, Authors and Publishers) award he picked up in April 1991 for the US version of *Dear John*. "I'm keen to do more music. I've got so much stuff down on tape that I haven't used," he once told me. "I'm always looking to do something with it."

I shall always remember John for his loyalty and kindness to me and his enthusiasm for the business he was in. I'd first met him back in 1990, a few months after *The Jolly Boys' Outing* had been screened, when I went to interview him about *Only Fools*. I was a young showbusiness reporter; he was already a legendary writer. To say I was in awe of him was an understatement. I'd grown up watching *Only Fools and Horses*, *Just Good Friends* and *Dear John*. As a teenager, because of *Only Fools and Horses*, I remember going to the market underneath the ugly concrete Tricorn shopping centre in my hometown of Portsmouth and being fascinated by the blokes selling stuff like sets of saucepans at knock down prices. Just like Del Boy they'd be doing all the old: 'I won't charge you £10, £8 I'm robbing myself, not £7 or £6 – £5 the lot' – and hands would go up all round the stall. They had the gift of the gab and I thought their spiel was brilliant.

To be honest, I was a bit nervous about meeting John that first time. But I needn't have been. He was warm, open and generous with his time. How lucky did I feel to spend a couple of hours chatting to the writer of my favourite television series in his lounge about how the show came about? He made tea and at lunchtime a platter of sandwiches arrived. I put a couple on a plate on a coffee table next to me. A minute or two later John pointed out that I was actually using an ash tray. It was my Trigger moment, although in my defence it was the poshest, shiniest ash tray I'd ever seen. Suffice to say, I felt like a total plonker. John thought it was very funny.

Before I left, I asked John if he'd consider letting me write a book about *Only Fools and Horses*, a behind-the-scenes history of the show. Yes, he said, a great idea – but he'd like to wait until the series had ended. We kept in touch and the following year he invited me to go out to Miami to cover the filming of the episode *Miami Twice*. Over the next twenty years I was lucky enough to work with him on my first book *The Only Fools and Horses Story*, two volumes of *Only Fools* script books, countless newspaper and magazine articles and his company's official website for *The Green Green Grass*. Professionally, he couldn't have been more helpful and personally he was kind, loyal and generous.

Despite his enormous success, John was a modest and unassuming man. His family was central to his life. He also was passionate about his work and, as you might expect, he had a dry sense of humour and was a master storyteller. He had a real talent for remembering idiosyncratic things about people and a great memory for logging funny things he observed.

John enriched the lives of those of us who were fortunate to know him personally and I feel incredibly lucky to have known him, let alone become a friend. His work has had a huge impact on the British way of life. His catchphrases from *Only Fools* have slipped into common usage and his comedies brightened – and continue to brighten – the lives of millions. For so many of us, a great family Christmas Day included watching *Only Fools and Horses*, when young and old could laugh and share in the humour together. John Sullivan had a rare gift – and he was good enough to share it with the rest of us.

JOHN SULLIVAN - A WRITING GENIUS

John would often write down potential jokes, scenes, characters and ideas on scraps of paper and put them away in a drawer. "When we first moved to our village and met new people and used to go out for dinner with them, I'd keep going off to the toilet," he said in 2010. "They thought I had a bladder problem, but actually I was making notes of things that had been said – and I'd think: 'That was a good line…' In the end I had to tell them: 'Basically I'm just ripping you all off.'" He would also store ideas in his head and so when it came to actual writing, he'd already plotted out an episode and could then write the first draft in under a week.

John was a keen observer of people and was fascinated by them. "I can be in a restaurant or anywhere and see someone talking in a particular way or displaying some unusual body language," he once told me. "They may be trying to be something they are not and you might be able to tell that by the way they dress or the way they are. They might be buying wine and know as much about wine as I do, which is very little, but have some quirky way of doing it. And suddenly you start to get a character forming. You obviously never meet these people but you come out of the restaurant and you have an idea for a character simply from that and you can imagine what they might be like at home or at work. The chances are if you met them you'd be a million miles away, but it doesn't matter – you've come out with a character. I remember doing it once myself. I ordered a bottle of Chablis and the bloke brought it over and I had it in the glass and I twirled it round and sniffed it and it went straight up my ******* nose. I never did it again.

"I remember being in the audience for *The Two Ronnies* one

night and there were a man and woman sitting in front of me. Now *The Two Ronnies* used to get a bit near the knuckle with their comedy. As they were doing the show, before the woman would laugh, she'd look at her husband and if he laughed, she laughed. And if he didn't laugh, she wouldn't laugh. That sort of thing interested me. You could imagine their home life and the dominance of this man."

John also had a great talent for realising the extra talents of the actors he was working with and then finding a way of using them in his programmes. Buster Merryfield recalled being at a rehearsal in Chiswick for one of his first episodes of *Only Fools and Horses*. "I got to this rehearsal hall first and there was this dirty old piano there so I just sat down and started to play – although I can't really play for nuts. I was banging out this old tune when David Jason walked in.

"He said: 'Hello Buster, was that you playing the piano?' I was shutting the lid and I said: 'Just tinkling for my own amusement.' He said it sounded quite good from outside. 'Does John know that you play the piano?' he asked. I said I didn't really play, it was just for fun. Then John walked in and David said: 'Did you know Buster played the piano? Go on play it!' So I did. I played *My Blue Heaven* and then everyone else came in so I stopped and that was that.

"Then we got the next script and the first lines of it read: 'Uncle Albert is in the Nag's Head playing the piano.' John had noted it, stored it and written it. He's got great powers of observation."

AN EYE FOR THE CAST TOO

John Sullivan wasn't just a dab hand at writing scripts. He also had a keen eye at spotting the right person to star in his shows. He cast Robert Lindsay in *Citizen Smith*, John Challis in *Only Fools and Horses*, Paul Nicholas in *Just Good Friends*, Ralph Bates in *Dear John* and Robert Daws in *Roger, Roger*. John Sullivan's wife Sharon also took an active role in his writing and made suggestions on casting and scripts, so much so that when *Only Fools and Horses* producer Ray Butt moved to a new job with Central Television he wanted Sharon to join him as a casting director.

JOHN SULLIVAN'S FAVOURITE MOMENTS

Del falls through the bar in a wine bar in *Yuppy Love* (1989)
It's a moment everyone talks about and I like it because it worked so well – and we managed to get it right first time. I'd seen a guy do it for real in The George pub, Balham Hill about fifteen years before I used it. The guy didn't go as flat as David did it but he went through the bar and stumbled through and then got up with a sheepish 'I meant to do that' grin. I'd saved it up because I didn't find the right time before. I'd thought about using it in an earlier episode of *Only Fools* but decided not to as if he was in the Nag's Head, Del would know where the bar flap was and wouldn't have made such a mistake.

Del Boy goes hang-gliding in *Tea For Three* (1986)
This is one of my favourite moments because I just think David Jason's and Nick Lyndhurst's acting was outstanding and so funny. Del gets himself into a situation where he's strapped

into a hang glider and although he really doesn't want to do it, his pride stops him from changing his mind and backing out. Because he's such a proud man he decides to take his life in his hands.

The Trotters ruin the chandelier in *A Touch of Glass* (1982)

This is another moment which a lot of people like but it's special for me because it's based on a story that my Dad told me and he's not around anymore so it's nostalgic for me. Whenever I see it it is almost like being in contact with him again, so I love that one. Obviously the real incident wasn't as funny for my Dad because seven men got the sack for that mistake – and that was back in the days when there was no dole.

The Trotters' voyage to Holland in *To Hull and Back* (1985)

Del, Rodney and Albert head to Holland on a rusty old trawler. During the journey Del starts philosophising about Britain being a nation of seafarers. He talks about his pride in British people doing things like going off to discover the New World. He then decides to sing but instead of singing a nautical song the best he can come up with is a song about Robin Hood.

Seeing Del and Rodney dress as Batman and Robin for the first time in *Heroes and Villains* (1996)

We filmed this scene in a street in Bristol and we went to a great deal of trouble to keep this storyline a secret. When we were filming we not only lit the set with lights, we also turned them round to try to stop photographers getting pictures and spoiling it for people. We knew it was a great gag and it was important to us for the reveal to be a very funny surprise for viewers and, as a lot of people talk about this scene, I think we succeeded.

JOHN'S 'HITCHCOCK' APPEARANCE

John Sullivan once appeared in one of his own shows making a Hitchcock-style cameo in an episode of *Roger, Roger*.

"I never ever dreamt of ever appearing on screen in an acting role because I'm too shy for all that," he told me. "It is just not something that ever crossed my mind," he told me. "But for episode two I wrote in a barman in a snooker hall and he just has three or four words to say and producer Tony Dow said: 'I can't offer such a stupid tiny part to a real actor. Basically we need someone with no talent who is incredibly cheap' and then he looked across at me. I suppose I made a cross for my own back by writing in this character.

"So I gave it a go and I quite enjoyed the acting and we managed to do it in only four takes – and the one people will see is the best one, which says a lot about the ones they didn't use. The good thing for the public is that I'm not on screen for very long – in fact people have longer sneezes than my appearance. I'm also very cheap - in fact the BBC didn't pay me a penny for it."

John joked that he didn't think many actors would be worried about him getting their work. "David Jason and Robert De Niro can sleep easy, as I don't think I'm going to be getting any of their roles," he said. "I've always appreciated actors but the experience did make me appreciate them even more because it isn't as easy to say lines and do something else, in my case for this, polish a glass, and be in the right place for the camera.

"I only had four words to remember and sometimes I give actors hundreds of words to remember and they get them absolutely right – I don't know how they do it, it's quite incredible."

THE TWO RONNIES

John Sullivan became a favourite writer for *The Two Ronnies*, penning a range of dialogue including news headlines and bar-room philosophers George and Sid sketches. In 1980 some robust conversations took place between a BBC executive and John's agent Roger Hancock (brother of the late comedy actor Tony Hancock) over John's fee for sketch writing on *The Two Ronnies*. Although keen to avoid increasing John's fee the BBC executive concluded: "The Ronnies particularly want Sullivan to write the 'two old men' sequences again. Therefore we appear to have no alternative."

David Jason - Del Trotter

Whenever he thinks about the circumstances that led to him landing the part of Del Trotter, David Jason chuckles to himself. It was, after all, pretty much down to fate, together with a fair measure of good luck.

It all began more than a decade before when David missed out on a role which would have given him his biggest television break and probably made him a major star. Back in the autumn of 1967 television producer David Croft and his writing partner Jimmy Perry were looking for cast for a new comedy series they were making for the BBC. The show, called *Dad's Army,* was all about the exploits of a group of old men who were members of a south coast town's wartime Home Guard platoon.

They had already cast most of the major parts for the show but there was one more part that needed filling – that of bumbling, elderly butcher Lance Corporal Jack Jones - and it was offered to character actor Clive Dunn. But he was busy at the time in *The Spike Milligan Show* and had to turn it down. Croft thought of David Jason, a young character actor who, although only still in his late twenties was well skilled at playing old men. Croft thought highly of Jason and had used him a couple of times before in a BBC sitcom he produced called *Hugh and I,* which starred Hugh Lloyd and Terry Scott as two friends who lived together in south London.

David Jason was called in to read for the part and two hours later his agent rang to tell him that he'd got the job. Three hours after that she rang back to say she had very bad news and that he hadn't got it at all. In the meantime Clive Dunn had discovered that no more Spike Milligan shows were being made at that time and he decided to accept the part in *Dad's Army* after all. Understandably David was hugely disappointed to lose a part that would have brought him his first big break into mainstream television and *Dad's Army* became a major success and ran for nine years. These days he's rather glad that it happened that way.

For life would have been very different for him if he had starred in *Dad's Army*. He would have been busy filming that series when the part of dopey corner-shop assistant Granville in Roy Clarke's *Open All Hours* came up. That would have meant that he would have never worked with Ray Butt on that show – or been cast in *It's Only Me - Whoever I Am* where he showed off his ability with accents by mimicking Ray's strong London accent.

Then he would have never even been considered for the part of Del Trotter – the role that has made him famous and let him demonstrate the brilliant acting skills that have since led to countless straight roles. "After I lost the part in *Dad's Army* and it started to become really successful there were times when I'd watch it and see Corporal Jones and I'd say: 'I was offered that bloody part!'" he recalled.

"You can't help thinking like that. At the time I thought it would have changed my life because I would have been recognised as a television actor, which I wasn't at that stage. Back then I was winning and losing parts like any other average actor. You'd go in and meet people who you didn't know and they didn't know you from Adam and they didn't really know your work and it was a struggle – but that's the way it is for anybody who is trying to forge a career and live as an actor. I was quite happy to go and do summer seasons, I was really happy on stage, I really enjoyed it.

"That's all history now but not getting that [the Corporal Jones] part had a major effect on my career. When I think about it, the whole thing that led me to getting the part of Del is littered with ifs and buts. Obviously if John Sullivan's other show hadn't been cancelled then he would never have written *Only Fools*. If Jim Broadbent or Enn Reitel had been free to play the part of Del then I would have never done it and if Ray Butt hadn't been determined to cast me then I would have never got the job at all."

David Jason was born David John White on February 2nd 1940. His father Arthur was a fish porter at Billingsgate Fish Market, and his mother Olwen was a charlady and the family, David, his elder brother Arthur and younger sister June, lived in a modest terraced home in Finchley, north London.

He did his first acting in a school play *Wayside War* at the age of fourteen. He only got the part when a classmate dropped out with measles. David had been a reluctant performer. "I didn't want to be in the school play," he said. "Only girls were in plays." He played a cavalier in the Civil War drama and to his surprise he loved every minute of it. Afterwards he joined an amateur dramatic society. "A friend asked if I wanted to join an amateur theatre group," he recalled. "I said no and my friend said: 'Pity, because there are twenty-five girls in the group and no boys...' I said: 'When do I start...' Then I fell in love with acting."

He left school at fifteen and, as his parents had always wanted him to get a trade, he worked in a garage as a trainee mechanic but quit after a year and became an apprentice electrician. Even back then he was a joker. "We used to play lots of practical jokes on one guy – like telling him to put his ear to a hole in a ceiling so we could call to him and then pour a bucket of freezing water through!" he recalled. By night he'd be treading the boards in a string of amateur productions and he set his heart on acting professionally, just like his elder brother Arthur.

By the time he reached his mid-twenties David was working as an electrician with his friend Bob Bevil, with whom he'd set up a company called B and W Installations. The urge to act professionally was too strong though and he began increasingly thinking about turning professional. His chance came in March 1965 when his brother Arthur was offered a part in the BBC police drama *Z Cars* which would earn him £25 and gave up a forthcoming £9 a week part in the Noel Coward play *South Sea Bubble* at Bromley Rep in Kent.

But before leaving, Arthur recommended his brother to the director who, after watching David in action in an amateur play offered him the job. It was the spur he needed. He gave his share in B and W Installations to his partner and took the plunge and made his professional debut on April 5th 1965. Other minor work followed, interspersed with long spells out of work, before he went back to Bromley Rep on a year long contract playing all sorts of parts with directors usually recognising his skills as a comic actor and casting him in comedy roles. "I was a resident so I had to do any part that came up in any play every two weeks," he recalled. "I was always playing something from a vicar to a Derek Royle lookalike falling over or jumping through hoops."

Derek Royle was an acrobat employed by the Brian Rix Company to appear in his West End farces and would forever be tumbling over or being knocked down. When Bromley Rep staged the farces the part Royle had played would inevitably fall to David Jason. "I enjoyed doing them and I could do all that stuff but in those days I couldn't get on the West End stage," he said.

It was while he was appearing at Bromley Rep that David first met Lennard Pearce, the actor who was later to become his co-star in *Only Fools and Horses*. They were in two plays together. In the first eighteenth century comedy *The Rivals,* David played country bumpkin Bob Acres and Lennard played Irish wheeler-dealer Sir Lucius O'Trigger.

In the second, Jack Popplewell's *Busybody* in August 1965,

David played Detective Constable Goddard and Lennard played a more senior officer, Detective Superintendent Baxter.

"He was a lovely character actor and one of many who would come in and play a part for a few weeks. We got on very well but after that I didn't see him for about fifteen years until we met again at the BBC," David recalled.

Afterwards David continued to work on the stage in a variety of roles and took a number of parts in summer seasons alongside stars like Bob Monkhouse and Dick Emery. In the autumn of 1967 he got his first television job in the children's comedy series *Do Not Adjust Your Set* alongside Eric Idle, Michael Palin and Terry Jones. It was around the same time that David lost out on the *Dad's Army* part. When *Do Not Adjust Your Set* ended in 1969 David landed a small role in the ITV soap *Crossroads* playing a gardener, but it was his next job that gave him a major break. London Weekend Television's *Hark at Barker* (starring Ronnie Barker) was produced by Humphrey Barclay, the man behind *Do Not Adjust Your Set* and he thought David would be great as Dithers, the hundred year old gardener.

"They were looking for a bloke to play Dithers who was capable of being knocked over and could fall down," said David. "You can't get old men to fall down for real because if you do they'll probably break something." The show was a success but more important for David was the impression he made on Ronnie Barker. The two got on famously and when Barker came to make a series of seven one-off comedies for the BBC in 1973 he recommended David for a part in one of them called *Open All Hours*, which later became a hugely popular series.

Similarly when another of the plays, *Prisoner and Escort,* by Dick Clement and Ian le Frenais was commissioned as a full series in 1974 and renamed *Porridge*, Ronnie suggested David for the part of aged prison lag Blanco Webb, a role he played in three episodes. Producers were reluctant but Ronnie Barker told them to watch a tape of David playing Dithers in *Hark at Barker*. In 1974 David gained his first starring role in the ITV comedy series *The Top Secret Life of Edgar Briggs* followed in 1976 by the series *Lucky Feller*. The same year the first full series of *Open All Hours* was made and some episodes were directed by Ray Butt and it was he who, five years later, spotted David Jason's potential as Del Trotter and cast him in *Only Fools and Horses*.

Immediately after being confirmed in the part David had gone off with his new co-stars Lennard Pearce and Nicholas Lyndhurst for a celebration drink at the BBC bar at Television Centre in Wood Lane, Shepherd's Bush. David had already spotted what Ray Butt and John Howard Davies had seen, not to mention the potential identified back in 1977 by Dennis Main Wilson when he backed *Citizen Smith*, that they were dealing with scripts by a rare talent.

David recalled: "I remember saying to Lennard and Nick in the bar: 'I think we've got something really unusual here and we're going to have to play this very differently.' They said: 'What do you mean?' and I said: 'Well I don't really just see it as a situation comedy. It's much more of a comedy drama. It isn't just obvious jokes, it's all about people and characters, there's much more to it than that.'

"It wasn't like your typical sitcom with very obvious in-your-face jokes, this was much more based around characters. It meant we'd have to approach it differently. I didn't realise at the time though that it had the potential that John Sullivan had seen in it and it would later grow and grow. John had this marvellous ability to make it move with the times and develop in a natural way."

David and Nicholas Lyndhurst had met before the meeting in Ray Butt's office when David was cast in *Only Fools and Horses*. Nicholas had interviewed him about his series *Lucky Feller* when he presented the LWT kids programme *Our Show*. "I'd forgotten that," said David. "Much later Nick reminded me of it." On meeting Nicholas again these were his first impressions: "Apart from him being too tall for himself, when he read I thought: 'This guy is a very good actor.' He'd instinctively got the sense of it and from that moment I realised that they had an excellent Rodney."

David's enthusiasm for the part and the world in which Del lived also came from the fact that he understood that world. "I came from the same sort of roots as Del," he said. "We both came from poor working class families and went to the same sort of school. But, from there on we go our separate ways. For example he's far more confident than I ever was. He's got more front than Blackpool and I'm not like that."

David, John Sullivan and Ray Butt were all working-class London boys and all talked the same language. "There was a tremendous amount of empathy between us that we could communicate quite quickly," he recalled. "Time and time again John would bring dialogue into the script that we'd used when we were lads, that wasn't heard anymore. I'd read a line in a script and that would spark off another one in me either that my father had said or we had said as kids."

With John Sullivan's script for the first episode, *Big Brother,* David had a decent idea of the character he was to play but he needed to flesh it out more and bring him to life. It was then that he remembered someone he knew from his days as an electrician. When they ran B and W Installations David and his partner Bob Bevil went to great lengths to try to get work. "One time we were so desperate for work that we did a mail shot," he recalled. "We sent out hundreds of letters to every builder, plumber and contractor in London and we got a letter back from this bloke called Derek Hockley. He ran a building firm and he had contracts to do up pubs all over East London and he called us down to his office at his builder's yard in the East End.

"He had a little goatee beard and was always terribly well turned out. He always had a clean shirt on that was immaculately pressed, a sharp suit, all the jewellery, highly polished shoes and a camelhaired coat and he just looked the business. He thought he was very smart and what I couldn't get out of my mind was a guy who looked as elegantly dressed as he did and yet he spoke like a gorblimey cockney. That really stuck with me and left a great impression on me.

"He looked like he could have been an accountant or an army officer or even a member of the royal family but he spoke like a barrow boy with an East End accent you could cut with a knife, very similar to Del Boy's. He was a great character and as I got to know him more it became clear that he was very much a ducker and a diver and his watchwords were very much 'What costs you nothing can't be dear' and 'Don't ask where it came from.'

"I think the reason why Derek Hockley stuck in my memory so much was that back then I'd never met anybody who spoke with a strong working class accent who looked like a posh person. He was a wheeler-dealer and a marvellous character. As far as I was concerned there was no way he did anything dishonest or illegal but you just knew - he was so sharp.

"We'd give him a price and we'd be making a little bit of a profit which he'd accept and then instead of putting on ten per cent he'd double or treble our price and put it in to his customer and get it accepted. His father had started the business and he'd expanded it and he was always after bigger contracts and we got involved with him after he'd become one of the major contractors for Ind Coope Brewery who had hundreds of pubs in the East End.

"He realised that in order to win contracts you didn't just turn up to meetings with brewery managers and architects looking like a wally, so he'd go very, very well dressed. They say 'Clothes maketh the man' and I think he was very wise to that and other rival builders hadn't quite got that panache. They'd go to meetings looking reasonably tidy but when Derek went people would remember him. He looked like money, he looked well dressed and he'd make an impression on people and I think that's why he did it. He was very clever like that.

"So when I came to do *Only Fools and Horses* I decided to have this character always trying to look the bees knees and trying to be elegant and smart, even if his taste wasn't quite as conservative as people might have liked. I decided to use some of Derek Hockley's attitudes and his dress-sense and I'd apply it to Del Boy. And all that smart, sharp dressing stuff in Del came from Derek. So even though Del, Rodney and Grandad were living in a Peckham council flat it seemed to be quite funny to find the head of the family spending a lot of money on his image.

"They could starve for the want of a slice of bread but Del would still have to have a new tie. Rodney, by contrast, always had the same clothes on and Grandad, well he wasn't really too worried. Even Del's jeans would have a crease put in the side of them because he thought that looked neat. He wasn't aware that he might look naff. He thought all these things looked smart. Some of them did but some of them looked just terrible."

"Del is so fastidious about his clothes and appearance and yet takes no notice of driving round in this funny old three-wheeler," David told the *Radio Times* in 1983. "So much time spent preening himself and yet he tries to pull the birds in the van! I find it all very amusing."

David discussed his ideas about Del with John Sullivan and costume designer Phoebe De Gaye and between the three of them the Del Boy, as seen in *Big Brother*, emerged. "John described him as a medallion man with a sovereign on each finger but I felt the medallion was too big and the rings were too many," said David. "I said I didn't think he'd have a ring on each finger, as that would look common rather than elegant. So we cut the number of them back to just a couple on each hand, the medallion became a chain with his initials on that he'd often wear over his shirt or jumper and we added a chunky bracelet."

Derek Hockley, who died some years ago, recognised the fact that David had taken some inspiration from him when he played

Del Boy in *Only Fools and Horses* and wrote to him. "He was delighted and very proud of the fact that he had been inspirational to me and that he was the original for Derek Trotter, if you like," David recalled. "He was flattered and pleased that I'd likened Del to him but funnily enough he was never known as Del."

"When I first read *Fools and Horses* scripts I remembered a building contractor who employed me as an electrician in the fifties," David told the *Radio Times* in 1989. "He wore a camel hair coat, lots of rings and he had that wonderful mannerism of twitching his neck. I've no idea what it means, but lots of them do it and it's a bit intimidating. I use those unconscious mannerisms to build up a character."

Del's confident swagger was David Jason's addition. "I'd seen it so many times with guys who fancy themselves," he said. "They develop a body language that is supposed to impress the birds I suppose. It's like a signal that 'I'm the business, look at me, I'm the cat's whiskers, I've got style, I've got class' which is really sort of wrong but it seemed to fit his personality because Del is full of it, especially when it came to chatting up girls. Like writers, actors are like magpies. They observe people and then sometimes pick things up from them and store them away and that's where that came from. It's just something I'd seen over the years. So you've got your character as created by the writer, then you pinch an idea from here, an observation from there and you hope that once you put it all together it makes a nice picture."

David has always had a soft spot for Derek Trotter. "He's a great character and I enjoy playing him so much because you can play all sides of him," he said. "Despite whatever happens to him he always bounces back, like a beach ball, however hard you push it down, Del will always bounce back."

"Del's heart has always been in the right place. In terms of human relationships he is a diamond because he'd give you anything ultimately and he cares for his family and his friends. His relationship with Rodney was wonderful – it was family life. They loved each other deeply even though they were always bickering about something."

"You can't help liking him," David said of Del in an interview with the *Radio Times* in 1983. "He is a little man trying to succeed against all the odds. He thinks that one day he will do the deal that will make him a millionaire. His education is of the streets so he does get spaced out sometimes by people who are well-read."

"I've always seen him as a sort of modern-day Robin Hood although he didn't really ever rob anyone," he said. "He's just into deals. It didn't matter if his gear was a bit hooky and he never asked where it came from. To him what was really important was how much he could knock it out for. One of the reasons why he was a failure was if he'd put as much energy into applying his brain to bigger things as he did to making a couple of quid on some bit of junk, then they would have been millionaires twenty years ago.

"In his manor he's the sort of bloke who knows everyone. There is no side to him and he didn't care who he sold to – black, white, Chinese, Jewish or whatever. Del treats them all the same. He'll rip off anyone he can – to him they are all equal. Having said that he treats people fairly. He'd never take money off the old, the infirm, the crippled. He'd never take advantage of people like that. And at the same time he would look after people. He cares about people and I think that's part of his charm – he had a real respect for older people. In a way he's a very moral character and very honest – well honestly dishonest!"

"The thing about Del is that although he's not honest, he's moral," David said in an interview in the *Radio Times* in 1985. "He'd sell you back your own watch, but if he made £500 and then bumped into a mate who was down on his luck, he's give him the lot. His other big problem is that he thinks small. But he's happy-go-lucky – the eternal optimist – and that's why people love him."

David has always rejected the suggestion that the series glamorised petty crime. "The whole point about Del Trotter is that he isn't that successful in what he does," he said. "It's easy come and easy go with him and some of what he sells is a bit iffy but most of it is just rubbish. How many times has he ever made any money out of the stuff he's sold? Hardly ever. He's forever getting burnt. Occasionally he makes a bit on a deal but then he loses it all on the next daft idea. So I can't actually see him glorifying living outside the law. It is a difficult one to quantify and I can't really defend him one hundred percent."

David's own theory is that most of the stuff Del sells is junk or fake rather than stolen. "If you go up to Oxford Street even now you'll see fly pitchers flogging their gear," he said. "You wouldn't believe that it still goes on. Just like Del Boy, they are there with their suitcases and a couple of lookouts selling something like dodgy scent. It's a tenner for three bottles. Everybody who goes up and buys it thinks it's knocked off but they don't say anything.

"The fact of the matter is it isn't stolen, it's fake. They buy it from a wholesaler, then sell it to people who think they are getting a bargain and that's the way I assume that Del Boy gets most of his gear. It's made somewhere like Taiwan or Singapore and they get it very cheap and so he doesn't mind selling it for a tenner because he's paid next to nothing for it and the punters are going potty for it. Sometimes when I'm in Oxford Street I stand there and watch and it just makes me laugh. I think: 'Who are the fools?' The guy has probably bought the fakes legitimately but he's giving people the impression it's knocked off to explain why he can afford to sell it so cheap!"

David has fallen prey to such a con himself. "I was on a tour once in the Far East with Derek Nimmo's theatre company and I went to this place in Dubai where they sell cheap perfume and aftershave," he said. "It was like a warehouse and it had every single scent in the world in exactly the right bottle with the right label and box. It was really cheap – it only cost me a fiver for half a dozen bottles.

"Later I found out why. What is in it is nothing more than water with a drop of the real stuff in. So that when you take the top off it smells ok but a few days after you've opened it it smells like cabbage water and it just stank. It had gone off and I had to throw it away. So much for my bargain aftershave!"

Del's family is central to his life. He's sacrificed a great deal, not least his chance of getting married as a young man, to bring up his younger brother Rodney when their father Reg walked out and Joan, their mum, died. "The family tie was always very strong for Del," said David. "He wasn't prepared to leave his family so if the girl didn't love him enough to take on the rest of the family then as far as Del was concerned she wasn't good enough for Del Boy and he'd elbow her. That would happen time and time again.

"At first Rodney was the younger brother who relied on Del to be fed. So Del was the breadwinner who had to go out and earn the money to put food on the table for him and Grandad. As they got older we'd see them bickering like all families do. It was usually something about Rodney not wanting to carry boxes round or be a lookout. It then became a battle of wits with Del trying to turn it all round to manoeuvre the situation to make Rodney feel important. Rodney would try to get out of the work and Del would have to use his brain and outwit him.

"Rodney would refuse to do something and then Del would say something like: 'But I can't do this without you Rodney, you are the brains of the outfit. You've got GCEs in Maths and Art. You are part of my design team and I need your artistic input into this.' He'd con him and then after a while Rodney would realise that he's being conned and being used. He'd started to see through Del but rather than say: 'Up yours' and walking out, he basically just does what Del asks. It's his loyalty back to Del, I suppose. The bond between them is stronger than any argument and ultimately they both recognise that."

Of course Grandad, and later Uncle Albert, would frequently get caught in the crossfire. "Grandad was family and yes Del loved him but it didn't stop Derek Trotter being Derek Trotter," said David. "If Grandad decided to take Rodney's side in an argument Del would say: 'Shut up you old git, what do you know? You're going senile.

You don't know what you're talking about' but if he took Del Boy's side then he'd praise him. It would be: 'There you are see, Grandad agreed. There you are Rodney, did you hear what Grandad said?' Grandad was used as a pawn. Del didn't mean any harm – it was simply that he wanted to get his own way and if it meant using Grandad then he'd use him."

The public have certainly taken David to their heart. He's undisputedly one of Britain's best-loved actors. He was awarded an OBE in 1993 and was knighted in 2005. However he's never courted publicity and avoids showbusiness parties, being happier at his home in Buckinghamshire with his family, wife Gill and daughter Sophie Mae. He loves his work, be it *Only Fools*, *The Darling Buds of May* or dramas like *A Touch of Frost* or *Porterhouse Blue*, but if he could choose, it would be without the attention he receives for it.

Not a hour goes by when David is out that someone doesn't shout something along the lines of: "Oi, Del Boy" or "You plonker". It's something that he's had to get used to. Nevertheless it means it's hard for him to lead a normal life. Having a quiet drink in pubs with friends has become impossible due to constant interruptions. And while David understands people's interest and is delighted that so many people love the show, it does become wearing when for the fortieth time that day someone asks him: "Where's Rodney?"

"I tend not to go anywhere that I don't have to," he said. "I don't go shopping or into pubs or the cinema much mainly because I know what's going to happen. It's part of the job and it is the downside but it is a small price to pay for the fun that we've had making the show and the enjoyment that it's brought people."

Indeed David is genuinely thrilled by the laughs he knows he and his colleagues on *Only Fools and Horses* have given people. "When you realise that you bring so much joy to people's lives, through television for Christ's sake, then it isn't all bad is it?" he said. "It's very satisfying and it makes me feel extremely privileged."

Only Fools and Horses has also given David the chance to make a difference in a way that few people ever will – and it's not something he has ever made public before. On several occasions he's helped bring people out of comas by recording tapes for them as Del Boy.

"Their families wrote to me asking me to do Del Boy on tape and asking me to talk to them in the character because it was their favourite show and they thought it might help," he said. "And it did, because they've written back to thank me. To me that has been the very best side of playing Del Boy. I felt very fortunate that I was able to help. It's an unbelievable power and shows just what a powerful medicine comedy is."

Fact file:

Name: David Jason

Born: February 2nd 1940 in London

Other TV work includes: Crossroads, Do Not Adjust Your Set, Hark at Barker, The Top Secret Life of Edgar Briggs, Lucky Feller, Open All Hours, A Sharp Intake of Breath, Porterhouse Blue, A Bit of a Do, Amongst Barbarians, The Chemist, The Darling Buds of May, The Bullion Boys, A Touch of Frost, March in Windy City, All the King's Men, Micawber, The Quest, The Second Quest, The Final Quest, Ghostboat, Diamond Geezer, The Colour of Magic, Albert's Memorial, Muddle Earth, Come Rain Come Shine, The Royal Bodyguard.

MY FAVOURITE EPISODES BY DAVID JASON

David Jason doesn't have an out and out favourite episode because there are so many to choose from. He loves *Heroes and Villains*, particularly for the Batman and Robin scenes. "I love visual stuff because I'm a visually orientated actor," he said. "So I like the chandelier episode and the bar hatch one obviously. They were all such great fun to do and when I was filming *Only Fools* I couldn't wait to get up in the morning to go to rehearsals because we just had good fun. We'd invent things and have wonderful lines to say. I remember something Ronnie Barker once said to me when we were doing *Open All Hours* which has stuck with me. We'd just done something in rehearsals that made us both laugh and he said: 'Isn't it marvellous?' and I said: 'What's that?' and he said: 'Well we get paid extremely well for making ourselves laugh.' And I've never forgotten that. He was right. It's a very fortunate life. You get paid very well to do something you love doing and to make yourself laugh. You can't complain about that can you?"

DAVID'S REAL NAME

David's real name is David White but he changed it to David Jason when he began acting professionally because there was already an actor called David White. "When I got my Equity card there was already a David White – so I chose Jason, after *Jason and the Argonauts*, a book I really loved at school," he said.

SOUVENIRS

David is no great collector of souvenirs but he has kept a few things to remind him of *Only Fools and Horses*. He said: "I've got a couple of bottles of Peckham Spring water. I'll keep them forever. I won't drink them. After all, it's BBC water and not only that, would you drink something Del Trotter had made? I've also got a few cast and crew T-shirts and I've got one of Del's flat caps."

Nicholas Lyndhurst - Rodney Trotter

 Nicholas Lyndhurst was sitting at home in his London flat at around 5pm on a Thursday in the spring of 1981 when he heard the double thwack of post landing on his doormat. The thick envelopes bearing BBC Television stickers contained six scripts and a covering letter from Ray Butt explaining that they were for a new series called *Only Fools and Horses* and asking him to read them with a view to him being considered for the part of Rodney.

Nicholas put the scripts aside. He was pushed for time as he was meeting friends for a drink at six o'clock. "I thought: 'I'll read them tomorrow' and I went out," he recalled. "I came home about 11pm that night, slightly the worse for wear and read the covering note again and noticed a line I hadn't seen before which read: 'Could you come and see us tomorrow afternoon.' I thought: 'Christ – an audition, I'd better start reading these things.'

"I had two options. To start reading them there and then or get up early in the morning. I decided to start reading one before I went to bed. That was it. I started reading the first one and I ended up reading the whole lot and didn't finish until about 2am. I just couldn't wait to turn over the page. I was laughing out loud."

Nicholas went off to the BBC the following afternoon thinking he was going to audition. He didn't know at that time that he was the first and only choice to play Rodney. Some weeks later he was called back to read with David Jason and a few days after that was asked to read with both David and Lennard Pearce. "I was oblivious to the fact that I was cast until the moment that they said: 'We'd like to go with you three' at the third meeting because that uncertainty was what I was used to," he said.

Nicholas liked the idea of playing Rodney. "He's very much an innocent and quite sheltered from the real world and had always had his brother to look after the real nasties," he said. "I was – and probably still am – quite awkward and gawky and I accentuated that for the character. I also based him on the younger brother of a friend of mine who was always trying to be one of the lads. Rodney is like that. He'd always be trying to be cool and failing miserably and you see that a lot with young blokes.

"Rodney relies on Del a great deal and, although in the early days he wanted to break free from him, he never knew how to. They were always rowing with each other but David and I decided that they would be scoring points off each other rather than shouting at each other all the time because that would just get boring for the audience. There's no real wonder though that Rodney never got his own enterprise off the ground. After all, who was his role model? Del Trotter and he's not really a great success. Poor Rodney was bound to fail.

"Rodney would moan about having to be Del's lookout or carrying boxes around but ultimately he owes Del a lot and he knows that. Del was sixteen years old when their mum died and Rodney was just two. Del could have cleared off and Rodney knows he could have gone into care and probably should have gone into care. These days he would be taken into care just like that. They wouldn't let a sixteen year old bring up a two year old.

"They fight like cat and dog but actually they care about each other deeply. Del also needs Rodney and as the series progressed we realised that more and more. In *The Jolly Boys Outing* there's a scene at the end of the breakwater where Del is saying he's never achieved anything and Rodney was saying: 'Yeah but you will.' There is a very strong bond with them and if the chips were down Rodney would die for him."

Rodney's relationships with girls never really worked out. "The trouble is, he's in a perpetual state of puberty," Nicholas told the *Radio Times* in 1985. "When he does meet a girl, he can't find anything to say to her. But he's got GCEs in Maths and Art and there's even a streak of honesty in him. If he'd been born into a middle-class family he'd probably have gone to university, but Del made him leave school early because he needed him down on the market."

Rodney eventually moved on and met and fell in love with Cassandra. "Up until he met Cassie he'd not had a lot of luck with girlfriends," said Nicholas. "He failed repeatedly and never had a steady girlfriend. Rodney was getting a bit old to stay that way so I was glad when he met someone and it worked out. Also, as far as viewers were concerned Rodney had always been in lust rather than in love and now he was really smitten.

"Their relationship was never easy though. Rodney got riled by her job at the bank in a childish way and Cassandra would give as good as she got and that's what started the fighting. She also teased him a lot hoping he'd see the funny side of it but often he'd just sulk. He didn't like the way her job at the bank took up so much of her time but he was never jealous of her success."

Nicholas began acting at the age of six, albeit only in a school nativity play. "I was a donkey and my only line was hee-haw," he laughed. "I don't think that was what got me interested in acting and I honestly couldn't tell you what did. I remember thinking I wanted to be in an advert, maybe because I thought it was a way of getting lots of chocolate, but I don't recall ever wanting to be in films or on telly. Eventually I did three adverts but only my hands were featured!"

At the age of eight he began asking his mum if he could go to drama school and after two years she gave in and he went off to the Corona Drama Academy in West London. "I think my Mum thought it would get it out of my system," he said. It didn't and he stayed there until he was eighteen using money he earned from adverts to pay his tuition fees.

His first television work came in two BBC Schools productions followed by lots of non-speaking work as an extra. His first big part came in a BBC production of *Anne of Avonlea*, a period drama. That was followed soon after by a leading role as Peter in an adaptation of the classic children's book *Heidi*, again for the BBC. Fame came at fourteen when he landed the starring role in *The Prince and the Pauper* which saw him performing the dual role of both peasant and royal.

Nicholas then had a lean time for a few years around the time he took his 'O' Levels. He was also growing at the rate of knots. "Producers were seeing me in *The Prince And The Pauper,* which was transmitted a year after we'd filmed it, and deciding to get that little lad Nicholas Lyndhurst in to audition for something. The trouble was by the time they did, that little lad was getting on for six foot and was a bit of a spotty Herbert by then!

"Work went a bit quiet at that age and I remember thinking that was it because a lot of kids don't make the transition to becoming an adult actor," he said. Fortunately Nicholas's quiet spell was only temporary and in 1978 he landed the role of Ronnie Barker's cockney son Raymond in *Going Straight*, the follow-up to *Porridge*, followed soon after by the part of Adam in the comedy series *Butterflies*. It was that role that led directly to him being cast as Rodney in *Only Fools and Horses*.

Nicholas has never forgotten his first day filming *Only Fools and Horses*. "We were at Chapel Street market and we had all these market stalls set up," he said. "We took a break from filming because it was pouring down with rain and I was standing there with an umbrella waiting for the rain to stop so we could continue.

All the production team were standing around, a lot of them without umbrellas, getting soaked.

"I saw a little girl hurrying to school using our stalls to keep out of the rain and then she suddenly ran and stood next to me using my umbrella to keep dry. She could see there was a camera and people standing about and she said to me: 'What are you doing, mister?' and I said: 'We're making a television programme' and she said: 'What's it called then?' I said: 'It's called *Only Fools and Horses.*' She considered that and she looked at us standing in the bucketing rain and she said: 'Where are the horses then?'

"I thought that was classic. She didn't know how funny what she said was but it was easy to interpret it that she meant: 'Everyone else in London is under cover and you bloody idiots are standing in the rain getting soaked.' It was pure John Sullivan!"

Over the years Nicholas has met more than his fair share of real-life Rodneys, but none of them sticks in his memory as much as the driver of a Capri who spotted him in Sloane Avenue in London. "I was walking home with a couple of bags of shopping one day and it was pouring with rain," he recalled. "I was soaked and there was a line of traffic waiting at a red light. Suddenly I was aware of the thump-thump of a loud stereo system. I walked past this Capri – a real Rodney-mobile – and then the lights changed and this car came parallel with me. I was aware of being clocked by this real geezer with a little earring and his two mates and I could hear them going: 'Yeah, it's definitely him.' The window came down and this voice boomed out: 'Rodney, you plonker.' He then laughed loudly. I heard a wheel spin and he drove straight bang into the van in front. This guy had seen the lights change again and the traffic move up a bit but the van in front hadn't got through and he was too busy clocking me and he wrote off his Capri.

"I then had the satisfaction of walking past him again and he was looking very sad and shocked. He had a look of total disbelief on his face not to mention worry when this very big van driver got out to have a word with him. I nearly collapsed laughing. I did want to stay and gloat but I didn't. For about a week afterwards I'd smile every time I walked past that spot!"

Away from the cameras Nicholas is nothing like the character he plays. Witty and articulate, he is good company and couldn't be more different from dopey Rodney. Like David Jason, he shuns the showbusiness party scene and likes his privacy. He lives by the sea in West Sussex with his wife Lucy and their son Archie and is a keen windsurfer, an advanced diver and has a private pilot's licence.

"It's not Rodney's sort of stuff at all," said Nicholas. "But I've always lived by the sea and love it and as a little boy I was always in love with anything that flew. I wanted to fly from way back when I was a kid. In fact at one stage when I was much younger I thought seriously about going into the Royal Air Force – until I saw what qualifications were required. I'd hate people to think: 'He does these things because he's made a bit of money now and he's just showing off.' I'd do these things whatever I did for a living."

Nicholas said he and David became friends almost straight away when the show began. "We hit it off from day one and I think that was down to luck and chemistry," he said. "I had been told that David might be a bit difficult to work with. I work with him fine so maybe I'm a bit difficult to work with as well. We've always got on well. We have never had any serious rows. Sure, we discuss things but I can't remember any problem other than something technical to do with filming. We give each other advice but we'd never tell each other what to do.

"*Only Fools* has always been a very happy show to work on and everyone gets on. I was nineteen when I started on it and it covered some very formative years and I do miss it and I always will miss it. I've had success with other things whilst I was doing *Only Fools* but it was always great to come back to it."

Fact file:
Name: Nicholas Lyndhurst
Born: April 21st 1961 in Emsworth, Hampshire
Other TV work includes: Our Show, Anne of Avonlea, Heidi, The Prince and the Pauper, Going Straight, Butterflies, To Serve Them All My Days, The Two of Us, The Piglet Files, Stalag Luft, Goodnight Sweetheart, Gulliver's Travels, David Copperfield, Thin Ice, Murder in Mind, Lassie, Rock & Chips

SAVED ON FILM

Lennard Pearce once said to me as we were walking past a shop: 'Of course, I won't ever die now' and I said: 'Why is that?' and he just pointed to a video recorder, which were quite new in homes then. That made him very happy and I often think of him saying that and I suppose he was right."

MY FAVOURITE EPISODE BY NICHOLAS LYNDHURST

"I've got more favourite moments than favourite episodes really," said Nicholas. "I love the Batman and Robin sequence from *Heroes and Villains*, the chandelier scene in *A Touch of Glass,* Grandad's 'war is hell' speech from *The Russians Are Coming* and all the stuff between Trigger and Rodney like when he asks him why he calls him Dave in *Homesick,* which was Rodney's first and last stand with Trig."

Lennard Pearce - Grandad Trotter

For an actor who had spent more than forty years in showbusiness, fame came late in life to Lennard Pearce. Becoming a household name as the Trotter boys' elderly Grandad gave him a great deal of satisfaction and, according to friends, a new lease of life when he had previously been thinking about retirement.

He was born Leonard Pearce (he later changed the spelling to Lennard) at Burlington Mews West, London on October 31st 1915 to Rose, a housekeeper, and Sidney, a rifleman with the King's Royal Rifles. Lennard studied drama at the Royal Academy of Dramatic Art and was in the armed forces entertainment unit ENSA during the Second World War. Afterwards he spent most of his professional life in the theatre. In the early sixties he understudied Doolittle in the original West End production of *My Fair Lady* and played the part for more than 150 performances.

He joined the National Theatre under Sir Laurence Olivier in 1965 and appeared in a string of plays there including *The Royal Hunt of the Sun*, *Much Ado About Nothing*, *Rosencrantz and Guildenstern Are Dead* and *Tartuffe*. He was also a member of the Royal Shakespeare Company and in addition played at many repertory theatres.

In 1975 Lennard was Owl in *Winnie the Pooh* at the Phoenix

Theatre in London and two years later he played Harper and Mr Witherspoon in a revival of the comedy thriller *Arsenic and Old Lace* at the Westminster Theatre. Leading television roles eluded him though until he landed the part of Grandad in *Only Fools and Horses* but he did appear in small roles in *Cathy Come Home, Take Three Girls, Dr Finlay's Casebook, Coronation Street, Crown Court* and *Minder*.

Sir Anthony Hopkins appeared on stage with Lennard and has fond memories of him. "He was a very nice man," he recalled. "A really gentle guy. I knew him at the National Theatre where he was playing a few small parts and I hadn't seen him for years until I saw him in *Only Fools and Horses* and it was nice to see him playing a major part in such a great series."

After being cast as Grandad, Lennard relished his work on the programme. "I have never been in a hit series before and it's nice being recognised," he told the *News of the World* during transmission of the third series. He said he had been dubious about doing the third series.

"The first two were so well constructed I didn't think John Sullivan could keep it up but I was wrong. The standards are just as high and I aim to be around if there is a fourth series. It's not only a wonderful part but the script is tremendous. There's so much for us all to get our teeth into." Sadly Lennard never lived to fulfil his wish and appear in the fourth series.

He had begun filming the series on location in December 1984 and had recorded scenes for the episode *Hole In One* in which Grandad was to fall down into a pub cellar in order to gain compensation from the brewery. But, ten days into filming and before the episode had been completed, he suffered a heart attack and was rushed to hospital where, a few days later on December 15th, he had a second heart attack which this time proved fatal.

Even as he was recovering from the first heart attack, Lennard's mind had still been on the job. He fully expected to recover and was anxious to get back to filming the show as his agent at the time, Carole James, recalled. "I remember going to see him in hospital after he'd had the first heart attack and he was in intensive care and he was sitting in bed surrounded by all the machinery," she said.

"We started chatting and he said: 'Darling, do you think you could get me the scripts in here because we've started filming and I want to be ready for when I get out.' And that was the kind of professional he was. He wanted to be preparing himself to carry on working. The job was very important to him and he didn't want to let people down. He loved going off to film the series on location."

Nicholas Lyndhurst recalled at the time of Lennard's death: "He was so thrilled at the reaction he got from the public. For the first time in his career he was being recognised in the street and approached by fans for autographs."

Lennard, who never married, lived in a small flat in London and his landlady and her daughter would always attend studio recordings and give him a lift home afterwards. He had been ill in 1980, the year before he was cast as Grandad in *Only Fools and Horses*. He nearly died and afterwards considered retiring from acting. At the time of his illness he was appearing at the Bristol Old Vic. "I lost my balance and kept falling asleep when I wasn't meant to," he told the *Radio Times* in November 1983.

"I had to give up. It was hypertension. I was a workaholic and never took a holiday. I never relaxed. I have a different philosophy now and I always urge young people, if they are too tense, to get away and relax. It was many months before I could work again and I nearly gave up. And then this series gave me a new lease of life."

It also earned him more than his jobs in the theatre and, although his pay cheques from the series were not huge, they enabled him to treat his friends. "I remember one Christmas he came in to the office with a very nice present for my assistant and I," recalled Carole James. "It obviously gave him pleasure to have money to spend like that."

Carole recalled accompanying Lennard to a BBC Christmas party. "He met several people he knew there including Jan Francis and then Lenny Henry came over," she said. "Lennard said to him: 'I think you're wonderful, I'm a great fan of yours' and Lenny immediately said: 'And I'm a great fan of yours too,' and that really thrilled him because Lenny had been a big star for some time."

John Sullivan remembered taking a phone call at home from Lennard. "He phoned to say that he'd just got home from doing his weekly shopping at a supermarket and some people had called him Grandad," he recalled. "After nearly fifty years in the business it was the first time he'd been recognised and he was absolutely thrilled, he really was. To me that was one of the saddest things about his death. He'd worked all his life in an attempt to really make it in the acting business and he finally made it for those brief few years and that was a real high spot for him and then fate took it away from him."

"We were very fortunate that Nick, Lennard and I got on so well," said David Jason. "We'd always said if we ever started not getting on we'd just walk away from the series because it's hard enough working in comedy. There is no point in trying to do it just for the money when you've got to work in an atmosphere where no one likes each other or doesn't talk to each other so we ensured that we avoided any form of conflict so it never came up. If we had anything to say about a scene then we would say it and we'd discuss it and work it out and when we'd decided whoever was right then that would be the way we'd play it.

"Lennard was great fun too because he was a man of great experience and when you had to say terrible things to him like 'shut up you old git' and he looked hurt you'd feel awful. But in real life it went straight over his head and he never took offence personally. He was just a lovely guy."

"He's sorely missed to this day," said Nicholas Lyndhurst. "He knew exactly how to say his lines so perfectly. David and I would often have lots of lines and he'd be sitting there watching telly and then he'd just have one line and he'd bring the house down. We used to say: 'You sod. We're giving you a twenty minute lead-in to what you are going to say' and he just used to sit there with a fag in his mouth and say: 'I know – but I'm old. I'm allowed.' He was great. He loved people calling him Grandad and even signed my twenty-first birthday card 'Grandad'.

"I remember first meeting him at the BBC. He was quite dapper and I wondered how this tidy man could be going to be our scruffy and smelly Grandad. But a bit of stubble and an old scarf and hat made a tremendous difference. He was also such an old giggler but he could get away with it by turning it into a wheeze or a cough. If you watch some episodes closely – like *Homesick* when he gave me a cigarette case and in the shelter in *The Russians Are Coming* - you can hear him wheeze, when he was actually giggling. He could laugh without shaking his shoulders but I can't do that."

Ken MacDonald, who played Nag's Head landlord Mike Fisher, knew Lennard from when they both appeared at the same theatre in Leatherhead. He recalled: "He was a lovely man and he couldn't believe it when he became a star in *Only Fools* because basically he'd retired after having a life in the theatre. Then suddenly his career was taking off in television and he was absolutely thrilled. It was so sad when he was taken from us so soon at a time when he was really enjoying what he was doing."

Fact file:
Name: Lennard Pearce
Born: October 31st 1915 in Paddington, London
Died: December 15th 1984
Other TV work: Cathy Come Home, Take Three Girls, Dr Finlay's Casebook, Coronation Street, Crown Court, Minder and Shroud For A Nightingale

MEETING HITLER

"Lennard told me he met Hitler once," recalled Nicholas Lyndhurst. "He was on tour in Berlin in the late thirties and he was in a room at a theatre and Hitler and all his cronies came in and he told me: 'Knowing what I know now, what I wouldn't have given for a gun.'"

Buster Merryfield - Uncle Albert

 This sounds like an outline for a novel: a man who always wanted to become a professional actor, but had to be content being in amateur shows because he'd vowed to his old mum that he'd stick with his secure job in a bank, retires and then lands a starring role in the nation's favourite TV show. Strange, but true. After all, that's just what happened to Buster Merryfield.

Born Harry Merryfield in Battersea, south London, in 1920, he was the second child of a caterer's porter, also called Harry, and his wife Lily, a part-time waitress. Their first child, Irene, two years Buster's senior, died when she was eight.

He was nicknamed Buster by his grandfather because he weighed more than nine pounds at birth. The nickname stuck and he always refused to give his real name. His parents were determined that Buster should have more opportunities than they had had themselves. They encouraged him to get a professional job and were delighted when, at seventeen, he was taken on as a junior clerk by National Westminster Bank.

He wasn't long in the job though, when the storm clouds of war gathered over Europe – and Buster was just eighteen when war began to look likely in the late summer of 1939. He immediately signed up to join the Territorial Army along with many of his colleagues at the Lombard Street branch of NatWest bank. On September 2nd 1939, the day before war was declared, he, along with thousands of young men, was called up to active full-time duty. "Day after day they'd been calling out all the reserves," he recalled. "As soon as they heard, people would down their pens and say 'cheerio mate' and they'd be off. Then it was my turn. Someone ran in the bank and said that the Territorials had been called out and everyone cheered and we all ran off and joined our units and I went off to mine in Fulham."

Buster joined the Royal Artillery as a gunner (their equivalent of private) but soon gained promotion to lance-bombardier, then bombardier and at the same time worked as a physical training instructor. Three years later he was offered the chance to train as an officer and he jumped at it.

His first posting as a newly commissioned lieutenant was in Windsor where he and his men formed part of a troop manning four Bofors anti-aircraft guns positioned on the edge of town. He must have impressed his captain because within weeks Buster was given command of his own troop but this time on four Bofors positioned inside Windsor Castle. While his men slept in the stables, officers were allowed to sleep inside the castle itself, albeit on the library floor.

Sometime later he was sent by train to Glasgow where he and 2,000 other men boarded the troop ship the SS Almanzora. "We still had no idea what our final destination would be even after we sailed," he said. "People would try to work out which direction we were heading by looking at the stars and some of them decided we were heading towards South America."

Later Buster learned why trying to work out where they were heading was so difficult; the ship had been zigzagging in order to put German U-boats off their scent. Weeks later they arrived at their final destination, Durban in South Africa. It was there that Buster came face to face with the enemy when he was put in charge of a ship containing 1,000 German prisoners of war before they were transported to Canada.

"There was only one German officer on the ship and the rest were men," Buster recalled. "He had a cabin to himself and was guarded by two marines and I had to visit him twice a day. He told me with a smile that he'd escaped three times since his initial capture and he'd continue to keep trying. He didn't manage to."

Weeks later Buster found himself aboard another ship which arrived in Bombay, India. That was followed by a five-day journey across India on a cramped train to Ranchi, which the British army used as a base from which to send men onto fighting units. Buster had to train newly arrived recruits in the art of jungle warfare. "It was very physical," he recalled. "My job was to train people to live and survive in the jungle. We'd be left in the jungle for weeks and have to survive. One time I was left on my own and told to work out where to take the troops. It was exciting because you never knew what you might come up against from snakes to tigers and I enjoyed all that.

"One day I nearly died. I'd discovered that the quickest way to travel was along dried up riverbeds because otherwise you'd have to cut your way through lots of jungle. On this particular day I was walking down a riverbed as wide as the Thames with monkeys swinging in the trees and beautiful birds flying around and sitting in trees. I turned a corner and saw all these vultures picking at the carcass of a cow. For some reason I decided to fire my pistol to see them all fly away. They all flew up then they saw me and down they came – like the film *The Birds* – and they were coming for me.

"I ran up the bank at the side of the riverbed and they were chasing me and when I got to the top of the riverbank I ran into the dark jungle knowing they wouldn't follow. I ran through and ended up jumping into a tributary. But because it was covered over by trees the mud in the bottom of it was still wet and I sank straight down into it. I was soon up to my waist. I panicked. The birds were all gathered nearby and I was up to my waist in mud. I thought I was going to die. I thought: 'No one will ever know what happened to me.'

"I tried to move but every time I moved my legs I went down an inch. I was too far in to reach anything to grab. I was sinking deeper and deeper. It was getting hopeless. I was miles from anywhere and there were no other soldiers nearby but I started to shout which was a risk in itself because it would let tigers know where I was.

"I was there for about an hour and still sinking gradually. I was almost asleep and suddenly I heard a branch crack and I thought that was it: a tiger was going to finish me off. But I was lucky – it wasn't a tiger, it was a young Indian girl dressed in a sari. She just stood there at the top of the bank staring at me. Then she turned and ran through the woods. Half an hour later a lot of people came through the trees and they threw a rope and pulled me out and took me to their village."

Afterwards Buster found himself back at his unit but soon fell sick with a range of illnesses including malaria and dysentery. One illness – thought to have been caused by an allergy to a jungle plant – caused his face to swell up massively so that he couldn't even open his eyes and he was sent back by train to Bombay. "I was declared unfit for tropical service and put on an Australian hospital ship HMS Wanganella back to England," he recalled.

Once recovered he was ordered to take charge of a battery of Bofors guns on a cliff top in Kent tasked with shooting down V1 doodlebug flying bombs that were wreaking havoc and considerably weakening morale in London. Buster's guns were the second line of defence after the bigger ack-ack guns and before RAF fighters had a go, followed by the last line of defence in London, barrage balloons.

"I believe about eight out of ten were destroyed before they could do any damage," he recalled. "They'd reach us in waves of thirty or forty a time and there were mid-air explosions every few seconds as the guns scored a direct hit. We were busy day and night with them and we slept in tents alongside our guns, always ready for action."

In 1946 Buster was demobbed and resumed his career with NatWest Bank. He'd married in April 1942 and in 1947 his wife Iris had a daughter, Karen. Buster wanted to become an actor but decided to stick with his bank job. "I wanted to leave but my Mum made me promise to stay there," he said. "She said that with a wife and baby to look after, I'd be stupid to give it up. My parents hadn't had the opportunities that I had and I felt I owed it to them to stay in my secure job."

Instead Buster threw himself into amateur dramatics performing in dozens of shows with various theatre companies before forming his own group which became known as The Merryfield Characters. With it he directed more than forty plays, starring in every one of them and winning many awards. Meanwhile, his bank career flourished and by 1978 he was manager of the Thames Ditton branch.

It was while working at the bank that he grew his famous whiskers - much to the anger of his boss. "I've had the beard on and off since the war," he said. "And I think I was one of the first people in the bank to have one. I grew it while I was working in the bank because I had to have it for a role I was playing. The day I turned up with about four days' stubble on my manager sent for me and said: 'What's all this you've got?' In those days you see there was never anyone in a bank with a beard. I said: 'I'm sorry, I'm growing this for a part that I'm playing' and he said: 'Well, if you want to look like a ruddy gorilla' and really gave me a wigging. But would you believe that after a few months all four cashiers on the counters had beards and I think they did it really to get at the manager because he told me off!"

Buster retired from his job at NatWest at the age of fifty-seven. Feeling that his late mum would have been satisfied with his forty years at the bank, he decided to give full-time acting a try. He wrote off to countless theatres and companies, trying to get work – to no avail. Even one of the more encouraging replies from Nicholas Young, artistic director at the Connaught Theatre, Worthing, indicated that he thought Buster's hopes were forlorn.

Buster recalled: "He wrote back saying that there was no way that a man of fifty-seven and an ex-bank manager could suddenly walk into rep," he recalled. "He explained that they only got two Equity cards per year and they gave them to drama students who helped out behind the scenes as assistant stage managers and who might just get a part in a play as a stand in if another actor fell ill.

"But he said I'd written an interesting letter and if I was ever passing to pop in and see him. It was the closest I'd got to an interview so I went down there and he said all that he'd said in his letter and I said, quite tongue-in-cheek: 'You surprise me. You're an artistic director and I thought the least you could do is to give me an audition because I could be the next Laurence Olivier and I'm really giving you first refusal!'

"He laughed and that was the catalyst that I think got him interested. 'Don't worry,' I said. 'Whatever the outcome of this interview, if you don't give me employment, that won't stop me becoming an actor because I'm going to do it whether you give me a job or not.' In the end he gave me an audition and he gave me a job and I had fifteen weeks of work with that theatre!"

Buster became one of the oldest assistant stage managers ever and spent the next few months sweeping up, making tea and emptying ashtrays – all for £40 a week. "I was the oldest 'boy' in the business," he laughed. "But I was just happy to be there and the whole cast were very kind to me." More importantly he also got small parts in three plays, *A Midsummer Night's Dream*, *Joseph and His Amazing Technicolor Dreamcoat* and *Equus* alongside actors like Bernard Bresslaw, Shirley Stelfox and Nyree Dawn Porter.

Buster's break paid off and he landed a few minor roles including parts in the BBC dramas *The Citadel* and *Hannah*. Another one of those early TV jobs came in 1983 when he got a small part in Anglia Television's PD James' drama *Shroud For A Nightingale*, which starred Roy Marsden as Commander Adam Dalgliesh. By coincidence while filming the drama Buster met Lennard Pearce who also had a small role in the production and whose untimely death the following year would change Buster's life forever.

"I was playing a pathologist and Lennard was playing the man on the gate of a big hospital. I had to drive up in a Rolls Royce and stop at the gate and Lennard put his head out and I'd say who I was and he'd open the gate and I'd drive in and that was the only contact on screen that we had together. He was a nice fellow, rather quiet and very pleasant company and we had lunch together. We talked a bit about what he'd done previously but we didn't talk much about *Only Fools and Horses*. Of course when I first went up for the part of Uncle Albert I was saddened to learn that he'd died."

After he'd filmed his first two episodes of *Only Fools and Horses* Buster had no real idea that he was going to be a regular in the show. "I'd done the part of Uncle Albert in *Strained Relations* and *Hole in One* and I thought that was probably it. I'd helped them out at a difficult time and I'd enjoyed doing it and didn't think I'd done badly and hadn't let them down which was always my main concern. It wasn't until several episodes later that I actually felt I was in it for good."

Perhaps inevitably for a man who only became a professional actor late in life, Buster always worried about his performance. He once told me that although he'd watch the show with his family, he'd also tape it and then watch it again on his own "to see what I've done wrong."

He loved playing Uncle Albert and was overjoyed by the response he got from the series. "The most pleasurable thing about playing Albert," he said in 1998, "is that I can walk down any street or get on any bus or train and people smile and go: 'There's Uncle

Albert' – and that's magic. It's like having a magic wand and that's lovely."

Only Fools and Horses viewers always saw Uncle Albert pinching Del's brandy on screen but off screen Buster never touched a drop. That said, he could rarely go in a pub without a rum appearing on his table. "'Alright Albert,' they go," he once recalled. "It's very kind of them but I swap it for an orange juice!" He explained "I'm tee-total and I don't smoke either. I wouldn't drink or smoke for the Queen. I've never had a drink in my life and I've never smoked in my life and this was largely due to my boxing career which I took up when I was about twelve.

"My gym master at school said: 'If ever you want to be a champion then you should never smoke and never drink.' Now I'm a pretty dedicated chap so I put the blinkers on and went for it and I wanted to be a champion. I'm pretty strong willed so I never touched a drop or smoked nor have even been tempted to since!"

And when Buster was in the army during the war his pals would always ask him to make sure they got back to barracks. He smiled: "They knew they could rely on me because I'd go to a party with them and if someone looked in then I'd probably be the liveliest without having a drink at all. I was a dedicated boxer and took it very seriously. My whole life was physical fitness. I'd never stay in at night as I'd always be out running round the block. It all paid off though and I became Schoolboy Boxing Champion of Great Britain and used to knock everyone out. Later during the war I became Southern Command Army Boxing Champion in 1945."

Sadly Buster died on June 23rd 1999, eleven days after being diagnosed with a brain tumour. His wife Iris was at his bedside. It was a loss felt across the country and particularly by his *Only Fools and Horses* co-stars. David Jason paid tribute, saying: "Buster Merryfield's death is a great loss to me personally, as well as to his family and the rest of the country. He was a great man, a joy to work with. I will seriously miss him, both as a friend and as an actor."

Nicholas Lyndhurst said: "He was a gentle, sweet-natured man and he will be greatly missed by everyone who knew him. He made the role of Uncle Albert a national institution."

"It is with a heavy heart that I pen these few inadequate words in memory of dear Buster," David Jason later wrote in the *Only Fools and Horses* Appreciation Society's newsletter *Hookie Street.* "As you may be aware we, the team who made *Only Fools and Horses* in real life, are like the Trotters in television life – we are family. So to lose Buster was like losing a real 'Uncle Albert', a real friend. Buster's cheery nature and natural good humour was always a joy to behold; a hard worker and talented actor was his CV. I, like the rest of the country, mourn his passing but thankfully 'Uncle Albert' will remain with us for a long time to come, giving us warmth and humour. We will miss you Uncle Albert."

Gwyneth Strong said: "I have many memories of Buster, not least that he was a true gentleman with lovely old fashioned manners. We often had long gaps between series or Christmas specials and during one of these breaks I had my second child Lottie. Buster, of course, congratulated me on this event. But every time we came back after a break he would tease me saying: 'How many children did you have this time?' My children loved him and Lottie thought he was Father Christmas for a long time. He will be missed by us all."

The first time I met Buster was in the lobby of a Bristol hotel in 1990. It was just after 6am but that didn't seem to worry Buster. I later learned he was a man who was enthusiastic about working, and indeed life in general, whatever the time of day. We joined around forty crew and extras on a coach and travelled a few miles through Bristol to the Broadwalk Shopping Centre where some early scenes for the 1990 Christmas special, *Rodney Come Home*, were to be filmed.

I was lucky enough to watch the filming of a number of scenes including the one where Del tried to flog some dodgy dolls to unimpressed punters with Albert unhappily acting as his look-out. Later, over lunch from the catering wagon, came my time to interview Buster for a newspaper series about *Only Fools* which was published in the *Daily Mirror*. We chatted about his life, particularly his late break into acting and his love of *Only Fools and Horses*.

What struck me most though, was what a thoroughly decent and friendly man he was, and how tenderly he spoke of his wife Iris, who he explained he'd married just a week after meeting her at an ice rink forty-eight years previously, and his daughter, Karen. During a subsequent interview he talked fondly of his grandsons, telling me: "They are smashing lads and I can't spend enough time with them." Quite clearly, his family were the mainstay of his life.

But it wasn't just his family who Buster cared about. He loved the fame *Only Fools* had brought him – and with his marvellous beard he was unlikely to go unrecognised. Many children thought he was Father Christmas, a role he was happy to play as he explained during another interview: "I always tell children when I meet them in the street that I'm not like one of these chaps in a shop with a false beard on - I am Santa Claus and let them have a pull of my beard and they usually turn to their mums and say: 'It is Santa Claus!'

"Then they ask me where I live and where the elves are and so I give them a whole story. It's wonderful going out during Christmas week with my big coat on and woollen hat and these kids see you and I do look like Father Christmas. They love it and so do I because I love children - I went to school with them!"

The last time I saw Buster was January 1998 when I went to see him at his home in Verwood near Bournemouth to talk to him for my book *The Only Fools and Horses Story*. Over several hours – which included a nice lunch of bangers and mash cooked by Iris - he told me much about his life and work, and in particular his wartime service and how he landed the role of Uncle Albert, his enthusiasm and zest for life being a clear theme throughout his life. I also found it somewhat ironic how, having become famous for playing an old sea salt whose war record was dubious to say the least, Buster by contrast had served his country with distinction during the war.

The BBC sent copies of the book to the cast, who'd generously given up their time to talk about the show they all loved so much. The following evening my mobile phone rang. It was Buster. He was just calling to thank me for the book and what I'd written about him, which was decent of him.

Buster was clearly adored by his family, admired by those of us who were lucky enough to have met him and loved by millions more who watched him on television. He was a man who achieved more in his lifetime than many others dream of, and his legacy lives on as dear old Uncle Albert in many episodes of *Only Fools and Horses*. I know that would have delighted him.

Fact file:
Name: Buster Merryfield
Born: November 27th 1920 in Battersea, London
Died: June 23rd 1999
Other TV work includes: Hannah, The Citadel, Strangers and Brothers, The Third Age, The World of Paul McKenna, Shroud For A Nightingale and A Tale of Four Ports

ALBERT'S TIPPLE

Albert's rum was really a mix of Coca-Cola and water. In real life Buster's favourite tipple was cream soda, which he only ever bought at Christmas.

Filming the first market scene

A ticket to an early studio recording

The first script

THE OLD DAYS

A signed photo of
Lennard Pearce

Fooling around for
a publicity shoot

In trouble
with Slater

Celebrating
the third series

A NEW FACE

Buster with Jamie Smith who played young Damien

Filming in the studio

More publicity shoots

NO PARKING

Ray Butt, David Jason and Buster Merryfield on location in Ipswich

Nicholas Lyndhurst takes a dive

asing a butterfly

The whole gang

THE JOLLY BOYS' OUTING

Going, going, gone

BEHIND THE SCENES

Continuity polaroids

The flat

That famous bar...

Roger Lloyd Pack - Trigger

Appearing as a builder in the West End play *Moving* in the spring of 1981 brought Roger Lloyd Pack a double helping of good fortune. Not only was his first son Spencer born while he was in it but it also led, by pure chance, to him landing a role that he would play for many years to come – that of dopey roadsweeper Trigger in *Only Fools and Horses*.

Producer Ray Butt had gone to see the play to decide whether actor Billy Murray, who was appearing with Roger alongside Penelope Keith, Miranda Richardson, Richard Thorp and Peter Jeffrey, would be right for the role of Del. Butt didn't think so but decided Roger was perfect for the part of Trig. "Ray called me in to see him and offered me the part of Trigger in this new series but he didn't know when it was going to start because he hadn't yet found the right person to play Del at that time," Roger recalled. "I was pleased because I knew it was good. It was a class above the rest."

In the script for the first episode Trigger is described as "a local part-time villain. He is in his early thirties, tough, but none too bright. He is wearing grubby jeans, shortie wellingtons and a donkey jacket." "Over the years Trigger has refined down to his essential self," said Roger. "He was a bit sharper at the start but after a while Boycie took over the villainy aspect and over the years

Trigger has become less and less involved in running the plot really and having anything to do with the action. He's just there!"

Roger has a big soft spot for Trigger. "The impact of Trigger is not commensurate with the amount of time that he's actually on the screen yet he retains this incredible mythology about him and I'm told he's become a bit of a legend," he said. "I played him as if he thinks he's quite intelligent and he thinks that it's the rest of the world that's out of kilter with him. He's a bit of a dreamer and he's just in his own world really. A lot of people tell me that they know people like him."

Roger loved playing him but admitted he sometimes finds the response he gets from some people in the street who assume he's as dim in real life as Trigger is on screen a pain. "You can imagine what it's like and it can be a drag but it goes with the territory," he said. "It's unavoidable and I deal with it as best I can. Some people are bloody rude and I swear at them or just ignore them. Most people shout 'Alright Dave' and then go off sniggering thinking they are the first to shout it at me.

"The upside of it is that most people are really nice and also that I earn a good living because of the high profile that *Only Fools* has given me. It also means I've been involved in some of the best comedy writing on television. It's also been lovely to be able to play a character for sixteen years because usually you only get to work on a character for as long as you do a play. It's also been extraordinary to have been in something that is so much a part of the culture of the country."

Some women it seems, have a thing about Trigger. "They seem to be quite fond of him and I'm told some of them find him quite sexy," laughed Roger. "I think they like him because they want to mother him and they find him rather loyal, trusting and dependable and they also probably feel rather sorry for him and they want to look after him. I don't get any rude letters from women though but ladies have rushed up to me on occasions and planted a kiss full on the lips so perhaps he's got more going for him than appears at first glance!" Roger might be famous for playing the fool but in real-life he's got a sharp mind and left upmarket private school Bedales in Hampshire with 'A' Levels in English, French and Latin, which would have allowed him to go to almost any university in the country. Instead though he chose to go to the Royal Academy of Drama Art to train as an actor. It meant following in family footsteps by becoming an actor as his father, Charles Lloyd Pack, had been a successful actor appearing in more than three dozen films.

"I hadn't always planned to be an actor," he said. "But I'd always messed around putting on shows as a youngster and I acted at school and eventually I decided that was what I wanted to do for a living. My Dad didn't particularly encourage me or discourage me. It's like people going into a family business. You don't want your children to go into it just because you did, you want them to go into it because they really want to."

Roger has made a considerable success of his career and is probably one of Britain's busiest actors. He lives in north London with his wife Jehane Markham. They have three sons and Roger also has a daughter, actress Emily Lloyd, from his first marriage. But despite his extensive list of other work, he thinks it will be for playing Trigger that he will always be best known. "I think whatever I do, when I die it will be a case of 'Roger Lloyd Pack, best known for his portrayal of Trigger in *Only Fools and Horses...*'" he said.

"But I don't mind though. Writers are always remembered for their one popular play even if they've done lots of other work. Bob Hoskins and Maureen Lipman will probably be remembered for their ads for BT despite all their other work. That's all down to the power of telly coming into people's homes. Sure I'd like be remembered for giving a haunting portrayal of Tartuffe or best known for playing King Lear at the Riverside Studios but only a few hundred people saw that. So I'm resigned to it and if Trigger has brought people pleasure then I don't really mind."

Fact file:

Name: Roger Lloyd Pack

Born: February 8th 1944 in London

Other TV work includes: Softly, Softly, UFO, The Survivors, The Professionals, Private Shultz, Boon, The Bill, The Chief, Inspector Morse, Selling Hitler, The Summer House, Lovejoy, 2 point 4 children, Murder Most Horrid, Knight School, Oliver Twist, Longitude, Murder Rooms, Dalziel and Pascoe, Vanity Fair, Harry Potter and the Goblet of Fire, Doc Martin, Agatha Christie's Poirot, The Living Dead, Doctor Who, New Tricks, The Catherine Tate Show, Survivors, The Old Guys, The Vicar of Dibley, Made in Dagenham, Hustle and Tinker, Tailor, Soldier, Spy

JUST WHY DOES TRIGGER CALL RODNEY, DAVE?

John Sullivan said: "In the first episode Del says to Trigger: 'You know my brother' and Trig says: 'Yeah, of course, how are you doing Dave?' It was just a little gag on the fact that Trigger obviously didn't know Rodney's name. Even after Rodney explained in *Homesick* that Dave isn't his name, Trig still gets it wrong. He's got in his head that Del's brother is called Dave and in the end nothing Rodney or anyone can say will budge Trigger from the fact that his name is Dave. I've had letters from people telling me that there are Dave Clubs around now where people all go round calling each other Dave."

Rodney to Del: Why d'they call him Trigger? Does he carry a gun? Del to Rodney: No, he looks like an 'orse!
Big Brother

John Challis - Boycie

It's hard to imagine *Only Fools and Horses* without John Challis as dodgy second-hand car dealer Boycie – but it could have happened. Back in 1980, a few months before the show went into production John was in America appearing in a string of plays. He enjoyed the experience so much that he nearly stayed there. "I thought America was the place to be at that time," he recalled. "But in the end I decided to come back which is just as well otherwise I'd have never got the part of Boycie."

On April 14th 1981 Ray Butt wrote to John offering him the role of Boycie in the second episode of *Only Fools and Horses*, *Go West Young Man*, and enclosing a copy of the script. Ray knew John's work as he'd previously cast him as a policeman, Inspector Colin Humphries, in an episode of *Citizen Smith* in 1979. "I read the script and thought it was very funny," he recalled. "It made me laugh out loud which is quite rare and therefore I had no hesitation about taking the part."

Writer John Sullivan had been so impressed with the character John had created as Inspector Humphries that he told him that one day he'd find him a part in another series. "He said: 'I really liked the character and I'm going to put him in a series one day' and I said: 'Yeah, yeah' and then the next year, true to his word, the part of Boycie came up which was smashing.

"It was only one day's filming and it was fun but I thought that was probably it. Then I came back to do one episode in the second series, two in the third and it progressed from there. The rest, as they say, is history. Boycie is a great character to play because he's so pompous. He's got aspirations and would like to climb the social scale so he pretends to be that bit more superior.

"But the only thing he had over Del Boy and the others – well up until they became millionaires – is that he has money, however dubiously he has earned it. At the same time he's quite lonely despite being married to Marlene and having Tyler and he'd really like to be one of the boys but his innate sense of superiority won't allow him to fully be so.

"He sees himself as a bit of the lord of the manor and sees the others as underlings. He's got money and he likes to show it off a bit and he also feels intellectually that he's superior whereas he's probably not at all; well except perhaps in the case of Trigger!

"He always thought Del was a little ducker and diver who would never make a success of anything and never have any real money and would always be scrabbling about to earn a living. He sees him as low-life, albeit charming and lovely but not really in his league. After all Boycie's got a mock-Georgian house with an in-and-out gravel drive and Del lives in a council flat.

"Of course all this went out of the window when Del and Rodney found the Harrison watch and Boycie then suddenly found that it had all been turned upside down and that they could actually afford the Rolls Royce he used to tease them about having their picture taken next to."

Boycie's voice comes from John Sullivan's lines. "When I first read them I could tell the way he spoke," said John. "I could also imagine this guy called Gordon who I knew from a local pub, the St Margaret's Hotel in Twickenham years ago, saying precisely the same sorts of things as Boycie came out with so I used him as part of my idea for the character. He would come in the pub and always be on his own and he'd have a little knowledge about practically everything and he'd bore everyone silly a lot of the time. He also said things with such utter certainty that people couldn't really refute what he said.

"Everybody nodded sagely at him and he always had this superior manner and was much derided because although he always wore a suit it was never as neat as Boycie's. It was always stained and his white shirt would always look slightly grubby. He would also have a scruffy little white dog with him, which he adored and he cried like a baby when it died.

"For a long time no one was ever quite sure what he did for a living. They'd say: 'What do you actually do, Gordon?' and he'd say: 'Well actually I can't really talk about it, suffice to say it's something to do with the electronics business.' People then assumed that it must be something top secret to do with rockets or something. It turned out that he was a travelling salesman selling video recorders and record players. He was a fantasist really but a riveting character who I sort of liked but thought was ridiculous as well."

Gordon may have had the gift of the gab but it didn't work when it came to chatting up women. "He loved women but they weren't very interested in him," said John. "One night we were out on the River Thames on a boat having a party and everyone was a bit drunk and Gordon suddenly declared to this girl how much he loved her.

"He then stripped off down to his underpants and leapt into the river. He thought he'd impress her by swimming across to the other side but he'd forgotten it was low tide and he ended up hitting the bottom very hard and getting covered in mud. No one could believe what they'd seen and a few of us had to go and pull him out. He was covered in blood and fairly incoherent and we dressed him and he wandered off home. Everyone was rather concerned for him."

Playing Boycie got John into trouble with the boys in blue

during the filming of *The Jolly Boys Outing* in the spring of 1989. He was dropping a friend home after they'd been out to dinner when he suddenly saw flashing blue lights in his rear view mirror and was pulled over by a police car. "I knew I was under the alcohol limit because I'd only had one glass of wine but they breathalysed me," he recalled. "Then they snatched it away from me, looked at it between the two of them and then said: 'Right, down the station with you.' They refused to let me see the test result and made me give them my car keys and wouldn't help my friend to get home, which I thought was wrong.

"The more I complained that they shouldn't leave her on her own late at night the tighter their grip became on my arm. They bundled me into a police car and whisked me off to the police station. I couldn't believe that it was happening to me." At the police station John was given another breath test, which, surprise, surprise came out negative. "The sergeant said to the two coppers: 'Well I don't know why you brought him in because he's under the limit.' One of them gave a hint of a smile, then I signed a piece of paper and they let me go – and they dropped me back to my car – but not before they asked me for my autograph!"

John reckons the two policemen were having a bit of fun with him because they knew the *Only Fools and Horses* team was in town and they had recognised him. Nicking Boycie, after all, would be a good tale to tell down the police station canteen. "I think they recognised me and decided to have bit of a laugh at my expense but to be honest I didn't think it was very funny at the time," he said.

Boycie might be a working class boy made good – or bad depending on your point of view – but John's upbringing is firmly middle class. His father was a civil servant and his mum was a teacher and he went to private Ottershaw School near Woking in Surrey. It was at school that John got his first acting role at the age of eleven. "I played Alison Elliot in *The Lady's Not For Burning* and very nice too I looked in a long blonde wig and a posh dress," he laughed. "Then I graduated to playing older women and then after my voice broke I started playing men!"

Neither John's headmaster nor his parents thought acting was a very sensible or secure job so at eighteen he started a job as a trainee estate agent in Surrey. "I sat there for about six months and eventually got sacked because I wasn't doing any work at all and spent a lot of my time impersonating the partners and doing fake deals." John's skill with voices has helped him to make Boycie one of *Only Fools and Horses'* best-loved characters – but his trademark laugh came about by accident. John, who has written his autobiography *Being Boycie*, recalled: "I just did it one day and John Sullivan liked it. In the next script it said: 'Boycie does one of his laughs' and from then on it became a regular thing."

Fact file:
Name: John Challis
Born: August 16th 1942 in Bristol
Other TV work includes: The Bill, Casualty, Doctor Who, Coronation Street, Wing and A Prayer, Soldier, Soldier and The Sweeney, The Tichborne Claimant, Heartbeat, Five Seconds to Spare, Subterrain, Dream, Doctors, My Family, Last of the Summer Wine, The Green Green Grass

MY FAVOURITE EPISODE BY JOHN CHALLIS
John's favourite episode is *The Sky's The Limit*. "It was just a brilliant script," he said.

Patrick Murray - Mickey Pearce

 Mickey Pearce had been talked about in *Only Fools and Horses* for two years before John Sullivan decided to bring him into the series as a proper character. Producer Ray Butt spotted Patrick Murray in a television commercial for Pizza Hut playing a similar character and called him in. "The guy I played was in a restaurant trying and failing to chat up these two girls," recalled Patrick. "It was quite funny but the ad got pulled by the company because apparently people were taking more notice of my character than the product!

"I saw Ray on the Friday and he asked me if I'd seen the programme and as I'm not a big TV watcher I hadn't," he said. "He told me about the character and I read a scene from *Healthy Competition* and Ray said: 'Can you start on Monday?' I was delighted and two days later found myself in Bournemouth filming my first episode. I struck up an immediate rapport with Nick Lyndhurst and all the lads and had a great time.

"Mickey is the sort of bloke who does a bit of what Del Boy does and is really a sort of understudy to him. Had he been Del's brother he would have been better at it than Rodney, who he sees as a bit of a gopher. Mickey is like Del in another way in that his antics always go wrong. Like Del, Mickey will try anything but he's not very trustworthy. He's always stitching Rodney up and Del is always threatening to clump him for it."

In the 1989 episode *Little Problems*, Mickey and his pal Jevon are roughed up by the dreaded Driscoll Brothers and turn up at the Nag's Head in plaster casts. That wasn't in the original script but was added by John Sullivan after Patrick had an accident that could have cost him his life. He fell over his dog at home and crashed through a pane of glass and cut his right arm very badly. He lost five pints of blood and had to have emergency surgery and was lucky not to lose his hand.

The first thing Patrick did as soon as he came to the following morning was phone the *Only Fools and Horses* office at the BBC to speak to production manager Adrian Pegg. It was a Wednesday and he was supposed to be back with the team for rehearsals of *Little Problems* the following Monday. "I told him I didn't think I was going to be able to make it and that my arm was in a cast," Patrick recalled. "He said: 'Can you get around and can you talk?' and I said I could and he said: 'I'll have a word with John Sullivan and I'll give you a call tomorrow.'"

Adrian phoned back the following day and gave Patrick the good news. John Sullivan had re-written a section of his script and had incorporated the plaster casts into the storyline. "I couldn't believe it," he said. "I'd been feeling very down in hospital, not just from the pain and the idea of going back to work really lifted me. It made me feel better just knowing that they wanted me back on the Monday.

"The day I went back everyone had been down to the props room and had borrowed false plaster casts and when I arrived all their legs or arms were in plaster. It was a nice gesture and really put a smile on my face and cheered me up because at the time, and through the recording of the episode, I was in acute pain. The doctors had said I'd never be able to use my hand again and although it was painful for a year afterwards I've got full use of it again now."

Patrick still gets a great deal of public response from playing Mickey. "Lots of people want to stop you for a chat and when I walk down the street I'm always getting tooted at by cars," he said. "The good thing about playing Mickey Pearce is that everyone loves *Only Fools and Horses* and the reaction is always a positive thing and people are always polite. I've met a lot of people who say they know someone who is just like Mickey but I've actually met more Rodneys than Mickeys! I've met more lanky wallies with nothing-between-the-ear expressions than anything else!"

Patrick, the son of an Irish tunnel miner and a Spanish dancer, became an actor after spotting an advert for an actor's agency in the *Daily Mirror* when he was fifteen. Three days after he signed up with them he landed a part in a play, which then led to a string of other roles. He made a television commercial for electrical giant Zanussi (which earned him that brand name as a nickname for the next five years) and then scooped a starring role in the acclaimed film *Scum*.

Patrick loved playing Mickey. "I like Mickey really because I like triers and he does try hard. He puts on his best suit and that said to me that he's having a go. He doesn't really want to stitch Rodney up particularly; it's just that he's just out for himself. That's the way of life where he comes from and so that's what he does."

Fact file:
Name: Patrick Murray
Born: December 17th 1956 in Greenwich, London
Other TV work includes: The Firm, Last Summer, The Terracotta Horse, The Bill, Lovejoy, Anna Lee, Keep It In The Family, The Upper Hand, Hale and Pace

Kenneth MacDonald - Mike Fisher

He might have been the butt of some of Del Boy Trotter's dodgier moneymaking schemes as the Nag's Head landlord Mike Fisher, but actor Kenneth MacDonald wasn't one for complaining. When he landed the part in 1983, he thought it was probably a one-episode role never dreaming he'd become one of the show's regulars and one of television's best-known pub landlords.

"I think they were looking for a foil for Del Boy at the pub," Kenneth recalled. "John Sullivan wanted someone there who Del could flog his gear to, have a bit of banter with and now-and-again stitch up. There had been several barmaids at the Nag's Head over the years but never a proper landlord who was there all the time."

Once again it was Ray Butt who cast Kenneth in the role. "I'd worked with Ray before when he directed *It Ain't Half Hot Mum* in which I played Gunner Nobby Clark and he remembered me and when he needed someone to play Mike I got the call," he said. "I was delighted because I'd always watched and enjoyed *Only Fools and Horses*. I didn't have many lines in my first episode, *Who's A Pretty Boy*, but I had a nice exchange with David Jason about doing up the pub and it was fun doing the show. I thought that was probably it and that I'd only be in the one episode. Then I went to the end of series party and got a hint that I might be back when

John Sullivan came up to me and said he'd liked what I done and that hopefully there would be some more episodes for me in the next series. I thought: 'Gosh I might be back' and I went home elated.

"Mike Fisher was a nice part to play because he's such a decent, reliable and big-hearted bloke. He's generous too, like when he paid for all the drink at the do at the flat after Grandad's funeral and of course, my last line in the series in *Time On Our Hands*, was 'On the house, Del.' He likes the Trotters and he's aware of what Del is like but he still allows himself to be stitched up by Del because he's gullible, there's no question about that. He's a real soft touch. He's a good landlord though and runs a happy pub – and the punters must like it because it's usually pretty busy."

Having one of the most familiar faces on television meant not a single day passed without Kenneth being spotted by fans of the series. "I get a tremendous response from *Only Fools and Horses*," he told me in 1998. "Mike is your typical landlord and everybody's friend and confidante and people seem to like him. I'd played some nasty characters on television like George Webb in *Brookside* but fortunately people seem to remember me most as Mike.

"They are always coming up to me or shouting things like 'Clean your pipes out Mike', 'Put an umbrella in it will you' or 'How's Del Boy?' to me and that familiarity is nice because you know the nation loves the show so much. Going into a pub is always amazing. The landlords usually say: 'You should be round this side of the bar' and I've actually gone behind the bar and served a few pints on occasions just for fun!"

Kenneth recalled in 1998 what it was like filming *Time On Our Hands*. He said: "It was very, very sad because you just couldn't believe it would ever really come to an end," he said. "By the end everyone was in tears. There wasn't an actor who didn't shed a tear that day and most of the audience were in tears too. It was a grief we all shared and it felt a bit like a funeral although it was a happy event as well."

Kenneth MacDonald was born in Manchester, the son of Scottish heavyweight wrestling champion Bill MacDonald, who died of kidney failure when Kenneth was just thirteen. "Dad was only forty-three and his death hit me very hard," he said. "I still think about him now and just wish he could have seen me grow up and have met my wife Sheila and our children William and Charlotte."

Kenneth left school at eighteen to help support his mum Emily and took a job at a Kellogg's Cornflakes factory. "I used to muck about during the night shift performing *Hamlet* and other Shakespeare plays that I'd learned at school and that earned me the nickname Hamlet," he recalled. "I'd also do daft things like fill a cornflakes packet full of free gifts and hardly any cornflakes. So a kid would open the packet up at breakfast and find loads of little Robin Hood figures. I used to think the kids would be delighted but their mums would have been rather less pleased.

"After about a year I'd had enough and I decided to go off and try my hand at acting. I knew I couldn't be stuck in a factory so I went to London and joined the National Youth Theatre. Soon after I was lucky enough get a couple of telly parts very early on in *Softly, Softly* and *Z Cars* and then shortly afterwards did the pilot of *It Ain't Half Hot Mum* which began in 1973 and ran for eight years."

Kenneth met his wife Sheila while he was appearing in panto in Crewe in 1976. "She was the costume designer and we met when she came over from college in Liverpool to measure me up for my outfit," he said. "It was love at first sight for me. As soon as I saw her that was it. I knew she was the girl for me and I was right and we've been together ever since."

Tragically Kenneth MacDonald died of a heart attack while on holiday with his family in Hawaii in August 2001. He was just fifty. David Jason said at the time: "It is a terrible shock. It is like losing a member of the family, because he was one of the warmest, kindest people that I have had the good fortune to meet in my career."

Roy Heather, who played Sid, told *Hookie Street*: "Ken was a consummate professional and probably the nicest guy I have ever met in this silly business of ours, although 'nice' hardly serves to describe his qualities."

As a journalist I've spent the past twenty-plus years interviewing actors. Ken MacDonald was one of the most decent and down-to-earth actors that I've had the pleasure to know. I first met him in 1990 when I was working on a series of newspaper articles on *Only Fools and Horses*. We had lunch in an Italian restaurant just off Regent Street in London and I soon discovered what a natural comedian he was.

Ken didn't have to try to be funny. He just was. But what struck me about him then and always did was his genuineness and his joie de vivre. His enthusiasm for life and for acting was evident to all. He adored acting and he loved being in *Only Fools and Horses* and he was extremely proud of the show. But he had a greater love than his career - his family. Ken's family was very clearly the centre of his life and that struck me most of all. That was the mark of the man.

Following that first meeting I interviewed Ken again regularly, usually coinciding with whatever he was doing on television. In the autumn of 2000 we talked about his latest role in the BBC drama series *The Sins* in which he played loveable rogue Oy. He had me in stitches as he told me how, after acting for three decades, he'd finally filmed his first nude scene, albeit a subtle one, when Oy had to climb out of a window naked when his lover's husband came home.

"I've been acting for thirty years without being asked to take my clothes off and then at nearly fifty they finally ask me to," he laughed. "And no, I didn't go to the gym to get in shape before filming it. My kids think it's hilarious! I thought it was quite ironic that I never had to take anything off when I was thinner and fitter and now I'm a big stocky middle-aged man they ask me to take my clothes off and get into bed with a pretty young girl!"

Not only did Ken love doing *Only Fools*, he also always paid tribute to John Sullivan's writing. He was a fan – and he didn't mind who knew it. He would have dropped anything to do the show. I always admired his willingness to support The *Only Fools and Horses* Appreciation Society and his genuine interest in the show's fans. At the fan club's first convention in 1998 I remember there was a bit of a crush while people queued for autographs. Ken went on the public address system. He said he and John Challis would be there to sign autographs all day, until everyone got what they wanted signed. He added: "No one will go home without their autographs. We'll stay all night if we have to." I bet he would have done too.

Fact file:
Name: Kenneth MacDonald
Born: November 20th 1950 in Manchester
Died: August 5th 2001
Other TV work includes: Softly, Softly, Z Cars, It Ain't Half Hot Mum, The Thin Blue Line, Silas Marner, No Bananas, Brookside, Crocodile Shoes, Moll Flanders and Touching Evil, A Rather English Marriage, The Mrs. Bradley Mysteries, The Peter Principle, Cor, Blimey!, The Sins, Time Gentlemen Please, Dream, Merseybeat, Peak Practice

KENNETH'S FAVOURITE EPISODE

Ken's favourite *Only Fools and Horses* moment was in *The Jolly Boys' Outing*: "When Del and the others are playing Trivial Pursuit and he's asked what a female swan is called. Rodney tries to help him by waving a pen at him and Del says: 'Oh, it's a Bic!'"

Paul Barber - Denzil

Denzil was conned by Del Boy the first time viewers saw him in the 1983 episode *Who's A Pretty Boy* and nothing much changed over the years. And however hard Del's lorry-driver school friend tried he never seemed to be able to keep out of trouble when Del Boy was around. That was probably down to Denzil's good nature and his inability to say no and stick to it. Take the time Del persuaded him to unload his consignment of dolls, which ended up nearly blowing the roof off Nelson Mandela House. Then there was the occasion when he had a breakdown after he kept seeing visions of Del and his little yellow van everywhere between London and Hull and even on the sea.

"Denzil is just a nice normal guy, who gets into trouble all the time with the help of Del Boy and Rodney," said actor Paul Barber, who played him. "He was always being stitched up by Del which I didn't mind. I loved the scenes when we argue a lot because they were great fun to do. When I first played him the character was already there. He's just a nice guy and that's his trouble. He always falls for it and then he knows he's landed himself in it."

Like almost all of the show's main supporting characters, Paul was cast by Ray Butt and only thought he'd be in one episode. But writer John Sullivan saw the potential with Denzil and brought him back time and time again. "It was like a family when we all got together," he said. "It was always a laugh." One of Paul's most memorable moments came when filming *The Jolly Boys Outing* episode. "We all had to get into the pirate ship ride at the funfair and nobody wanted to go in it," he recalled. "The idea was that everyone would get in it and then Del would say: 'Right lads' and lock the gate and start it and everyone would come out feeling very sick. But hardly anyone wanted to do it so it ended up with just me, Patrick Murray and Nick Lyndhurst in there. Tony Dow, the director, told us to look as if we were having a fun time and we all laughed. Then the machine started to move and by the time we got to the top we weren't laughing any longer!"

Paul grew up in Liverpool and was brought up in care until he was eighteen after both his parents died before he was six. "I shipped around from step-parents to step-parents, foster-parents here, foster-parents there and I had a great time at school. Despite its ups and downs I loved my childhood and I treasure it." One of Paul's first jobs was at Lewis' department store in Liverpool and while he was there he and a friend formed an accapela band. One afternoon his friend spotted an advert in the local paper for auditions at the Liverpool Empire for parts in the musical *Hair*. "I went along to keep him company but decided to audition too," he recalled. "We sang and the next day I had to go to Manchester to re-audition and I got a part – and my friend didn't."

Paul ended up starring in the show alongside people like Paul Nicholas, Joan Armatrading, Floella Benjamin, Angela Bruce and Richard O'Brien. He was twenty-one when it finished and afterwards gained a part in the musical *Jesus Christ Superstar* followed by the lead role in a TV play called *Lucky*. Away from *Only Fools and Horses*, Paul is best known as Horse in the hit film *The Full Monty* but he readily admits that it is because of *Only Fools* that he's famous. "I get people calling me Denzil pretty much every day and families wanting their pictures taken with me," he said. "That's been the same since my first episode went out. Someone shouted 'Denzil' in the street. I thought to myself: 'That's funny because I've just played a character called Denzil.' I didn't realise they were shouting at me. About two weeks later it happened again and I realised I was going to have to live with it for the rest of my life – the same as John Challis has to live with Boycie and Roger has to live with Trigger - and it's a good thing to live with." When *Rock & Chips* was being filmed Paul was invited down to the set by John Sullivan to meet Ashley Gerlach who was playing young Denzil. "John thought I could give Ashley some words of encouragement and some scouse accent even. It was brilliant seeing it all – and Ashley was a great choice as young Denzil." Paul, whose autobiography *Foster Kid* was published in 2008, was a huge fan of John Sullivan. "You'd watch an episode and just think: 'Where on earth does he get these ideas from? I'd love to know the original stories behind some of the episodes. John and I got on really well and would text jokes to each other all time – almost every day. He was the most loyal person I've ever met. He was always on your side. He was like family – a big brother. It was great to be part of his gang."

Fact file

Name: Paul Barber

Born: March 18th 1951 in Liverpool

Other TV work includes: Lucky, The Brothers McGregor, Gangsters, The Front Line, Chancer, Needle, Brookside, The Boys From The Blackstuff, Tom Jones, Casualty, Harbour Lights, Taggart, The 51st State, The Hidden City, Holby City, Single Voices, Nice Guy Eddie, Babyfather, Mad Dogs, Doctors, The Green Green Grass, Dalziel and Pascoe, Dead Man's Cards, Splinter, The Invisibles, Coronation Street, Caught in a Trap, Going Postal

Sue Holderness - Marlene

Sue Holderness joined the cast of *Only Fools and Horses* in 1984 to film one episode *Sleeping Dogs Lie* as Boycie's wife and that, as far as she was concerned, was that. She never expected that she'd be back the following year and from then on become a regular member of the team.

She was cast after producer Ray Butt and director Susan Belbin spotted her in the TV sketch show *End Of Part One*, a sort of forerunner to *Not The Nine O'Clock News*, written by *One Foot in The Grave* creator David Renwick and *2 point 4 Children* writer Andrew Marshall.

"Prior to that I'd really been known for playing middle class or posh women on television," she said. "So playing downmarket Marlene made a nice change. I didn't audition for it, they just gave me the part and it was supposed to be one day's work." Up until then Marlene had been referred to in the script – and so had her reputation. There had been gags along the lines of: "Do you remember Marlene? Oh yes, all the boys remember Marlene."

"Marlene and Boycie fight but then they also get on quite well and I think she likes him really," said Sue. "It's just that Marlene also loves everybody else. She's much too sweet really to say no to men and because of that she's become known as the Peckham bicycle. I think she's probably had flings at some stage with most of the regulars at the Nag's Head – but I doubt she can remember exactly who.

"I thought that one episode was it and then the following year John decided he liked the idea of seeing Marlene on screen and wrote her in again quite a lot," she said. "That was great for me because I like playing her. She's actually very sweet and quite daffy, although she can be quite shrewd with Boycie. She's also got much more money than sense."

Marlene reappeared in the first episode of the following series, *From Prussia With Love,* in which Del tries to sell her and Boycie a newborn baby. John Sullivan had already worked out that Marlene and Boycie didn't have children and had been trying to start a family for years. In *Sleeping Dogs Lie* it was clear that their dog Duke was really a baby substitute for Marlene and in *From Prussia With Love* Marlene's desperation to have a child was clear.

Later, in the episode *Video Nasty*, the couple discover that it's actually Boycie who has the problem, with hospital tests discovering that he had a low sperm count. "That gave me one of my favourite lines," said Sue. "'He's been firing more blanks than the territorials!'" and led to John Sullivan's infamous description of Boycie as a 'Jaffa – seedless.'

"Marlene was bloody angry when she found out that it was his problem because for the past twenty years she'd been blaming herself for not getting pregnant when actually it was him," said Sue. "Then later she managed to get pregnant and that changed their marriage too and she dotes on little Tyler."

A character's desperation to have a baby isn't a subject most sitcom writers would risk trying to tackle, but John Sullivan bit the bullet and the poignancy of both Marlene's sadness and Boycie's embarrassment comes through the laughter. For Sue it meant a bulging postbag of letters from women facing the same plight in real life sharing their own experiences. Ironically, though, Sue couldn't share their suffering very easily because in real life when she filmed *Sleeping Dogs Lie* she was three months pregnant with her first child and by the time the infertility storyline was screened Sue had had two children.

"It was surprising to me just how many members of the public took it so seriously," she said. "They wrote to me asking for advice about what to do about infertility. That was very awkward for me to answer because by that stage I'd had two babies. So all the time I was playing this character who was desperate to have a child, I was in fact reproducing like mad. I found all that quite tragic because my situation was the reverse of Marlene's and these other women. It was very sad.

"It was quite hard for me to communicate with these women because I'd experienced the joy of having children myself and that was after previously not being particularly maternal. Once you get them you understand much more strongly how desperate it is for women who can't do it."

Sue was still single in her mid-thirties and had begun to wonder whether she'd ever settle down and have a family. Then she met her husband, Mark Piper, and they decided to start a family soon after. "I'd left it very late – I was thirty-six when I had my first child – because I'd been busy and had an exciting career and it wasn't until those hormones started churning at thirty-five that I thought I'd better get on with it.

"Prior to that I hadn't been maternal at all. If anybody had handed me a baby I'd have run away because babies used to scream as soon as I held them. I had no rapport with them and I didn't like them at all. Now that's all changed and I'm mad about them and I'm a hopelessly besotted mother."

Sue is frequently asked to open fetes and charity events as Marlene, which she does when she can, sometimes together with John Challis. "They want me to dress up as Marlene and so over the years I've bought various outfits in junk shops including a wonderful leopard skin jacket which is just up Marlene's street," she said. "They are the sort of things I'd never wear out normally, but are perfect for the character."

Sue lives in Windsor with Mark and they have two grown-up children, Freddie and Harriet. As a child she studied dancing and did her first acting at school. She caught the acting bug and after 'A' Levels she went to Central School of Speech and Drama. "From the first time I acted at school I knew that was what I wanted to do," she said. "My parents wanted me to go to university but I was hooked on acting and thankfully I've been able to make a career out of it and to this day I've never had more than three months without knowing what the next job is."

Fact file:
Name: Sue Holderness
Born: May 28th 1949 in Hampstead, north London
Other TV work includes: The Sandbaggers, The New Avengers, End Of Part One, Girls About Town, Canned Laughter, It Takes a Worried Man, The Cleopatras, Dear John, You Me and It, Heartbeat, Out of Sight, Colour Blind, Cold Feet, Murder in Suburbia, The Green Green Grass, Doctors

Tessa Peake-Jones - Raquel

Going shopping has never been the same after Tessa Peake-Jones appeared in *Only Fools and Horses* for the first time on Christmas Day 1988. The climax of the episode saw her character Raquel being revealed as a part-time kissogram girl who had been booked to peel off for Albert's birthday at the Nag's Head. Del was humiliated and their romance hit the rocks in a big way.

For Tessa, appearing in the episode had quite a dramatic impact on her life. "I lived in the East End of London at the time and round there *Only Fools and Horses* is like the flagship programme. It's hugely popular. Straight after the episode was transmitted, I got a lot of attention which I wasn't used to at all and it wasn't always easy.

"For the first time in my career I got recognised a lot and people would stare at me in the bank and when I went to Safeways someone even said: 'Are you going to take your clothes off!' In the episode I sang *Slow Boat To China* and when I walked into my local one night someone started playing it on the piano for a bit of fun. The main comment I got – and still do get – is: 'Where's Del then?' People think that they are the first person to have said it when in actual fact they are the nine hundredth! The great thing about *Only Fools and Horses* though is that all you ever get from people is how much they have enjoyed it. It's quite rare that the only feedback you get from the public about something is praise and that's rather lovely and makes you feel very privileged."

Tessa was booked to play Raquel in the autumn of 1988 and back then it was solely for one episode. "John Sullivan had wanted to write more for a woman but I don't think he ever intended to match up Del with her long-term," she said. "It was a one-off Christmas special and in the end they split up and that as far as I was concerned was that. It was a great script and I had great fun doing it. I never expected to do any more. Comedy was quite a male-dominated area then and I thought the part of Raquel was fabulous. Suddenly John Sullivan, a man who you thought wrote brilliantly for men but hadn't written much for women had created this fab, well-rounded part. Raquel was a little bit lost and was trying to make enough money to keep herself going. She wanted to be an actress and she has a heart of gold and then she meets a similar man in a way. The script touched on things like loneliness and marital problems and seemed to me to have real depth."

Four months later Tessa was filming another television series in Norfolk when a call came through from her agent asking her if she would call *Only Fools and Horses* Director Tony Dow. "I spoke to Tony and he explained that John wanted Raquel to come into the series full-time and how did I feel about it," she recalled. "As you can imagine I was really chuffed but I had no idea I'd still be playing her years later. Over the years Raquel developed as a character and grew as a person. When she and Del first met she really lacked confidence and Del has given her the boost she needed. Since then she's become tougher and tougher, probably partly due to living with him, and she now doesn't take any truck from him. Having a baby has probably made her stronger too." Tessa first saw an episode of *Only Fools and Horses* in 1985 when she watched the Christmas special *To Hull And Back*. "My Godmother, Auntie Renie, used to watch it and it was her favourite programme in the world," Tessa recalled. "All my family had gone on for years about how good it was and I was a student at that time and never really caught much telly. Then I watched *To Hull And Back* and I thought it was hysterical. It was like this whole new world opened up to me and I suddenly became a huge fan."

Tessa grew up in Harrow, Middlesex. When she was nine she began going to dancing classes and later began doing drama at school. After school she gained a place at the Central School of Speech and Drama in London. She left after three years and landed her first television role in the drama series *Telford's Change*, before appearing with Alan Ayckbourn's theatre company in Scarborough for a year. Then she landed the starring role in a BBC adaptation of Iris Murdoch's *The Bell*. It was while acting in *Romeo and Juliet* at the Birmingham Repertory Theatre that Tessa and her partner Douglas Hodge met. They were starring as Shakespeare's doomed lovers in the play and fell in love for real. *Only Fools and Horses* holds a special plaxce in Tessa's heart. "I loved doing it and even though I came in much later than the others they were so welcoming and friendly that going back each year to film was like seeing members of your family again," she said. "It's also been great for my career and I know it has led to other work."

Fact file:
Name: Tessa Peake-Jones
Born: May 9th 1957 in Hammersmith, London
Other TV work includes: Telford's Change, The Bell, Pride and Prejudice, Up The Garden Path, So Haunt Me, The Demon Headmaster, Tom Jones, Midsomer Murders, Births, Marriages and Deaths, Summer in the Suburbs, Holby City, The Bill, Waking the Dead, The Lost World, Dalziel and Pascoe, Heartbeat, Agatha Christie's Poirot, Casualty, Cosi, Doctors, Marchlands

Gwyneth Strong - Cassandra

Gwyneth Strong went to audition for the part of Cassandra in *Only Fools and Horses* not really expecting to land the part. Four months earlier she'd had her first baby, Oscar, and she was feeling ready to work again. Going for interviews was a gentle way of getting going again. "I really didn't think I'd get the part because I was so wrapped up in the baby world," she said. "I met Tony Dow and the interview went like a dream and then I got called back and this time met Gareth Gwenlan. After that I walked from the BBC to my Mum's house at Notting Hill and while I was there I got a call to say I'd got the part.

"I was delighted because I loved the show but back then I thought I was just going to be in one episode *Yuppy Love* and because of that there was no pressure. My brief for Cassandra was pretty much as she is. Her dad is a working class bloke made good and like him she's quite ambitious and got a good job in a bank, which has made her quite middle class. She was not the sort of girl that Rodney had been out with before.

"Rodney and Cassandra are mad about each other and that gets them through any crises they face. He's loyal and sensitive and I've seen surveys that say the character of Rodney is what most women adore. He's popular because mothers want to mother him and girls want to look after him and they love the fact he gets things wrong because he's not nasty at all."

Despite being thrilled about getting the part Gwyneth was nervous about starting on the show. "I was quite overawed when I started on it," she admitted. "I mean, who wouldn't be? I was suddenly part of something that I had watched and enjoyed for years. Fortunately everyone was very welcoming. I'd also never done a sitcom before and rather naively thought it would be just the same as theatre acting of which I'd done quite a lot. That wasn't the case so I learnt on my feet very quickly and lucky for me because I was able to learn from two of the best - David Jason and Nick Lyndhurst."

Some of Gwyneth's first scenes as Cassandra were romantic moments with Rodney. "They were supposed to be a bit nervous and shy – and so were we for real!" she laughed. "I think most actors are like that but they don't admit it. Over the years we've got to know each other better and have become much more relaxed with each other as Rodney and Cassandra have."

After filming her first episode Gwyneth was asked back to do the next one *Danger UXD* and soon discovered she was to become a regular in the show. "And by the end of that series Cassandra and Rodney got married," she said. "It was amazing that it all happened that fast and for me it was wonderful. It was quite a whirlwind."

Gwyneth already knew that appearing in *Only Fools* would have quite an impact on her life – certainly in terms of public recognition. "The Monday after my first episode went out I was banging my pram down the steps outside my house and I hadn't reached the bottom one when someone shouted: 'Look there's Cassandra!' and it has continued from then on. Since then I don't think I've walked down a street without someone shouting that or 'Where's Rodney?' or 'Oi plonker!' if they are really drunk.

"Usually you have to be in a show a while before you are recognised but *Only Fools* has such a high profile. It's quite good at parties though because I never have to say what I do for my living because so many people watch it. I've got lots of friends who are wonderful actors or actresses and do great work and it's awful at a party to say 'I'm an actress' only for them to say: 'Oh, have I seen you in anything?' which is really boring when you've been doing the job for twenty-five years."

Gwyneth received a lot of fan mail from *Only Fools* fans – particularly teenage boys. "If you're a teenage boy and it's not going easily for you then the idea of Cassandra being with Rodney I think gave them hope," she said. "I'd had fan mail before but not on that level."

Admirers of *Only Fools and Horses* point to John Sullivan's inter-weaving of serious moments – like the hospital scene in *Modern Men* after Cassandra's miscarriage – with humour. "He was a genius," she said. "It's quite unique to take a subject like that and give it everything it deserves in terms of emotional pain and also make it funny. If you describe that, it sounds impossible, but John managed to do it."

Gwyneth's favourite episode though is one of sheer comedy – *The Unlucky Winner Is…* - when Rodney wins a foreign holiday in a painting competition. It was also one of the hardest to film with David and her having a long scene filmed in one take, interrupted by Rodney's return from a bout of skateboarding. "It felt like it went on for about twenty minutes but it can't have been," she said. "We walked the whole length of the set and went in and out of different rooms and then Rodney and another character come in. It was like filming a piece of theatre and I was so frightened that I'd be the one to mess up halfway through. Fortunately no one did!"

Gwyneth has been acting since the age of ten when she and a childhood friend Murray Dale, son of *Carry On* star Jim Dale, who lived round the corner, wrote to an agent enclosing a photograph of them together. It worked – and they both ended up getting acting work, with Gwyneth gaining a small part just months later in the play *Live Like Pigs* at the prestigious Royal Court Theatre in

London. "I was so lucky," she said. "It was such a great place to start." A year later she landed a part in the film *Nothing But The Night* with Peter Cushing, Christopher Lee and Diana Dors.

Her parents had been less than keen about her going into acting but nevertheless Gwyneth left school at sixteen determined to make a career in the profession and she hasn't looked back since. "I've had quiet patches but if you are lucky no-one really notices," said Gwyneth, who is married to actor Jesse Birdsall. Gwyneth and Jesse have two grown-up children Oscar and Lottie. Gwyneth considers herself very lucky to have survived the 'curse' of being a child actor and is as passionate about acting now as she was on day one.

Despite being watched by millions in *Only Fools and Horses* Gwyneth has managed to avoid being typecast and even appeared with her *Only Fools* co-star David Jason in his ITV drama *A Touch of Frost*. "That was great," she said. "I played a senior officer to David's DI Frost who was investigating him and the hardest part of it was to be very dominant with him because that was a big role reversal from *Only Fools and Horses*."

Fact file:

Name: Gwyneth Strong

Born: December 2nd 1959 in East Ham, London

Other TV work includes: Shadows, Angels, It's a Lovely Day Tomorrow, Inside Out, King of the Ghetto, Shrinks, Living With Dinosaurs, From A Far Country, Paradise Postponed, Nice Town, Waiting On The Line, 99-1, The Missing Postman, A Touch of Frost, Real Women, Real Women II, Forgotten, An Unsuitable Job for a Woman, Brand Spanking New Show, Lucy Sullivan Is Getting Married, Casualty, Suzie Gold, Murder in Suburbia, Doctors, New Tricks, Midsomer Murders and In Love with Alma Cogan

ALSO STARRING...

Roy Heather - Sid

Roy Heather joined the cast of *Only Fools and Horses* in 1982 as café owner Sid in *The Long Legs Of The Law*. "Sid is just a scruffy greasy spoon café owner," said Slough-born Roy. "The whole place was a bit down at hill and the thing about Sid was that he smoked incessantly and you wouldn't really want to eat anything that he'd cooked," said Roy. "Filming the show was never like work. It was always great fun and was really like just meeting old mates again." Roy's other credits include: *Return to Treasure Island, The Bill, Bottom, Cadfael, Frank Stubbs Promotes, Birds of a Feather* and *My Family*.

Denis Lill - Alan Parry

Denis Lill first appeared in the series as Cassandra's dad Alan Parry in the 1989 episode *Little Problems* in which Cassie and Rodney married. He became a regular face and went on to feature in a further six episodes. In addition to *Only Fools,* Denis has appeared on Denis' other credits include: *Sherlock Holmes, Outside Edge, Blackadder, Red Dwarf, Highlander, Heartbeat, Berties and Elizabeth* and *The Royal.*

Wanda Ventham - Pam Parry

Wanda Ventham, mother of *Sherlock* actor Benedict Cumberbatch, played Cassandra's mum Pam Parry and made her first appearance in *Little Problems*. Wanda's other credits include *The Lotus Eaters, UFO, The Saint, The Prisoner, The Sweeney, Doctor Who, Casualty, Boon, Executive Stress, Men Behaving Badly, Heartbeat, Midsomer Murders* and *Lewis.*

PART 3
Series One

After weeks of planning, work began on the first series of *Only Fools and Horses* on Wednesday May 6th 1981. Then, just a few days into filming, the production team was hit by a huge problem. On the morning of the third day of shooting, producer Ray Butt, who had been working on the show since its conception, awoke at his west London flat in agony, having suffered a slipped disc during the night. Ray was not only the show's boss, but he was also to be directing the six episodes that made up the first series.

Writer John Sullivan recalled the moment he got the bad news. "I was the first person Ray phoned," he said. "He was so worried about the show that he phoned me before he even rang a doctor or the hospital. There was this agonised voice on the line, obviously in great pain. With Ray off we were in deep trouble. Our producer and director had been taken into hospital and all the actors were sitting around down in a market somewhere waiting to start filming and wondering what the hell we were going to do."

It was the last thing David Jason could have done with so early on, for although he was relishing getting into the character of Del Boy, he was nervous about it all. "I think you are always a bit nervous when you first go into something because you don't really know the character or where you are going," he said. "You are desperately trying to settle down and for the first few days you are still finding your feet.

"Eventually it all starts to gel and then you start doing it

129

instinctively and begin to feel you know what a character would or wouldn't do in a given situation. Like everyone else you are scrabbling round desperately hoping it will be funny."

Ray Butt's injury resulted in a three-week stay in London's Charing Cross Hospital. For the production it meant a major upheaval. Another director, Martin Shardlow, was rapidly called up to fill in and a senior producer in the comedy department, Gareth Gwenlan, later to become the show's main producer, stood in as producer during Ray's absence and filming was able to continue.

The first episode, *Big Brother*, was screened at 8.30pm on Tuesday September 8th 1981 and was billed rather flatly in the *Radio Times* as the story of "two brothers living with their grandad in a south London flat and existing off shady deals". The episode cost around £28,000 to make, which was about average at the time for a sitcom, was transmitted the same week as the BBC also began showing a six-part adaptation of John Wyndham's *The Day of The Triffids*, a new drama series *Blood Money* starring Bernard Hepton and Michael Denison and the fly-on-the-wall documentary series *Fighter Pilot*, which tracked the progress of new would be RAF top guns.

It was sandwiched in between a repeat of the American private eye drama *The Rockford Files* (starring James Garner) and *The Nine O'Clock News* and was up against a documentary about new French President Francois Mitterand on BBC2 and a drama, *The Flame Trees Of Thika,* starring Hayley Mills and David Robb, on ITV. Its impact with television critics was negligible and few even bothered to review it, although one, Stephen Biscoe, writing in the *Yorkshire Post*, backed it from the start. In a review the day after transmission he said that Mary Whitehouse might not approve of the language used. "This viewer, on the other hand, will be watching it because he likes its earthy characters and therefore forgives them their earthy behaviour," he added. "There is, in fact, more than a touch of that earthiest of couples, *Steptoe and Son*, in this new series."

The episode, in which Del tries to sell a batch of briefcases that don't open, attracted a respectable 9.2 million viewers but it's fair to say that it didn't set the world alight. "We didn't really get any publicity and the show went out in a very bad slot," said John Sullivan. "I kept hearing about the BBC publicity department but to me it was like something out of mythology. They never contacted us and therefore the boys didn't do any interviews. The show just went out without that sort of promotion."

Later on during transmission of the first series, John and David Jason complained about how the show was being treated inside the BBC. "In the BBC Television Centre foyer each month were displays of massive photographs from different departments," John recalled. "One particular month it focused on comedy and they were all up there: *L For Lester* (starring Brian Murphy), *To The Manor Born* and lots of others but no *Fools and Horses*.

"So we made enquiries, wondering if we'd missed it and we were told there was one up on the sixth floor of BBC Television Centre which was the sort of place only executives go to for a bit of lunch sometimes. We definitely felt then that we were a bit of an embarrassment to them and they wanted to hide us away. It was nothing you could put your finger on but we just had this feeling that we were the black sheep of the family. We ended up having a meeting with John Howard Davies about it and he said he'd get it moved to somewhere a little more noticeable."

"We felt desperately unloved for a good couple of years," said Nicholas Lyndhurst.

The second episode **Go West Young Man** sees Del deciding to try his hand at the second hand car business after cadging an old banger from Boycie, making his first appearance in the show. Del sells the clapped out Ford Cortina GT convertible to a mouthy Australian, played by actor Nick Stringer, who was to return in the episode *Who Wants To Be A Millionaire?* in series five as Del's old pal Jumbo Mills.

Filming on location for the episode on a council estate in North

Acton, north west London was a worry for producer Ray Butt. After all, the script called for Rodney to drive the car at high speed and nearly run Del over. Keeping the public away from filming was no problem but Nicholas Lyndhurst hadn't passed his driving test and therefore wasn't allowed on public roads. "But I needn't have worried," recalled Ray. "Technically we weren't on a public road where we filmed it but even so I told Nick not to go too fast because I was going to undercrank the film – which meant it would come out looking like it had been speeded up.

"He came round the corner and it looked unbelievable. The tyres were screaming and black smoke was pouring out the back (because we'd put smoke canisters under it) and the car was on two wheels. He did it far faster than I'd asked him. Even though Nick hadn't passed his test he was still a superb driver." Nicholas recalled: "In the script the car was supposed to have spongy brakes but I made damn sure they worked because I had to stop just before a parapet and if I'd not stopped I'd have had a forty foot drop!" David Jason recalled: "Nick came round the bloody corner like a bleedin' bat out of hell and stopped within a couple of inches of me."

Cash and Curry sees Del getting embroiled in a deal with two Indian businessmen – and at one stage he kicks a burly minder between the legs. Del then delivers one of David Jason's favourite lines. David said: "The businessman goes on about having a big house and lots of land and then Del says: 'Yeah, and he's got a couple of acres an' all, hasn't he!' It's a brilliant line. You can't go wrong with stuff like that. We always tried to play it straight because the jokes are there in the script. I always used to say: 'Don't put a joke on a joke,' then it works better."

In *The Second Time Around* Del met up with his old fiancée Pauline Harris, played by actress Jill Baker. Rodney has bad memories of how she dumped Del and he's not at all enthusiastic about them getting together again, particularly when he hears that both her previous two husbands died. "I remember how she treated you when you was engaged," Rodney tells Del when he accuses him of being hostile to her. "I may have only been a little nipper Del but I remember how she screwed you up."

Soon after Del announces that he and Pauline are going to get married and she moves into the flat and causes uproar by serving Rodney and Grandad corned beef while she and Del have best steak, hiding Grandad's false teeth and suggesting they put him in an old folk's home. When she starts talking about Del having life insurance, Rodney and Grandad decide to leave home. Fortunately Del realises before it's too late that she's really only after his money. The trio flee the flat for five days only to return to find her having gone but not before she's run up a huge phone bill by leaving it connected to the speaking clock – in America.

Del's entrepreneurial flair takes a new turn in *A Slow Bus To Chingford* when he starts his Trotter's Ethnic Tours. He decides that tourists want something new. "Your average tourist gets fed up seeing the same old places – the Houses of Parliament, Buck House, the National Gallery," he tells Grandad and Rodney. "Once you've seen one Rubens you've seen them all – this is where a dynamic person like me steps in."

Rodney meanwhile is far from happy with his new job as a night watchman, particularly with the impact it has on his romance with Janice, not to mention his traffic warden's uniform. Del's £17 ethnic tours fail to catch on – but that's perhaps not too surprising when the itinerary includes the Lee Valley viaduct, the glory of Lower Edmonton at dusk, a walkabout in Croydon, the birthplace of Sherlock Holmes and the summit of Mount Pleasant. It might have helped though if Grandad had actually sent out the advertising handbills as he was supposed to have done, but he had a good excuse. "It wasn't me, Del Boy, it was me brain," he explained.

With US-Soviet relations taking a turn for the worse in the early eighties, the timing of *The Russians Are Coming* was very appropriate. Del buys a pile of old bricks that Rodney discovers is actually a prefabricated nuclear fallout shelter. Del's all for selling it but politically aware Rodders reckons World War Three is just round the corner and wants to build it. "It only takes one little rumble in the Middle East and them missiles are gonna start flying," he says. "And what have we got in this country to combat the might of the Soviet Union? Three jump jets and a strongly worded letter to the Russian Ambassador."

Getting to the shelter when the four-minute warning goes off is a problem, but not as hard as it would be if they built it in Grandad's preferred location – the New Forest in Hampshire. In the end they decide to put it up closer to home – on the roof of Nelson Mandela House. There Del offers his theory about the younger generation not having had the chance of going off to war. This angers Grandad who launches into an unexpectedly profound speech about war and the treatment of the young men who fought in the First World War. After the armistice, he recalled, "As the nation celebrated they were hidden away in big grey buildings far from the public gaze." Then he added: "They promised us homes fit for heroes; they give us heroes fit for homes."

The first festive episode *Christmas Crackers*, which was added on to the six-part series as an extra, takes place on Christmas Day in the Trotter's flat but was actually screened on December 28th. It saw Grandad cooking the Christmas dinner and Del and Rodney complaining about it. The episode was not a classic but nevertheless has some fine moments, like Del trying to cut the turkey with a electric carving knife minus its plug and some great gags like Del insisting they couldn't go out and leave Grandad at home – and then the old man himself goes off out.

The fact that it was totally studio-based and that most of the action takes place only in the flat brought home the idea of a real Christmas for a very close-knit family. There's the boredom, the arguing and the reliance on watching television. And when Rodney complains that he's bored, as many youngsters do on Christmas Day once present opening is over, Del tells him: "Everyone's bored. Christmas is a religious festival. It's meant to be boring."

John Sullivan had originally written a slightly reworked section of dialogue in the nightclub scene as part of a *Two Ronnies* sketch called *Pills and Ills*, which featured the characters Sid and George. When the scene was cut from *The Two Ronnies,* John altered it and rewrote it for *Christmas Crackers*. After it had been recorded the BBC reinstated the scene into *The Two Ronnies*. "I suddenly heard that the Ronnies thing had been re-edited and these lines had gone back in. I rang Roger my agent and said: 'What do I do? They are now in two different shows...' I don't know what happened. I think the programmes went out and nobody noticed."

After the first series ended the BBC did an audience survey to gauge what viewers thought of the series. The BBC Broadcasting Research Viewing Panel Report of January 22nd 1982 found that the majority of the respondents had enjoyed the series. "They found it entertaining, amusing and well written on the whole," it said. "Several people commented on the witty dialogue, credible situations and originality of the idea of the series. Nevertheless, there was a fairly general feeling that it had got off to a slow start, although it had improved by the end. Also, some of those reporting complained of only 'sporadic humour', 'weak storylines' and 'a poor theme'. These views were outweighed, however by those who felt that *Only Fools and Horses...* had been one of the funniest comedy series for a long time.

"The characters in the series appealed to most reporting viewers and the standard of the acting was very highly thought of; indeed, in the opinion of some, the acting was considered to have far surpassed the material. David Jason received widespread praise for his performance as Del; he was excellent in any part he played. Nicholas Lyndhurst as Rodney was also well liked: it was generally thought that he provided a good foil for Del, yet was amusing in his own right. In fact, the three main characters (including Lennard Pearce as Grandad) were considered to complement each other very well, and the whole cast was commended for working together with great success.

"The production was praised throughout the sample audience, particular approval being expressed about the use of outdoor locations. In addition, the sample members felt that the production had achieved the right 'tone'; in the words of one viewer, 'there was skilful direction to bring out the absurd in the series'. Asked if they would, personally welcome a further series of *Only Fools and Horses*..., the reporting viewers answered: Yes, very much (41%), Yes, quite (35%), Not particularly (20%) and Definitely not (4%)."

Traditionally the BBC had always prided itself on nurturing programmes even if they weren't instant hits. It would commission a second series even if the first wasn't a major success simply because someone had a hunch that it might take off. The viewing figures for the first series of *Only Fools and Horses* were disappointing averaging just 7.7 million and clearly someone senior at the BBC didn't think *Only Fools and Horses* had much potential and didn't deserve to be re-commissioned for a second series.

"After the first series finished I had a meeting with John Howard Davies and he asked me what I was doing next because at that stage I was under a contract with the BBC," John Sullivan recalled. "I definitely got the feeling, although he never actually said it, that they'd probably rather I went off and came up with something else. That was a bit of a shock because at that stage the BBC had this policy whereby they'd give something a second chance unless the writer or principal actors didn't want to do any more. The way John was talking to me, saying things like: 'I liked that other idea of yours' I felt I was being steered towards forgetting *Fools and Horses* and doing something different instead."

Ray Butt still thought the show could work and John had another strong ally in David Jason who was very confident about the show. "David and I had many meetings, drinks and dinners and he was very, very supportive," recalled John. "He was really eager for it to work."

"I had total faith in it," David recalled. "I could see that it was very funny, there was no question about that. One problem we had though was the title, which no one understood and the fact that it didn't have anyone in it. I mean it had Nick, Lennard and me in it but it didn't have anybody in it that was so well known that people would want to switch it on just to see what they were doing. For whatever reason, people weren't tuning in and we weren't really building an audience."

At a further meeting with Howard Davies, John Sullivan insisted that he really wanted to give it another go and Howard Davies agreed to give the show a second run. At the same time it was decided to dump the original theme tune in favour of one written by John Sullivan that explained the show's title. During transmission of the first series the BBC had been bombarded by letters from viewers wanting to know what the *Only Fools and Horses* meant. The new title track would explain it all. John Sullivan had always been unhappy with the show's original theme tune, which had been a very typical piece of seventies-style sitcom music.

"The script had described the music to be Chas and Dave-style rockney," he said. "What we got was Ronnie Hazlehurst's version of that and to be honest I didn't like it that much. My version had already been written for the first series and I thought they'd use it but for some reason Ray had decided to go with Ronnie's. No one was very happy about, it including the cast, so between series one and series two it was changed to my version, which is the one people are now familiar with. I'd written the theme music for the closing credits on *Citizen Smith* and *Over the Moon* and just got in the habit of doing them." John also sang it. "I wasn't supposed to," he said. "Because Chas and Dave were going to do it. Then they had a number one hit called *Ain't No Pleasing You* and they became very busy and couldn't do it. That was a bit of a choker because if they'd done our theme it might have gone to number one too. I'm sure they'd have done it better than me. I'd recorded it originally just to get the tune, so Ray said to me: 'You do it'. I wasn't keen and had to be persuaded with lager! Going into a studio and singing with a band was not really my kind of thing." Of course, the theme music – for which John was paid £250 (£125 for the opening tune *Only Fools and Horses* and the same for the closing credits, *Hooky Street*) - is now iconic and in 2009 was voted the greatest television theme music ever – beating *Minder*'s *I Could Be So Good For You,* sung by Dennis Waterman.

HOW DID DEL END UP WITH A COMPANY CALLED TIT?

Something that has always fascinated David Jason is John Sullivan's ability to hide gags for them to be exploited later. David said: "For example, did he do the TIT gag first or did he invent Trotters Independent Traders and then afterwards realise that the initials spelt TIT?" "It was an accident," said John Sullivan. "I had the name Trotters Independent Traders and I put it on the van and suddenly I looked at it and thought: 'Shit, the abbreviation spells TIT!' and wondered if anyone else had noticed. I pointed it out to Ray Butt and he just said: 'Great!' I'd love to say it was a deliberate idea from the start but it wasn't, it was a pure accident."

FOREIGN SALES

It isn't just the British who love *Only Fools and Horses*. It's also been sold all round the world and dubbed into a host of foreign languages. Among the countries who've bought the show are: Ireland, Hong Kong, Spain, Yugoslavia, Belgium, New Zealand, Croatia, Australia, South Africa, Israel, Poland, Cyprus, Greece, Pakistan, Serbia, Barbados and Malta. The Netherlands went one better and in addition to buying the BBC original also made their own version.

Series Two

The second series went into production in April 1982, the same month as Argentina invaded the Falklands Islands in the South Atlantic and Britain dispatched a large task force to retake them. The opening episode, *The Long Legs of the Law,* sees Rodney committing a cardinal sin in Del's rule book by going on a date with a policewoman, played by actress Kate Saunders, who went on to become a journalist on the *Sunday Times* and later a successful novelist. "That's what started the whole thing of Rodney having a thing about uniforms," recalled David Jason. "Rodney dating a policewoman was like a poisoned chalice to Del. You couldn't really bring anyone in the police round to the flat because there were always one or two things in there that he wouldn't want them to see."

In *Ashes to Ashes* Del tries to sell Trigger's Gran's antique urn – but comes a cropper when he and Rodney discover that it contains the remains of Trigger's Grandad. They try all sorts of methods of disposal – scattering them on a bowling green, dumping them in the River Thames, even adding them to a cement mixer – until the ashes finally accidentally disappear up the vacuum pump of a roadsweeping lorry.

David Jason recalled: "Nick and I had to rush up to the bloke in the cab and say: 'Stop, you've just sucked up our urn,' then the driver would say: 'Oh my God! What was he, a little kid?' The cameraman was in the cab looking down at us and every time we said it he just fell about laughing. The camera would then shake and we'd have to do it all again. When that happened we'd crease up. We ended up doing it about six times and in the end he had to give it to his assistant to do. It was very funny." Nicholas Lyndhurst hasn't forgotten being out on the Thames in a small rowing boat for one scene in the episode. "It was high tide and it was very rough out there," he recalled. "David had to row very hard to keep up with it and we were very nearly swamped. I doubt they'd let us do it these days."

A Losing Streak sees Del and Boycie play a high stakes game of poker and was inspired by John Sullivan's own knowledge of the game. "I'd been to all night card sessions even though I was no big player myself," he said. "What fascinated me was how friends fell out in games and not just over money. A game would be like a duel and people took it very seriously and would sometimes accuse friends of cheating. My father was a big gambler and that was why I never gambled because as a kid I saw how much money you could lose and the rows it would cause at home. I remember one night he came home drunk after a game of cards. With him was a greyhound he'd bought off some guy in a pub. The next night he took it over the common. He threw a tennis ball and the dog zoomed off after it and got the ball and carried on. He never saw him again. He came home and I remember him saying: 'I tell you what, he was bloody fast so he was still a good buy.' We had the dog just one day!"

"That was a great episode," said David Jason. "It had a brilliant ending – where Boycie had been cheating and so had Del. When you have endings like that you have a wonderful feeling of elation because John's script surprises right at the end – and you never saw it coming. A truly great writer."

No Greater Love demonstrates the real bond between Del and Rodney. In the episode Rodney falls for an older woman called Irene while selling clothes door-to-door. Del does his best to dissuade Rodney from continuing with the relationship, reminding him that she's got a dodgy husband Tommy MacKay who is about to be released from jail. Rodney takes no notice but it's Del that suffers the wrath of Tommy (played by David Daker who would later go on to find fame as Michael Elphick's pal in the ITV drama *Boon*). He catches up with Del on a dark night and mistakenly thinks he's Rodney. But instead of saving himself from a beating Del keeps quiet and takes a vicious beating on his brother's behalf. "Del didn't want his brother to take a good hiding so he took it for him," said David Jason. "That episode showed a lot of the strength and depth of how good the series was going to be because John wasn't frightened of having a serious moment – and treating it seriously, as we all did, so that you have those moments of surprise. I always think about entertainment: if you can make your audience laugh and cry at the same time then you are on to a winner."

In *Yellow Peril* Del sends Rodney off to decorate a Chinese restaurant with yellow paint and later the pair decide to spruce up their mum's ornate grave. It's only later that they realise that the paint they've used is actually luminous. "They wanted to brighten it up because it was looking tired," said David Jason. "It wasn't a very subtle memorial!" "It looked really gaudy," said Nicholas Lyndhurst. "We filmed the scene in a park and the tombstone was made of fibreglass and to make it glow the electricians had put lights inside it. It was so bright that traffic nearby kept slowing down to see what it was. We were lucky we didn't cause an accident."

Location filming for a whole series was always done in one or two blocks before any interior studio recordings took place. This made planning easier for the production team and cut out the need to keep transporting cast and crew back to locations. Right from the start of filming David Jason and Nicholas Lyndhurst got on well so it came as a bit of a shock to the production team one day during their first week on location for a new series to hear the pair having a blazing row in their caravan or winnebego, which was used as a mobile green room (the place where actors wait before they are called onto a set).

As they lined up to get their lunch, the crew could hear cutlery and plates flying about along with insults. They listened in horror it seemed that their stars were falling out in a big way. Suddenly the caravan door burst open and Nicholas stormed out shouting: "Don't you speak to me like that" at David who responded by telling him rather bluntly to "piss off and don't come back!" before shouting after him: "Go on - bleat to the bloody production crew."

It was every director's nightmare and it happened to be the first day as director for Mandie Fletcher, who had worked on the show from the first day as assistant floor manager and would later have great success as director of the hit series *Blackadder*. She and the crew stood around mortified. Someone approached Nicholas Lyndhurst to try to find out just what had gone wrong and why the pair had had such an enormous bust-up. All they could get out of him was: "I'm not bloody working with him again." The production team, including Tony Dow who had joined the crew as a trainee assistant floor manager and would later become the show's director, were going spare. How could they produce a series when its two stars wouldn't speak to each other?

It was lunchtime and phone calls were made to Television Centre and then to writer John Sullivan who got on well with both men. Could he come down and have a chat with them and see if he could smooth things over? Eventually David came out of the caravan to get his lunch and still the two of them wouldn't speak to each other. During the whole of the afternoon they would only converse through other people and the unit's morale was plummeting.

What the crew didn't know was that the whole thing was an elaborate hoax that David and Nicholas had come up with for a bit of fun. At the end of the very tense afternoon the pair collapsed into fits of laughter during the four o'clock tea break and there was relief all round – mixed with a little anger. John Sullivan recalled: "I got a phone call asking me to come out to where they were filming which was quite a way out from my home. I was told that there was a big problem between David and Nick because they weren't talking to each other and they won't work together again. So I was just about to get in my car and drive down there when I got another call from one of the production team thankfully explaining that it was just David and Nick mucking about. That call was quite a relief and saved me a bit of petrol too!"

David recalled: "We were a bit bored and Nick had said: 'Why don't we have a pretend row – that will wind everyone up.' We thought it would be a bit of a wheeze to have these two actors who suddenly appear to not be able to abide each other. So we started the shouting and stuff and we could see out of the window that everyone could hear and they were all looking a bit panicked. We could see out but they couldn't see in. After Nick had stormed out and I'd gone to get lunch I could see they all thought it was real. Their faces were white! I said: 'I don't want to talk to him. I won't have him in the same caravan.' In the end we both started laughing but it had gone on for a few hours by then and some people were rather annoyed."

It did also demonstrate very early on how David and Nicholas could react to each other instinctively – and on screen this made them convincing as brothers. Off-screen they became good friends and wind-ups became an effective way of keeping stress at bay. Over the years the pair of them became masters at wind-ups along with members of the supporting cast. "If we had a bit of spare time on our hands we'd come up with some plan or some scheme to wind someone up," said David. "But we'd never let a wind–up go on too long so that people get really hurt. That would be cruel and we couldn't do that. We'd just have a little bit of a laugh about it, wind it up and then let the cat out of the bag!"

When the script for *It Never Rains...* arrived at David Jason's home he was rather pleased. The episode saw the Trotters going off to Spain on holiday. "Great." he thought. "A trip to somewhere hot." He was sadly mistaken. Studland Bay near Bournemouth in

Dorset was as far as he and the team got for the filming of that episode. "Cheapskate productions," David recalled thinking. "We weren't famous enough then to warrant tickets abroad so we had to make Bournemouth look like Spain. It was cold and windy and we were laying on the beach pretending it was hot when it was bloody freezing and people kept having to hammer down our goose bumps!"

Location filming began on April 19th 1982 – the day before Nicholas Lyndhurst's twenty-first birthday – and although everyone in the cast and crew knew about it they decided to try to pull-off a major wind-up on him. "Someone came up with idea of pretending that we'd all forgotten – or didn't know – that it was his birthday," David recalled. "So for the whole day of filming no one said anything about it to him. Everyone was sworn to it so there were no cards and no 'Happy Birthdays' and as the day went on he was getting more and more morose. He was away filming so none of his mates were around and it was his twenty-first and he should have been having a bit of knees-up."

"I was racking my brain and thinking: 'What have I done?' Nicholas recalled. "After we finished I went and had a shower then came down to the bar for a drink. There was no one around except for David. I asked him where everyone was and he said they'd gone off to Bournemouth for the night. A couple of the crew went past and I asked them if they wanted a drink and they just said: 'No, you're alright, we're going out.' David said he wasn't staying long. We just had a drink and sat there for about twenty minutes with me thinking: 'Some bloody twenty-first birthday this is going to be. David is going to go off in a minute and I'll be stuck here on my own.'

"Then David said: 'Why don't we go and play a trick on Lennard? Why don't we go and screw his shoes to the floor?' Thinking about it now you'd wonder what the hell would we want to do that for. We'd only get into trouble with the wardrobe department and

Lennard wouldn't be too pleased but by then I was up for any form of entertainment whatsoever. So we went down to the gym which was being used to store costumes. It was pitch black and David said: 'I'm just going to find the light switch.' Then he went off and I was trying to find the switch when all the lights suddenly came on and there was about seventy people there – the whole unit. I got quite choked up about it. There was lots of champagne and presents and we had a great night. We all drank a little more than was good for us!"

David Jason added: "Nick was very touched by the fact everyone had made the effort – but that didn't stop him going round calling me – and everyone else 'rotten bastards'. 'You really had me going,' he laughed. It was a great night and everyone got very drunk. At the end of the night we adjourned to Nick's room to finish off drinking and someone brought his birthday cake up – which hadn't been started and Nick had planned to take home - and John Sullivan accidentally sat on it."

A Touch of Glass was one of those episodes that few people forget, with its master visual gag involving a priceless chandelier. The idea for the episode came about from a story told to John Sullivan by his father. "Dad was a plumber and was always trying to instill in me that I should check and double check things," he said. "I don't think he really realised the difference between writing a scene and putting in a hot water system. If he did it wrong someone would get scalded whereas I could correct it in rehearsals!

"One day he started telling me this story about this accident with a chandelier at this mansion house when he was an apprentice. They were putting in a new heating system and they had to take this chandelier down to protect it when they ran the pipes over the joists where it was. My dad was up on a ladder with his mates waiting to catch the chandelier. But they hadn't properly organised which chandelier they were all working on and the young guy upstairs undid the wrong one; it came crashing to the ground. They'd assumed he knew which one they were working on but he'd gone to another one. Seven men got the sack including my Dad. When he told me about it I roared with laughter but Dad being an old socialist didn't see the funny side of it because these guys had lost their jobs during the depression in the thirties.

"A few days after Dad had told me the story I had a drink in the BBC bar with David and Ray and I told them about it and David said: 'You've got to use it' and I said: 'I know, but how? Why would the Trotters be in a mansion?' so I went away and for the first time I wrote a story back to front. I wrote the end when the chandelier fell and then I had to figure out how to get them there."

When it came to it, they clearly only had one chance at filming the chandelier crashing to the ground scene. "It was planned very carefully," recalled David Jason. "It had to be done in one shot with the falling chandelier in the background. So there was Nick and I up a ladder ready to catch the chandelier trying to keep a straight face.

"All the crew were hiding out of shot and were under strict orders not to laugh. After the chandelier crashed to the ground Nick and I had to keep a straight face. But all we could see in our peripheral vision was the crew jiggling about with laughter. One person was biting their script so as not to laugh. After what seemed like about an hour we finally heard someone blurt out: 'cut' and the whole place exploded and people were coughing and crying with laughter. Nick and I were just relieved that it was over – and we'd got it in the can."

"Before we did the shot Ray Butt took me to one side and threatened me with the sack if I ruined it by laughing," said Nicholas Lyndhurst. "He scared me because I thought he meant it because although the chandelier was fake it was a very elaborate and expensive fake, which I think cost £6,000, and we only had one. We had to get it right first time. He had been thinking about putting the end credits over the film of David and I looking at each other after the chandelier had crashed and that needed to be thirty seconds. That meant we had to stand and look at each other for all that time having just witnessed something very funny happen, and not laugh.

"Out the corner of my eye I could see Ray standing behind me giving me daggers. The seconds ticked by and then very slowly and very quietly I saw him reach into his parka pocket, pull out a handkerchief and stuff it into his mouth and leave the room. That was funny in itself but I knew I couldn't laugh. After we cut I gave him some very well-chosen words I can tell you!"

John Sullivan's father would always be the first one to phone him after an episode had transmitted and after *A Touch of Glass* was screened John was worried. "The phone rang and I thought: 'Here we go…he's going to disown me' and say: 'You're no son of mine…' and he said: 'Alright, it was funny.'"

That Christmas *Fools* fans got a double dose of the show. First there was a short six-minute episode which formed part of an eighty minute special presented by Frank Muir called **The Funny Side of Christmas**. Broadcast on December 27th, it also featured mini episodes of other BBC hits including *Yes Minister, Sorry*, *The Les Dawson Show*, *Smith and Jones*, *Three Of A Kind*, *Last of The Summer Wine*, *Reggie Perrin*, *Butterflies* and *Open All Hours*. The *Fools* story, *Christmas Trees*, was all shot on film over three days starting on November 10th and shows Del trying to sell the latest Christmas trees at £6 a throw with a telescopic motion that makes them easy to fold away. They were not proving popular with the punters and Del tells Rodney, with a topical joke for the year which had seen conflict with Argentina over the Falklands: "These are going down as well as Union Jacks do in Buenos Aires." With nearly a hundred and fifty trees to sell Del comes up with a neat little scheme – he donates one to the local church and then starts flogging the rest at £7 as "The only Christmas tree used and recommended by the Church of England itself."

Three days later saw the screening of **Diamonds Are For**

Heather which saw the real possibility of Del getting married to a single mum called Heather and featured the classic moment when Del pays carol singers to sing the Clinton Ford song *Old Shep*. "Del had been engaged so many times and I wanted to show that underneath this flash, confident exterior there was a man who most probably would have loved to have got married and had a couple of kids," said John Sullivan. "And this episode was a way of showing it."

Despite the two Christmas episodes the future for *Only Fools and Horses* was not looking good. The viewing figures for *A Touch of Glass* had gone up to 10.2 million (the highest ever for the show at that time) but overall, despite a series on series increase they remained relatively poor with an average of 8.85 million. These days that figure would be considered very reasonable but back in 1982 there were only three terrestrial TV channels, with Channel Four becoming the fourth on November 2nd, during the run of series two.

There was no competition from the satellite and cable companies like there is now and even domestic video recorders were still some years away. The *Only Fools and Horses* viewing figures were being compared unfavourably with the other big hits of the time like *The Two Ronnies, Last of The Summer Wine* and *Dallas* all regularly attracting around 16 million viewers. Comedies like *Hi-De-Hi* and, ironically *Open All Hours,* still featuring David Jason alongside Ronnie Barker, were also being watched by about 14 million people every week.

For John Sullivan it was a time of great disappointment. He felt the show had still not received the backing it needed from the BBC. "I'd hoped they would have thrown their weight behind it more," he said. "But it hadn't happened and we'd still got no publicity. I wanted David and Nick to go on a chat show to let people know we were out there but we didn't get any noticeable support. The viewing figures did improve slightly but they didn't really take off. I was disappointed it hadn't really worked out and began thinking about what I could come up with next.

"I'd tried one pilot script after series three of *Citizen Smith* called *Dear Old Pals* about the pal's regiments in the First World War with the idea of Ronnie Barker and David Jason starring in it. It was about two old boys who'd been in the First World War together having being born in the same street, growing up and now living in a very modern world. But Jimmy Gilbert didn't seem to like it and that was quite a disappointment."

Then, on July 5th 1983 a repeat run of the second series of *Only Fools and Horses* began and something changed. It wasn't broadcast in a noticeably better slot, going out at 7.45pm after a new lifestyle show called *Looking Good, Feeling Fit.* But even though the repeats were screened during the summer, when traditionally fewer people watch television, the ratings peaked at a respectable 7.7 million viewers. That, combined with the fact that the original run of the second series had seen a week by week increase in viewers, suggested to BBC executives that they perhaps ought not to axe the series after all. Perhaps, against the odds, the previously dead-in-the-water show was showing signs of life. Head of Comedy John Howard Davies decided to put his neck on the line and commission a third series.

"Sharon and I took the kids to Hastings and we were staying in a caravan when I picked up a paper and glanced at the TV ratings and there was *Fools and Horses* at number five and then it went up to two or three," recalled John Sullivan. "And I had no real idea why. It was as if the public had finally noticed the show. If that hadn't happened we would have been dead. There was no way a third series would have been commissioned. By the time I got back home I was offered two more series. Prior to that, for three or four months, I couldn't get arrested at the BBC!"

John was called into John Howard Davies' office and asked if he had seen the ratings and would he be willing to write a third series. Smiling to himself, he agreed. The BBC later improved the offer – and added a fourth series. "As you can imagine I was delighted – and very relieved from my own financial point of view. Up till that point I'd been getting increasingly convinced that I'd have to come up with something new. I remember David, Ray and I chatting about it and thinking 'About bloody time – they've realised this thing they've got here is quite strong.' We felt we'd proved a point particularly because prior to that we thought we were down and dead."

The success of the repeat of series two gave John a great boost to his confidence. "If you are working class background and you are fortunate enough to crack this business, until you've actually had that success you are writing for your money," he said. "You write scared almost and you worry about every idea you get, and you tend to think that some of them are just too outrageous, and that can make you think of holding back and doing a nice script that doesn't offend because your money relies on it.

"It meant I could take the shackles off a bit and open up. Not long after I wrote *Just Good Friends* and I felt myself doing better. The fear I had had began to disappear along with any inhibitions I had with my writing." The BBC began to take note of just what a valuable product they had in *Only Fools and Horses* and just what a talent they had in John Sullivan. *Just Good Friends* was instantly commissioned for a full series and became a hugely popular show, starring Paul Nicholas and Jan Francis as Vince and Penny.

Series Three

Location filming on the third series began on Friday September 2nd 1983 for scenes for the first episode *Homesick*. The story sees Grandad having a health scare and the Trotters trying to get a new council bungalow to save the old fella from walking up twelve flights of stairs (because the lifts were broken). Rodney's new position as chairman of the local housing committee helps him persuade the council that they are a case in need and, with help of council official Miss Mackenzie, they are offered a new home.

Lennard Pearce had some priceless moments in the episode, with the best one coming as Grandad lies in bed looking very poorly after collapsing on the lounge floor. He calls Rodney over, shows him the old cigarette case with a big dent which he says he wants to leave to Rodney, explaining that his Grandad had it with him during his army service in the Boer War.

"One night my Grandad was on sentry duty standing there alone in the middle of Africa when suddenly a sniper fired at him. The bullet was aiming straight for my Grandad's heart but he had that cigarette case in his breast pocket and the bullet hit that instead." "Jeez. It saved his life," exclaims Rodney incredulously. "Well not really," says Grandad. "See the bullet ricocheted up his nose and blew his brains out!"

That scene took ages to film because the cast couldn't stop laughing. "However many times we did that scene we couldn't do it for laughing," recalled David Jason. "We ended up doing it about three or four times and in the end Ray Butt was becoming seriously annoyed. I said to him: 'If you think it's so ******* easy you come down and do it.' If you watch it very carefully you can see me trying not to laugh – and I think it's the same for Nick."

For Lennard filming the episode reminded him of his own real life health scare a few years before, as he told *The News of the World* in December 1983. "I had a supposed deathbed scene in that episode," he said. "It brought back memories of my time in hospital when I wasn't playing it for laughs."

The next episode *Healthy Competition*, Rodney leaves Trotters Independent Traders to set up with Mickey Pearce, but Mickey jets off to Spain for a holiday using their company money. Rodney is too embarrassed to admit to Del that he's been ripped off and tells him that Mickey has gone there to look into setting up a self-catering holiday division.

Del can't quite see how they do this on just £200 and Rodney says: "We're starting in a small way" to which Grandad pipes up with the line: "What have you got? A Wendy house?" The line brought the house down and the laughter from the studio audience was so loud and long it almost brought filming to a halt. "It got a huge laugh and both Nick and I could barely get the next lines out," David recalled. "It just floored us. It stopped Nick and I in our tracks.

"We thought it was a good line but the huge response took us by surprise. When we got to the end of the episode people were still talking about it. Just for fun I said to the studio audience: 'I'm going to resign. That's it. I don't want to be in this show any more. Do you realise that Nick Lyndhurst and myself have spent twenty minutes in this show working our socks off? Lennard Pearce hasn't said a bloody word in the whole show and he just says "Wendy House" and it gets the biggest laugh I've ever heard.' Nick and I were laughing old Lennard was chuckling away. He really enjoyed it."

From then on any line in the script that the cast thought would get a big laugh would be judged on its Wendy factor, as David Jason explained: "If it would get the biggest laugh of the show then it would be termed a Wendy. A sub-Wendy would be just below that, a mini-Wendy would be an average laugh. When someone got a line we thought would bring the house down then we'd say: 'Look out, Wendy alert!'"

Shades of Hammer horror films came to *Only Fools* in the guise of the classic episode **Friday The 14th** in which Del borrows Boycie's West Country holiday cottage as a base for a spot of poaching. From the start the gags come thick and fast. When the Trotters are stopped by a policeman who they think is after them on suspicion of poaching. Of course, they deny all knowledge, despite the fact that the roof is packed with fishing rods. One scene sadly didn't make it to the screen due to the episode over-running. It saw the Trotters enjoying lunch at a country pub and meeting an old country yokel, played by actor Michael Bilton.

Even when he's left alone with the mad axe man, Del seizes an opportunity to capitalise on his situation when his captor challenges him to a game of snooker, to be played on an imaginary table. The madman, we discover, hates winning – and wants Del to beat him, so ever-sharp Del Boy decides to play the game for cash. "That was just brilliant," laughed David Jason. "The whole script had some great lines in it but that ending was just fantastic."

Clearly people at home thought the same too. That episode attracted 9.7 million but even more significantly the following week's episode was watched by 10.6 million – a week on week gain of close to a million. *Only Fools and Horses* was becoming a show that people would watch and then talk about down the pub with their friends and that sort of word of mouth praise can help to add tens of thousands to the ratings. The winter of 1983 saw it beginning to become a 'don't miss' programme and noticeably from that week on it never once attracted less than ten million viewers.

Yesterday Never Comes sees Del apparently scoring with posh antiques dealer Miranda Davenport, played by Juliet Hammond. What he doesn't know though is that she's really only interested in a painting he's got hanging on the wall at the flat. The episode featured one of Del's most cringe-making chat-ups when he slaps her on the bottom and says: "Fancy a curry?" "Of course we didn't know that she only said yes because she was after his picture," said David Jason. "And Rodney nearly faints with shock when Del tries this approach with her and it works – or rather it seems to at that time."

Nicholas Lyndhurst can't forget the time a party of Finnish directors came to see how the BBC made comedy shows. "They came to a studio recording and didn't understand the gags at all," he recalled. "They had an interpreter but because of that their laughter came through fifteen seconds after the British audience. There was a whole row of them and it was quite disruptive to our timing and in the end we asked them to move further back so we couldn't hear them."

May The Force Be With You saw the first appearance of Jim Broadbent as Detective Inspector Roy Slater, who turns up at the Nag's Head like a bad penny looking for trouble and Del Boy in particular. Ray Butt had been keen to use Jim ever since he'd had to turn down the part of Del. "I was very pleased to play Slater," said Jim, who has gone on to become a hugely accomplished star with roles in films like *The Gangs of New York, Bridget Jones's Diary, Moulin Rouge and Iris* and on television in *Blackadder, Any Human Heart* and *The Peter Principle*. "It was a nice role for me."

Despite his other successes there's some irony in what the public remember him most from. "*Only Fools and Horses*," he laughed. "Whenever I'm spotted they say: 'All right, how's Del Boy?'" He has no regrets about turning the job down. "I never really took it as an offer at the time because I was busy working," he said. "And if I'd done it I'd only have done two or three series because I like to constantly move on and do different things."

Wanted is one of those episodes in which John Sullivan demonstrated his ability to weave comedy and pathos together with perfection. The plot sees Del winding Rodney up to believe that a woman he helped in the street has accused him of being a pervert.

Del, as is par for the course, takes the joke too far, telling Rodney that he's been dubbed the 'Peckham Pouncer' and that vigilantes are after him. Poor Rodney decides to go on the run. The denouement comes when Rodney is found by Del hiding at the top of Nelson Mandela House. In an emotional scene Del admitted that it was all a huge tease and Rodney agreed to come home. But unusually it is Rodney who comes off best – with the last joke being on Del. He's been drinking from the tower block's water tank all day only to find that Rodney has peed in it. "It was Rodney's turn to win," said David Jason. "It was a very emotional scene trying to coax Rodney down from the tower."

Who's A Pretty Boy? rounded off the third series and sees the first appearance of Paul Barber as Denzil and Kenneth MacDonald as new Nag's Head landlord Mike Fisher. In the episode Del cons Denzil into allowing the Trotters to decorate his lounge after warning him off over the workmanship of Brendan, the local Irish painter and decorator.

Denzil's plan is very much against the wishes of his wife Corinne, played by Eva Mottley, who according to the story, still hasn't forgiven Del for the disastrous catering he arranged for their wedding. As she says in the script: "What was it we were supposed to have Del? Lobster vol-au-vent, game pie, kidneys with saffron rice, beef and anchovy savouries... and what did we end up with? Pie and chips all round!"

Meanwhile, a Trotter from another generation shows it's not just Del who can pull a fast one. Grandad proves he's not as daft as he looks when he buys a canary for £45 and charges Del £50 for it. But it's Del who ends up smiling at the end by roping landlord Mike Fisher into a con on the brewery. He offers to decorate the pub for £2,000 when Brendan has said he'll do it for £1,000.

Del then explains why Mike should plump for the higher offer. "Because of all the advantages it has to offer like my specialised profit-sharing scheme," he says. "Let me explain how it works:

'The £2,000 would be dispersed thus. There would be £500 for vous and £500 for ve.'" To which Mike replies: "What you mean I get 500 quid?" "Oh yes," says Del. "And what happens to the thousand that's left over?" asks Mike. "We give that to the Irishman and let him do the job," Del explains.

Sadly the episode was to be the only appearance in the show for Corinne, although John Sullivan had planned to bring back both her and Denzil in later episodes. But tragically actress Eva Mottley, who played her, died of a drugs overdose on St Valentine's Day 1985.

Barbados-born Eva, who was just thirty-one, had found fame as Bella in the hit ITV drama series *Widows* but had later left the series suddenly after a row with producers. "Her death was a great shock and suicide is so terrible," said Ray Butt. "She was a very vivacious lady and great fun to have around and didn't seem to have a care in the world. I'm sure she would have been back in the show at some later date because she and Denzil were good characters and were nice people and there was a lot of scope with them."

"It was a terrible shame," recalled David Jason. "Eva was lovely and was going to be a good team player and Denzil and Corinne would have worked well in the future as a couple. She was obviously the one with the get up and go in that relationship and he was the hen-pecked husband. She was very strong and would take no truck from Del Boy and had him completely sussed. Del knew this and tried to treat her with kid gloves and he'd try to ingratiate himself with her and he was all slimy and creepy-crawly with her, trying to get on her good side to no avail."

Christmas 1983 saw the transmission of the first Christmas Day special of the programme *Thicker Than Water* and the only appearance of the Trotter boys' father Reg, played by actor Peter Woodthorpe. Woodthorpe had been cast by Ray Butt because of his likeness to David Jason, something David himself could never quite see. "I couldn't see a likeness at all," he said. "But then others did think he looked like me. To me he just looked just like himself!"

Del was out when Reg turned up at the flat and was furious on his return when he found him in his [Del's] favourite seat, smoking one of his best cigars. Reg then proceeded to cause a family rift after revealing he was suffering from a hereditary illness and then calling into question Del's paternity after he and Rodney received the results of blood tests. "I never brought Reg back because he'd turned up and blotted his copybook so badly that I couldn't see Del ever accepting him back again so I never attempted it," said John Sullivan. "I thought there was no way I could ever persuade an audience that Del would let him back in again after that or that the others would want him back so I just left it that he was there and now he's gone."

"It was good having Reg Trotter come into the series because it showed what a total shit he was," said David Jason. "The character had left them and their mother and he was a real rotten bastard and it was good to remind people of that." As if to reflect the series' hugely increased popularity, in April 1984 the programme won the Television and Radio Industries Club Top Situation Comedy Award.

During 1984 a special episode of *Only Fools and Horses* called **Licensed To Drill** was filmed as a schools programme. In the episode Del has big plans to become an oil baron with his own company called Trotter Oil. John Sullivan recalled: "We were approached by an American company called Phillips Petroleum in 1984 because the head of their European Division Philip Caudill was a big fan of *Only Fools and Horses*. He wanted to make an episode featuring Del trying to get involved in the oil business, which would be screened as an educational programme. I wrote the script and it was filmed at a studio in south west London by an independent company called Topaz because the BBC didn't want to make it. It was great fun to do but we had to be a little bit more careful with the script than usual as it was being aimed at children."

The nineteen-minute episode, which had a different theme tune, written and sung by John Sullivan and arranged by Ronnie Hazlehurst, featured Lennard Pearce's final appearance as Grandad.

DEL'S LINGO

John Sullivan's inspiration for Del's daft foreign phrases came from anywhere from sauce bottles to clothes labels. "Del would read things, think that they were impressive and then he'd start to use them very inappropriately," said John. Other words – like 'cushty' – which means great or smashing - is an old London saying which comes from Britain's colonial days, when a posting to a town in India with a similar-sounding name was considered to be easy. 'Lovely jubbly' comes from an ice lolly sold called Jubbly popular in the fifties, which was advertised with the slogan 'Lovely Jubbly'.

Here are some of the best of the rest - and what Del means when he uses them:

Fabrique Belgique:	I agree
La plume de ma tante:	Actually means 'my aunt's pen' but is used by Del when he's exasperated instead of something like 'Gordon Bennett'
Bonjour:	Goodbye
Au revoir:	Hello
Allemagne dix points:	Such is life
Pucker/Pukka:	Perfect
Twonk, Dipstick, Plonker, Pranny, Wally and Div	Idiot

Series Four

Location filming began for the fourth series in early December 1984 at a pub just off Ladbroke Grove in west London for the episode *Hole In One*. In it, Del and Rodney are so strapped for cash that Grandad decides to 'accidentally' fall down into a pub cellar and then claim compensation from the brewery.

The following Sunday filming moved to the Magistrates Court at nearby Kingston for scenes when Grandad and the boys go to court to win compensation for his injury and he's later exposed as having pulled the same trick quite a number of times before. Shooting ended around lunchtime and the cast and crew went their separate ways. Ray Butt jocularly asked Lennard Pearce: "When are you with me again, you lazy old sod? He said: 'Next Sunday,'" Ray recalled. "I said: 'I'm buggered if I'm paying you for a whole week when I'm not seeing you because we're all still working!' and he laughed and I told him to take care and that I'd see him the next Sunday."

It was to be the last time they saw each other. Lennard suffered a heart attack on the Wednesday and was rushed to the Whittington Hospital at Highgate, north London. Lennard's landlady phoned John Sullivan to tell him the bad news. "Jan Francis (who knew him well) and I went up to see him," John recalled. "He had lots of wires going into him and he showed us what he said was a support machine. It was just a small box and I thought he'd got it wrong, because I thought they were these big things."

John took with him a lucky charm pig just like Trotter, the

pink China one that took pride of place in the control box during studio recordings of the series. It had been bought by Ray Butt's secretary Penny Thompson and after she'd showed it to Lennard Pearce before a studio recording and he'd gone on to have a really good show, he'd always go and touch the pig for good luck before a recording. "I couldn't find the original Trotter," John recalled. "So I bought another one that I called Son of Trotter and took that along for him."

At around 8am on Sunday December 16th, the day when Lennard had originally been due back on location for his next block of filming, Ray Butt received a phone call at home from Lennard's agent Carole James telling him that he had died. "We were due to start at 9am and I had to go up there and tell them that Lennard had died," he recalled, clearly still moved by the memory. "Everyone was absolutely gutted and there were lots of tears.

"To most people – cast and crew – Lennard was Grandad. They all called him Grandad and hardly anyone called him Lennard and he loved that. So we cancelled filming. No one was in a mood to work that day. It was a very sad time." David Jason and Nicholas Lyndhurst were in make-up when Ray came and told them the dreadful news. "Ray came into make-up and stood in the doorway and just shook his head gently and then walked out again," recalled Nicholas. "He didn't say anything and he didn't need to. We knew. Lennard had been on our minds all the time since he'd suffered his first heart attack. No one had been thinking about much else all week. David and I followed Ray out and it started snowing really heavily just for a few minutes, and I stood facing a shop window and cried my eyes out. After a while we went back to our trailer and I remember David very gently swearing under his breath every so often. We were both very upset."

"We'd been shooting some scenes that didn't involve Grandad and we were in make-up when Ray came in with the news," David recalled. "That was it. We just all went home. We couldn't even think about working that day. It was just too upsetting."

John Sullivan recalled: "Apparently a few days after Jan and I visited him they took him off the machine and he had another massive heart attack. Without the support of the machine he couldn't live. My wife Sharon took the call from Ray saying that Lennard had died and she was in tears. We were devastated because he was such a lovely old man and such a kind man and was always sending things for the kids like dinosaur books for Dan.

"He was like a third Grandad to our kids. It got very confusing for them at school and I think they thought someone had married twice because both the boys had Grandad John, Grandad Charlie and Grandad Trotter. The boys thought they had three Grandads too because at Christmas they'd get presents from all three and Lennard would just sign the card 'Lots of love from Grandad' and they'd ask which one and we'd say: 'That's from Grandad Trotter.'"

The following day Ray Butt went to his office at BBC Television Centre and had meetings with John Sullivan, David Jason and Gareth Gwenlan, the new Head of Comedy, and between them decided that, despite the tragedy, the series would continue. "We were committed to transmission dates and, Christ knows how, it had to be worked out," recalled Ray. He announced that filming would start again on January 2nd. The team was due to have had a Christmas break anyway and it was extended to give John Sullivan the chance to write new scripts.

Lennard Pearce had made the character of Grandad very much his own and neither Ray nor John had any great desire to see it played by another actor, because really as far as they were concerned Lennard was irreplaceable. "No one was very keen on the idea of re-casting the part of Grandad," recalled John Sullivan. "Because the show was like a family and it seemed disrespectful to Lennard."

David Jason recalled: "Someone higher up in the BBC pecking order said: 'We understand that it's difficult but you've got to make the series. Why don't you get a look-alike? The audience will soon accept it and forget the change.' I said: 'Yeah, they may do but I wouldn't' and John Sullivan said: 'I'm not going to do that because I wouldn't insult Lennard's memory' so that put the kibosh on that. But we realised we needed to have a third element because it wasn't a class war, it was a war of ages. It was Rodney the younger, Del in the middle and the elder, Grandad."

"There was a real need for the new character and one from an older generation," said Ray Butt. "We needed him to complete the triangle with Del Boy and Rodney. I thought I had problems but my troubles were nothing compared to John's. He had the big headache. He had to turn his scripts upside down and write out the character of Grandad and bring in a new older character."

David Jason said that at one point it was suggested that the new character should be a woman. "Someone said: 'I know, just to make it different, why don't we make it an old aunt that comes and lives with them?'" said David. "And someone else said: 'Yeah, good idea, it's about time we had a woman in it.' I could see this idea looming in front of me like some sort of monster. Everybody was fired up with it and John thought he could make it work and I said: 'It won't work. How are you going to bundle her into the back of a three-wheeled van. How are you going to say "Shut up you old git" to a woman, you'd have to get rid of all of that.' Don't ask me why, but you could push Grandad into the back of a van. Or drag him out or do anything you like, even though he's a little old man – and get away with it. You just couldn't do all that with an old woman, nor could you use the language. It would never have worked."

Then the conversation moved towards the new character being an Uncle. "John was keen to keep the war references going," said David "So it was decided to go with the idea of him being an Uncle, who'd been in the war and been away at sea a lot – and that's how we came to have Uncle Albert."

"It was a gigantic re-writing job," John admitted. "We wanted to do a funeral because the Trotters were a real family and if Grandad dies then we should reflect that on screen. It was a bad time. The rest of the series had been written but I had to write *Strained Relations*, the funeral episode. Then we all agreed we couldn't start the series with a funeral so I had to write another episode, **Happy Returns**."

John didn't like it when, if an actor in a television programme died, it was explained on screen by the character suddenly moving somewhere. "I'm glad we didn't do that," he said.

"We felt it was right to have a funeral for Grandad, like a real family would, just as we had had a funeral for Lennard," said David Jason. "The episode was superb. I don't think any other writer would have taken the challenge that John did to bury one of your central characters in a comedy series. It just doesn't happen. But he rose to that challenge and delivered a brilliant script."

John had to write the two brand new episodes in double-quick time so that filming could begin again straight after Christmas. Amazingly, despite the rush effort, the quality of his writing stayed the same and *Happy Returns*, in which Del thought he'd found out that Rodney's new girlfriend was actually his daughter by his old flame June, won a Bafta award.

"My problem was finding an actor who we thought was right and who would fit in," recalled Ray Butt. "The chemistry had to be right with David and Nick. The relatively short time we had for casting the first series now seemed like a luxury. I had the problem of finding an actor without actually having a part for him firmed up because John was still writing the scripts and coming up with ideas for the third guy. Then John hit upon the idea of having a long lost Uncle of the boys who'd been away at sea for years. It was a great idea but we still had the same problem with finding the right man for the part."

Before going away for Christmas Ray had gone back to his office at the BBC to find himself faced with a mountain of mail from out-of-work and unknown actors putting their names forward for the part. "There were all these people saying that they knew

Lennard and they'd like to take the part. They were all bloody no-nos, they really were," said Ray. "It made me very angry. I had this pile of letters about a foot high and I picked them up and threw them into a pile in the corner of the room and left the office. It was not a good time and I wasn't interested in them."

He returned to his office on New Year's Eve knowing that he had to find a new actor – and fast. He picked up the pile of letters he'd chucked on the floor and began leafing through them. "After a while I spotted this photograph with a letter from a bloke called Buster Merryfield who looked a bit like Father Christmas and a bit like Captain Birdseye with a big round face and a big white beard. It caught my eye so I read his note.

"It wasn't full of all the bullshit like the others. He briefly outlined the facts that he'd been a bank manager and had only started acting professionally after he had retired. It was quite a bizarre story and it made him stand out from the other, frankly, has-been actors. His letter was very straightforward and almost the sort of business letter that you'd expect from a bank manager!"

Buster Merryfield was driving back to his home at Byfleet in Surrey after two performances as the King in *Jack and the Beanstalk* at the Theatre Royal, Windsor. He was tired out and, after removing his stage make-up, went straight to bed. It was about midnight and his wife Iris woke up as he climbed into bed and told him that some producer at the BBC had phoned and wanted him to ring back in the morning.

"That was nothing unusual because I wrote off for jobs all the time," Buster recalled. "Being the man I am – quite enterprising – I was always trying to get work. The message was to call a chap called Ray Butt. It hadn't said what it was about but before I went off to the matinee performance at the theatre I rang him up.

"He told me he was the producer of *Only Fools and Horses* and, believe it or not, I'd never seen the show because when you are acting in the theatre you don't get much time to watch television what with working evenings. I knew of the show and I knew it was a comedy and that it was successful because people would talk about it but, apart from that, I didn't know too much about it. I was just flattered that he'd called me because it was a known show and he was the producer and, being optimistic, I thought that maybe he had a small part for me so I was quite excited. He said: 'Do you think you could come up and see me tomorrow morning?' and I said: 'I'm sorry but I'm in pantomime' and he said: 'Oh yes, we know that but you don't start until 2.30pm.

"'What if I sent a car to pick you up, bring you up and then we'll get a car to take you back to the theatre in time for your matinee?' I said: 'Fine' and besides, the idea of being driven up in a chauffeur driven car quite appealed to me!" The following day the two men met at the reception of BBC Television Centre. They took the lift to the fifth floor and went to Ray's office where Buster was introduced to Gareth Gwenlan.

"They told me that Lennard Pearce had died, which I didn't know until then. I immediately thought that they must be wanting someone to play his part and I interjected and said that I wouldn't fancy stepping into the shoes of someone who had just died. They explained that the writer was accepting the death as part of the series and that the Grandad would die in the series, and he was creating a new character - his long lost brother called Uncle Albert.

"That perked me up. They asked me if I'd be interested and would I read a bit of the script for them. They didn't have any lines for Albert yet so I had to read some of Grandad's lines with Ray and Gareth reading Del and Rodney's. I asked them what accent to do and they said: 'He's a south Londoner' so I read about four lines before Ray interrupted and said: 'Right, thanks, that's enough. I thought: 'Oh dear, something's gone wrong.'

"They thanked me and said that they'd better be getting me back for the matinee. I didn't feel I'd done too badly but I had no idea what they thought. Ray took me back down in the lift and said:

'We'll ring you this afternoon.'" Buster was on stage when Ray Butt phoned him and he rang him back during a short break. "My old heart was going," he recalled. "I thought: 'This is it!'" It wasn't. Ray Butt simply asked Buster to come back up for another meeting the next day.

"It was a complete anti-climax," he recalled. "I asked Ray if there was something wrong and he said not at all but that he'd like me to meet David, Nick and John Sullivan because he wanted to find out if the chemistry would work." This time Buster was taken to a hospitality room at Television Centre where he was greeted by a sea of faces including David Jason and Nicholas Lyndhurst, who were due to be back filming an episode later that day.

John Sullivan was also there along with a handful of executives from the comedy department, all anxious to see if Ray's wild hunch about this bank manager turned actor being right for the show was correct. "There was coffee, cakes and sandwiches and we chatted and David asked me what I'd been doing, work-wise and asked me about the pantomime I was appearing in," Buster recalled.

"We didn't talk about *Only Fools and Horses*, we were chatting about general things and nothing in particular and it was all sort of geared towards seeing if we spoke the same language. Again I read a bit of script, just a page I seem to recall, but this time with David and Nick playing their proper roles and after that it was time for me to once again head back to Windsor and the panto."

Again Ray Butt walked Buster to the lift and told him that he'd call him later that day. "He was very nice and considerate," said Buster. "He gave me some encouragement and said: 'You did very well, Buster. Before you go back there's something I'd like to tell you. If you get this part – and I repeat *if* – you will become famous and I say that because you must tell your wife. Once people get to know you, you might find it alters your life and her life as well. It could disrupt your normal way of life and you ought to be aware of that before deciding what to do.' He said he'd ring me later."

With Buster back in the car and on the way to Windsor, Ray and the others began discussing the pros and cons of casting a relatively inexperienced and certainly unknown actor in a top-rated sitcom.

"David and Nick weren't a hundred percent happy and I think that was mainly because they were still thinking about Lennard," said Ray Butt. "It was the same for all of us really. I had all the same emotions as them but the job had to be done and the show had to go on. It was as simple as that. We had to make it work. Buster had read OK and he looked the part but nevertheless it was a terrible gamble but I thought we could mould him and get away with it and it really was desperation time."

Buster tried not to build up his hopes as he waited for the call at the Theatre Royal, Windsor. "I'm not a stupid fellow and I knew they might just turn round and say: 'Sorry, you're not quite the chap for us'. I'd had auditions before and then afterwards they'd say that I wasn't tall enough, or fat enough or whatever so I was quite used to the way that the business worked.

"Nevertheless when one of the girls at the theatre came up to me during the matinee and said: 'Can you phone the BBC back?' I was shaking. I thought: 'This is going to be the answer one way or the other.' So I phoned Ray back and he thanked me for coming up again and I was thinking: 'Please get to the point!' Then he said: 'We'd like you to join us.' I couldn't believe it!

"He said: 'We're filming tomorrow' and I thought: 'Oh Lord.' Ray then added: 'And we will need you on set for filming at seven-thirty. We'll send a car for you. Is 6am all right?' I'd thought I wouldn't be needed for a few weeks and by then I'd have finished in the panto. But I was wrong so for the next fortnight I'd start at 6am filming *Only Fools and Horses* and then go and do the panto and finish at ten at night."

The following morning Buster found himself on location outside a pub which was doubling as the Nag's Head to start filming the story *Hole In One*, the episode the team had been shooting when

Lennard Pearce died. "When I arrived they were all ready to start filming," Buster recalled. "Ray came out and said: 'You better go over to the costume van and get yourself some gear for Albert's costume.'

"We knew he was an old sailor so were sort of looking for stuff that would suit him. There was a costume designer there who suggested this old peaked cap and we spotted a duffel coat, so I put that on and tracked down an old pair of cords. Everything was done in a great hurry and not much research went into it. We were just trying to pick something suitable for that day.

"We topped it off with a scarf, mainly because it was so cold. When I arrived on set I had no idea what I was going to be doing. Of course it turned out that I was filming what would be my second episode but I had no script as such - just had a sheet of paper with my four or five lines on it. I wasn't that nervous because it wasn't like being in the theatre where once you leave the wings then you are on your own. I'd done a small bit of telly beforehand and I knew if something went wrong then we could cut and do it again. My first scene was where Del speaks to Mike, the Nag's Head landlord, who is down in the pub's cellar. Albert then has a word with Mike and Del then drags him away when he mentions a dodgy deep fat fryer that Del has sold Mike. That was pretty much it for that day and then I had to dash off and get back to Windsor for the afternoon's matinee performance of the panto. It was quite hectic!"

Buster's first day had gone quite well. He'd enjoyed it but worried unnecessarily about lines he'd got wrong, even though no one else was unhappy with his performance. He still had no real idea that he was to become a regular member of the team. Nor did John Sullivan, who was really writing the series on the hoof. The more he could see Buster what was capable of then the more lines he'd give him.

Two weeks later, on Sunday January 27th, Buster was wondering whether he'd taken on more than he could cope with and starting to doubt his own ability. It was the studio recording of the episode *It's Only Rock And Roll*. Recorded in the large TC6 studio at BBC Television Centre in front of a live audience, including his family, it was a daunting experience for Buster. Despite his vast amateur theatre work, he'd faced nothing like this before. "I was dreading it," he admitted. "I was frightened to death because I knew there would be an audience of two or three hundred people. I was very apprehensive because I'd never done a recording in front of an audience before.

"I was so keen not get it wrong. I remember I made my entrance at a particular point and I forgot my lines. I felt terrible. I never usually forgot my lines and compared to some of my big theatre parts, I had relatively little to say. We did it again a couple of times and I got it right but I still went back to my dressing room and sat there thinking: 'You fool. You've blown it!' I thought that forgetting your lines was the most serious thing in the world.

"I was really panicked. I felt terrible and I didn't think they'd want me. I was so inexperienced myself and I held people in television in such esteem that I thought that they never dried up. I was very intimidated by it all and all the cameras moving about but I had to go back on again and make another entrance and do my next scene. I must have been ashen.

"I was terribly nervous and I was probably shaking a bit and I think they noticed how worried I was. I said a line and got it right and David Jason as Del answered me and he got his words wrong. He forgot his line and he was saying: 'What's the line? What's the line?' All the audience started laughing and he said: 'What are you lot laughin' at? You didn't pay to come in, you're getting it for nuffink aren't ya? What do you expect?'" For Buster it was a moment that helped enormously. He could see that even seasoned performers like David Jason could fluff their lines and that perhaps it wasn't such a great sin after all.

It wasn't until after the recording had finished that Buster realised that David's 'gaff' had probably actually been deliberate. "I reckon he saw how nervous I was and did it deliberately to put me at ease. He knew I was shaky and I think he did it to reassure me that it didn't really matter and to give me my confidence back. I never knew for sure but I think that's what happened – and that's the kind of man he is. Of course now I realise that getting lines wrong is a regular thing that can happen to anyone but at the time I had no idea. It was a necessary thing to experience and now I don't worry about it."

David and Nicholas Lyndhurst would later tease Buster about his letter to Ray Butt that got him his part in the series. "If he complained it was cold or something on location we'd joke with him by saying: 'You shouldn't have written in then!'" said Nicholas.

Days after shooting his first scenes for *Hole In One*, Buster was filming exterior shots for his second episode, ***Strained Relations***, although it was screened first as episode two of the series. It was the episode that dealt with Grandad's funeral and was the hardest script John Sullivan had ever had to write. Having just lost a much-loved friend and colleague, he had spent his Christmas re-working the next series. To his credit, John had decided to tackle Lennard Pearce's death directly and kill off the character of Grandad. Not only that but he chose to include the funeral in an episode, rather than just refer to it. "It was a terrifying idea," said Ray Butt. "To open a comedy show with a funeral would normally, to use a terrible pun, be death. But John was brilliant. He engineered it so well."

With consummate skill Sullivan wrote a brilliant script, which I believe is one of his finest ever. Not surprisingly the funeral scene wasn't littered with jokes. It was dark and gloomy, much as the cast and crew felt at the time. But Sullivan knew he couldn't make the whole script downbeat, so he broke the mood with a gag which was a master stroke.

Rodney drops Grandad's trilby hat into the grave before it's filled in by gravediggers. As far as Del and Rodney and the viewer is concerned that's that - until the vicar sets off for home and asks if anyone has seen his hat. This was a typical Sullivan twist which lightened the moment completely and lifted the gloom. "You had all the pathos and all the sadness which is an important element of comedy and then he pricked it by the fact that Del and Rodney had thrown the wrong hat into the grave," said Ray Butt. "It was a brilliant idea by John and he engineered it so well and put it in exactly the right position and it lifted the whole episode."

David Jason agreed: "It was a brilliant way of lightening the scene. And I have to say it's a tribute to the brilliance of John Sullivan's writing that he could handle something as delicate as a death in the family with such skill that one minute you are laughing and the next minute you are crying."

Nevertheless, there were problems during rehearsals of *Strained Relations*. The episode could not be squeezed into thirty minutes and was running consistently at thirty-five even after pages of scripts had been dumped. "Whatever we did it would not run to time," John recalled. "And we were already down to just the bones of the thing. Everyone was very fed up – and still upset over Lennard's death. I asked Gareth Gwenlan for an extra five minutes and he said it was impossible because they couldn't shave five minutes off the preceding programme, *Top of The Pops* nor the following, *The Nine O'Clock News*."

In the end John stormed out of the rehearsal room. He needed to cool off. The pressure had finally got to him. When he saw John leaving, Ray Butt jumped out of a kitchen window - the quickest route - and chased after him before he could drive off. The men talked but there was no row. After all they were on the same side and were both under great strain. Back home John called his agent to talk about the problem. Calls were then made to the BBC.

Minutes later BBC1 boss Michael Grade was on the phone to Sullivan telling him: "You've got your extra five minutes. I'm telling *Top of The Pops* they'll have to lose a bloody record." Back at rehearsals the following day the relief was huge, and amazingly the next run through ran to just thirty minutes. "It just picked up," John recalled. "Perhaps it was because the pressure was off but in the end I had to ring Michael Grade back and tell him that we didn't need the extra five minutes and we even put some cut material back in!"

For the production team and the cast, though, these were the hardest days of filming they'd ever experienced because just a fortnight before they'd buried Lennard Pearce for real. Now they were at a cemetery in Acton filming his character's burial. "I can't think of anything worse than that day," recalled Ray Butt. "It really was hard and it's still difficult to think about it." "It was a bitterly cold day and all our thoughts were with Lennard," said Kenneth MacDonald. "It was very difficult."

"It was a very difficult time because we'd only buried Lennard for real a few weeks before," David Jason recalled. "Yet we still had a few laughs because that was the best way to get through. Someone, and I can't remember who it was, which is probably just as well, said: 'Lennard must feel lucky' and I said: 'Why?' and they said: 'Well he's the only man I know who has been buried twice!'"

Indeed, Lennard Pearce's real funeral wasn't without laughter and that's something by all accounts he would have wanted. John Sullivan was sitting directly behind David Jason and seconds after the vicar announced hymn number 187 John saw David's pew begin to shake. David was having a fit of the giggles. David turned round to show John that the page was missing from his hymn book and the two men smiled. "John realised why I was laughing," David recalled. "We were both thinking the same thing: 'Had Del Boy supplied the hymn books?'

"All our emotions were so stirred up and suddenly something like that happens and you do see the funny side of it. It wasn't an insult to where we were or to Lennard's memory. And I think Lennard would have seen the joke in it too." *Strained Relations* also featured an exchange between Del and Rodney that must be one of the best sitcom scenes ever. It comes when grief-stricken Rodney asks Del how he can have got over Grandad's death so quickly. Of course he hasn't:

"Get over it? What a plonker you really are, Rodney. Get over it? I haven't even started yet, I ain't even started bruv. And do you know why? Because I don't know how to. That's why. I've survived all my life with a smile and a prayer. I'm Del Boy ain't I. Good old Del Boy, he's got more bounce than Zebedee. 'Ere pal what you drinkin'? Go on darlin' you 'ave one for luck. That's me, that's Del Boy isn't it. Nothing ever upsets Del Boy. I've always played the tough guy. I didn't want to but I had to and I've played it for so long now that I don't know how to be anything else. I don't even know how to….oh it don't matter. Bloody families, I'm finished with them. What do they do to you, eh? They drag you down and then they break your bloody heart."

"John Sullivan wrote so many great scenes in *Only Fools and Horses*," said David Jason. "But that is certainly one of the best as far as I'm concerned. He was just brilliant at expressing real emotion in his characters. It was a very difficult time. We put our energy into that episode in Lennard's memory. We were all a bit sensitive at the time for an episode or two. We were careful to defend Lennard and would make sure that Buster didn't take on any of the moments that belonged to Lennard and slowly that all began to relax and anyway Buster then made it his own, so that didn't matter.

"We weren't against him in any way. He was great. He was different but it wasn't Grandad, it was this character and it was taking us a bit of time to cross over that bridge. Buster had to learn, because he hadn't got the experience of television that Lennard had so it was a difficult time for Buster too because he was taking over somebody's role and he didn't know any of us. It was a difficult time but we all crossed over it and formed a new and happy relationship with Buster which was great.

"He played it very, very differently and because he was playing it differently that gave John a chance to exploit his way of carrying on which was very funny. Joining the show like he did must have been very hard for him and we tried to give him as much support as we possibly could and tried to make him feel relaxed. We didn't want him to feel like an outsider and he responded to that. It was potentially very dangerous to bring someone new in like that but, bless him, he rose to the occasion. He made the character his own quite brilliantly."

After *Hole In One* came ***It's Only Rock And Roll***. This episode sees Del deciding to go into music management and taking on Rodney and his mates' band, which he dubs 'A Bunch of Wallies.' Not surprisingly everything goes wrong, with Del getting bookings in the most inappropriate places. Sadly for Rodney it's only after he quits the group, after rowing with them over Del, that they have a big hit with *Boys Will Be Boys* and get to appear on *Top of The Pops*. Actor and writer Daniel Peacock, who played psychotic singer Mental Mickey, had a great time filming it. "I was twenty-six at the time and being on *Only Fools and Horses* and *Top of The Pops* was a double coup," he said. "I thought they'd just build a set for the *Top of The Pops* appearance but I was wrong. We rehearsed the song we had to sing, *Boys Will Be Boys*, for a couple of hours and then were whisked over to the actual *Top of The Pops* studio to record it while they were filming the real show. It was great. We were up there in front of all these screaming girls and Radio One DJ Mike Read introduced us."

Sleeping Dogs Lie saw the first appearance of Sue Holderness as Boycie's wife Marlene in the episode in which the pair went on holiday, leaving their new dog Duke in the less-than-safe hands of the Trotter family. The dog fell ill and later it was discovered that Albert had mistakenly taken Duke's vitamin pills instead of his own sleeping pills and vice versa. The climax of the episode saw Del and Rodney mischievously calling to Albert: 'Here boy...'

The day after it was transmitted Buster was walking along the road at Clapham Junction, south London and was spotted by some fans. "I heard someone call out 'Albert, Albert' and I looked over the road between the buses and saw three shabbily dressed chaps in their twenties smiling away. Suddenly they got in a line and shouted: 'Here boy, here boy!' They copied just what had been on the programme. It was lovely and it made me laugh."

Nicholas Lyndhurst had a lucky escape during filming. For one scene he had to carry the dog and then fall over with it on top of him and Duke got a little bit frisky. "They cut just in time otherwise in a another few seconds it would have become a very different show," he said. "I couldn't get the dog off me and it was only with crafty footwork that I got it off in the end!"

Watching The Girls Go By focuses on Rodney's continuing lack of pulling-power. When Mickey Pearce teases him about not being able to bring a girl to a party at the Nag's Head, Rodney ends up betting him that he'll have a girl on his arm that night. Egged on by Del, the bet gets as high as a 'round fifty'. Rodney is in a fix and Del decides to buy the bet off him. He's now got an interest in Rodney's success and gives old friend Yvonne, a stripper and would-be singer, £20 to go on the date with Rodney. Everything goes wrong when Yvonne gets drunk and takes her clothes off and Rodney is humiliated. But it's Del who ends up most upset as Rodney's bet with Mickey was for 50p not fifty quid!

The final episode of the series *As One Door Closes* was inspired by an article John Sullivan read in the *Sunday Times* about climatic changes in Britain. "It said some famous butterfly that had never been seen here before had been spotted and a big cash reward was being offered by a collector to whoever caught one alive," he recalled. "If Del had read the article it was just the sort of thing he'd have gone for." The last scene saw Del catch the butterfly only to have his hands slapped by Denzil - with obvious results. In rehearsals Paul Barber suggested he did the scene on roller skates –

an idea he soon regretted. "I couldn't skate at the time and then had to spend two weeks going round my local park trying to learn how to," he recalled. "But I did get to keep the skates after we finished the episode!"

ONLY FOOLS AND HORSES - THE STAGE SHOW

The success of stage versions of hit comedies like *Dad's Army, Are You Being Served?* and later *Bread* and *'Allo, 'Allo* led the *Only Fools and Horses* team to consider doing a stage version of the show in 1985 to be put on either in the West End or at one of the big regional theatres for a summer season. Producer and writer David Croft had done well with his shows on stage, which he co-wrote with Jimmy Perry and later Jeremy Lloyd, and they were known to be a great way of making money.

"None of us were making much money in those days and it was a case of what could we do to make some more money," recalled Ray Butt. "I suggested to John that we cobble three or four scripts together but John didn't want to do that. He liked the idea but the theatre wasn't a medium he had any experience of. And. by that stage, he was also busy writing both *Just Good Friends* and *Only Fools and Horses* and was always behind the clock with them. David, Nick and Buster were all keen but we just never got it together."

"It would have been very successful financially," said David. "But I've never done anything for money, it's always been the work first, then I try to discuss money afterwards. I think it would have worked brilliantly but I was getting to the point where people were beginning to only think of me as Del Boy and that was beginning to worry me, as much as I was enjoying playing him.

"I needed some space to do other things and I felt that if we went and did a summer season or a West End season we'd be doing it every night and we'd be doing it more for money than anything. It was bit of everything really. When it started to be quite heavily mooted, before it went any further I personally was pouring cold water on the idea and perhaps everybody else was too. Or maybe if everyone had really gone for it then maybe I would have been sucked along with it."

1985 Christmas Special

Christmas 1985 saw the first ever feature length *Only Fools* special, **To Hull and Back**. The previous Christmas, the BBC had enjoyed a huge hit with a ninety minute episode of John Sullivan's comedy *Just Good Friends*. The fourth series of *Only Fools and Horses* had been a big success despite the upheaval following the loss of Lennard Pearce and the introduction of Buster Merryfield as Albert.

So in April 1985 BBC1 bosses decided to follow the previous Christmas hit and commission a festive feature length episode. As John Sullivan started working on a script, producer Ray Butt set about budgeting for it. It was then that they hit a major snag that nearly sank the whole production. "I prepared the budget, which was a normal procedure, and put it in to my manager," recalled Ray Butt. "He said: 'We can't afford that' and I said: 'Well if you can't afford that then you ain't gonna get it mate. It's as simple as that because that's what it's going to cost.'" John Sullivan's script saw the Trotters hire a fishing boat and travel to Amsterdam on a very dubious diamond smuggling expedition arranged by Boycie and his shady business contact Abdul (played by actor Tony Anholt) while being chased by Detective Inspector Roy Slater, again played by Jim Broadbent.

By the time the episode was screened on Christmas Day Tony Anholt would have become a big star and a very familiar face to television viewers as ruthless tycoon Charles Frere in the BBC sex and sailing drama *Howards' Way*. "The foreign filming made it expensive and it was to be a six-week shoot, all on film and shot in late summer," said Ray. "I told my manager: 'If I spent that much last year then with adding a bit on for inflation it's going to come to at least that much and for less than that I can't do it.'

"He said: 'We just haven't got that sort of money.' Some five weeks later Ray Butt, who was directing and producing a series of *Just Good Friends* at the same time, went to the Montreux Television Festival in Switzerland. At a BBC dinner one night Ray found himself sitting next to Michael Grade, a high-flying television executive, who had recently joined the BBC as the Controller of BBC1. The two men hadn't met before, although Butt knew Grade was a fan of *Just Good Friends*, and they introduced themselves to each other. "He asked me how it was going and what was the news on *Fools*," Ray recalled.

"I said: 'Well, frankly mate we've got this great idea but the firm tell me it's too dear.' He said: 'Well, tell me about it' so I did and told him how much we needed and he said: 'You've got it. If you've got a problem then ring me.'" Grade's high-level intervention saved the show – or at the very least it gave Ray Butt the budget he needed. Grade added almost £250,000 to the budget, taking it to around £850,000.

By August 1985 the BBC had discovered that ITV's big Christmas Day hope was a feature length episode of its hit drama *Minder* called *Minder On The Orient Express*. Michael Grade moved quickly and revealed that he would be putting the *Only Fools and Horses* special in direct competition to the *Minder* special and the press began billing it as a *Minder* versus Del Boy clash. Of course, this all took place back in the days before most households had video recorders and PVRs were many years away. In the *Daily Mirror* Tony Purnell pointed out that it would be viewers who'd suffer and quoted an unnamed BBC source as saying that: "It's another case of the viewer losing out yet again." "Millions of fans will be forced on Christmas night to choose between loveable London rogues George Cole and Dennis Waterman and equally loveable London rogues

David Jason and Nicholas Lyndhurst," Purnell wrote.

The *Daily Express* said it presented an "agonising choice" for viewers and called on both the BBC and ITV to repeat the shows early in the New Year to give viewers a chance to see the one they missed. The paper decided that Michael Grade's move was connected to the BBC's loss of its popular American drama *Dallas* to ITV company Thames, which made *Minder*, and it said he was still smarting at its loss. It quoted Grade as saying: "We are in direct competition with ITV. That's the way it is and always will be." In early December even David Jason joined in the friendly rivalry when asked who would pull in more viewers. "It's got to be us, innit," he was quoted as telling the *Daily Mirror*. "We will be funnier and better... no doubt about that my son. I will put my feet up with the rest of the country. Poor Arfur will have to make do with *Minder*, along with his three regular fans."

George Cole, who played wheeler-dealer Arthur Daley in *Minder* hit back: "There is already talk of an ITV blackout. Obviously Del Boy is behind it because he's so worried." Away from the joking, the two actors clearly felt sad that the viewers would have to choose which to watch with David Jason saying that TV bosses who engineered the clash are "buggers, aren't they? It's bound to cause rows in families up and down the country. There is nothing we can do about it, I guess." George Cole said: "It's a shame. We must have a similar following and not everyone has got a video to record one of them for later viewing. Millions of fans will be disappointed."

Nevertheless the viewers made their choice and the BBC gave ITV a thorough pasting in the ratings with 16.9 million tuning in to watch *Only Fools and Horses* compared to a few million less for *Minder*. It was a great confidence boost for John Sullivan, a second-in-a-row Christmas hit for Ray Butt, a tribute to the acting of the cast and a successful gamble for Michael Grade. "It proved to be money well spent," said Ray Butt. It was the start of *Only Fools and Horses'* dominance of seasonal TV and from then on the show became as much a key part of the British Christmas Day as the Queen's Speech. For David Jason, Nicholas Lyndhurst and Buster Merryfield, along with Ray Butt and his production team, it made some tough days filming on the North Sea seem well worthwhile.

"We shot a lot of it at sea on this terrible old ninety foot boat and travelled up and down the Yorkshire coast," Ray Butt recalled. "At the start we were ferried out to the boat that was moored off Spurn Head. I was one of the last to arrive as usual and as I got alongside Buster and Nick were waving and they said: 'Christ, Ray have you got a problem. David is in the aft cabin and he's feeling terrible.'

"There was a bit of a swell and it had always been a worry to me how everyone would react to filming at sea. We had about a five or six day shoot to do on this boat at sea and David feeling really lousy was all I needed. I climbed aboard and I said: 'Right I'll go and see how he is' and I walked down to this stinking old cabin and there was David laid up on one of the bunks. He looked terrible.

"I said: 'All right, mate?' and he just groaned. I said: 'Is there anything I can get you?' and he groaned again. Then he burst out laughing – he couldn't keep it up. It was a wind up and I'd fallen for it hook, line and sinker. I shouted a few rude words at him and said: 'Get out of that bloody bunk – or I'll throw you over the side of the boat!' It was very funny – and later I found out that one of the make-up girls had got at him to make him look so poorly!"

"I'd been made up to look seriously ill," recalled David. "And they told Ray that I'd been really sick. Ray was obviously thinking: 'How am I going to finish the filming?' and he pokes his head round the door and I'm going: 'Arhhh, ahhh' and he says: 'Oh Christ' and I made more groaning noises. And then he sussed me because when he got close he could see my colour wasn't real – and we all fell about. But we'd had him going."

Ironically it wasn't the cast who were caught out by seasickness; instead Ray found his crew strength massively depleted as one by one they became ill. "The weather wasn't that bad but we had quite high seas," he recalled. "The boat did roll a bit and there was one time when the whole of the costume department were sick and one make-up girl was having to do the lot, costume and make-up.

"All the sparks [electricians] were gone, Tony Dow was holding the lamps, the poor cameraman was having a horrible time trying to film the actors with the whole background going up and down. He had to keep stopping and was as sick as a dog. I think in the end, of the eighteen or so crew we had aboard only about four of us were still operational plus, fortunately, the actors." Ray, a keen sailor, added: "I loved it though. It was great fun."

Buster Merryfield loved being at sea, despite being quite seasick. Albert, being an old sea salt, was rather worryingly in charge of the boat. Buster had no such trouble. "I was on the helm and I found it quite easy," he recalled. "And the real skipper was there, just out of sight of the camera in case I got anything wrong."

One of the most memorable moments of the episode was when Del calls to a man working on a gas rig and asks directions to Holland. The scene was only a few seconds on screen but took nearly a day to film. "We actually shot it on a British Gas rig in the North Sea," recalled Ray Butt. "It was a six hour sail to get there, then we shot it quite quickly. Tony Dow was on the boat with a camera looking up at the rig and I'd gone out to the rig by helicopter with another camera looking back at the boat.

"It was all controlled by walkie-talkies and we did it all in about six takes, then they had a six hour trip back to Hull. But although they had the longer journey, they had the last laugh on me because before they'd left port they'd filled the boat up with booze and on the way back they had a bit of a party and got absolutely plastered, whereas on the gas rig there was no booze at all and I was sat there waiting for a helicopter! But it was a good gag and worth doing and it's something everyone seems to remember."

"One critic said: 'Do they honestly want us to believe that that old heap of a boat could sail to Holland?'" said John Sullivan. "Well before we used it it had just sailed across the Atlantic from Canada!"

Christmas week 1985 saw the screening of a special spoof film on BBC1's *Breakfast Time* in which its Consumer Editor Lynn Faulds Wood did a Roger Cook-style report on Del Boy. In the short Cinderella-themed sketch Lynn confronted Del over his sale of a pumpkin which was supposed to have turned into a coach, and four white mice which were supposed to have become horses. "It was a lot of fun and I remember thinking David was very attractive!" said Lynn, who went on to present the BBC's *Watchdog* programme. "Del was supposed to be outraged that I could have possibly thought that he was selling dodgy merchandise."

HOW ONLY FOOLS AND HORSES NEARLY WENT TO AMERICA

An American TV network once considered making its own version of *Only Fools and Horses* starring *M*A*S*H* star Harry Morgan, who played Colonel Sherman Potter, as Grandad. "*M*A*S*H* was coming to an end and they wanted a new vehicle for Harry," said Ray Butt. "They wanted to develop the Grandad character as the lead as opposed to Del Boy being the main character and I don't think John liked the idea very much."

Series Five

In April 1986 the *Only Fools* team were back together for a new series. ***From Prussia With Love*** was the first episode and featured actress Erika Hoffman as German au pair Anna who had been sacked from her job and thrown out by her employers after falling pregnant. Del senses there is cash to be made and takes Anna in so that he can then sell her baby to childless Boycie and Marlene.

The episode brings the Boycie and Marlene infertility storyline, hinted at in *Sleeping Dogs Lie,* to the fore and actually ends rather poignantly. It again demonstrated John Sullivan's ability to mix comedy with serious subjects. For Sue Holderness, who made her second appearance as Marlene in the episode, it remains a favourite.

"It was very touching," she said. "It was as if everything Marlene had longed for in her life was going to come true and it was going to be perfect. And it was very sad when it all went wrong. As an actress it was very rewarding to work on the episode - Marlene went through a great deal of emotion because having a baby had been the overriding thing in her life since she was sixteen. Then she'd got the chance of having one and then it was taken away again. It was beautifully written - as good as any Chekov or Shakespeare play."

A good deal of fun was had by David Jason and Nicholas Lyndhurst while filming the next episode, ***The Miracle Of Peckham***, in which Del fleeces a string of gullible journalists after conning them into paying him large wodges of cash to film a statue of the Virgin Mary apparently weeping. John Sullivan recalled arriving on the set near a church in Bermondsey, south London to find David waiting for him. Herding John into his caravan, the mischievous star explained what he and Nicholas were up to.

"We've convinced Buster that you are writing an episode where there is a flashback sequence to when Albert was thirty," David explained. "And we've told him he's going to have to shave his beard off!"

"Now that beard is Buster's trademark," said John. "Not to mention his fortune when it comes to the pantomime season. So I was lumbered with the task of breaking this 'news' to Buster. He was sitting in the make-up van and as I walked between David's caravan and where Buster was I had to make up a tale of what it was I was actually writing and why he had to shave his beard off.

"Now David and Nick are good at keeping straight faces in such circumstances but I can't. So I'm standing there telling him and Buster is taking it very seriously and saying: 'Couldn't we just sort of brown it and trim it?' I was saying: 'No mate, it's got to come off. The make-up people have said to me they can make you look so much younger and that's how it's got to be.' Buster looked quite sad about it and I thought: 'This is getting cruel'.

"Then I looked out of the window and outside were David and Nick laughing and in the end I just broke down into fits of laughter. I couldn't keep it going and Buster was mightily relieved. And it didn't take him long to work out who the perpetrators were. After all he didn't have to look far with them two around!"

"Nick and I had got bored waiting to start filming so we came up with this idea," smiled David Jason. "Buster got quite worried about it but being such a professional he was prepared to do it. We said to him: 'It's all right, you could get a false one while yours grows back' and he's saying: 'No, it takes years' and we said: 'Well you could get a false one for years.'"

The Longest Night includes a guest appearance by actor Vas Blackwood as Lennox, who'd been hired to pull off a fake robbery at a supermarket by the debt-ridden manager and aggrieved security boss. He gets into the manager's office after getting caught shoplifting, an idea that from came a real event.

"A friend of mine heard about this bloke in prison who got to the manager's office and the store safe by deliberately getting caught shoplifting," said John Sullivan. "He then pulled a gun on them and told them to open the safe. I liked the idea of that for a story but I needed to take the sting out of it. I didn't want to show somebody with a real gun and so I came up with the idea of the three men being in league and the Trotters became their witnesses – with the extra twist that Lennox was late because his mum had bought him a dodgy watch from Del and the safe was on a time switch."

Tea For Three sees Rodney and Del fighting over the same girl, Trigger's pretty niece Lisa (played by Gerry Cowper). Del had been bragging about his exploits as a paratrooper and Rodney decided to stitch him up when he was offered the chance to go hang-gliding – and make him live up to his boasting and actually do it. David Jason, an enthusiastic glider pilot, was keen to do his own stunts as Del took to the skies, over Butser Hill in Hampshire. "I wanted to do it," he said. "But they wouldn't let me for insurance reasons so they got a stunt man instead. I could see their point of view because when you are filming a series you'd be in real trouble if your leading man broke his leg or something because it would delay filming."

In *Video Nasty* Rodney gets a grant from the local council to make a community film and Del then tries to earn money by selling endorsements on it. The idea was inspired by the largesse of the Greater London Council. "Ken Livingstone had given out money to various art classes to make minority films and the papers and people were complaining that it was a waste of money," said John Sullivan. "Rodney is a bit arty and it would have been right up his street."

The episode also revealed Boycie's infertility problems and Del dubbed him 'Jaffa' because he was seedless. That led to a number of complaints to John Sullivan from viewers who thought it was insensitive. "They came from people trying to have babies who had the same problem and I wrote back apologising and explaining that it was mainly aimed at making Boycie uncomfortable and not to hurt anyone," he recalled.

The week John was about to begin writing the final episode of the fifth series he and his wife had dinner with David Jason and his girlfriend at Le Caprice restaurant in London. During the evening it became clear that David felt five series was enough and wanted the series they were working on to be his last. John went home saddened but understood David's desire to pursue other acting projects. After discussing the situation with Head of Comedy Gareth Gwenlan, he went away and wrote *Who Wants To Be A Millionaire?* In it Del is offered the chance to head out to Australia with his old friend Jumbo Mills (played by Nick Stringer) and takes it, leaving Rodney behind because he is refused an immigration visa due to his minor drugs conviction.

"The last scene was to have seen Del flying out the country to become a millionaire and Rodney walking out of the airport looking a bit lost," John recalled. Contingency plans would then have seen the programme continue with the new title *Hot Rod* without Del but with the option of him coming back at a later date. "*Hot Rod* would have featured Rodney trying to continue the business but being constantly stitched up by people like Mickey Pearce and all the others. I never wrote that ending though, because in the meantime David changed his mind and talk of him leaving the show was forgotten and we started discussing the next series. By then I was too far into the episode so I just changed the ending so that Del says no to Jumbo's offer."

1986 Christmas Special

Filming for *A Royal Flush* the 1986 Christmas special, was interrupted by cast illness when David Jason lost his voice for three days and shortly afterwards Nicholas Lyndhurst came down with a bout of flu. Filming had begun during the second week of November in Salisbury, Wiltshire and the episode centred on Rodney's blossoming romance with Sloane ranger Victoria, daughter of the Duke of Malebury, supposedly a cousin to the Queen. Before they've even had their first date at the opera at the Theatre Royal, Drury Lane, Del can see pound signs and is already planning to marry Rodney off.

The entrance, foyer and bar scenes were shot at the actual Theatre Royal but for the lengthy auditorium scenes and the shot of the performance, the production moved from Salisbury to the Opera House at Buxton, Derbyshire. "If I'd used the interior of the Theatre Royal, Drury Lane, it's such a big house that I would have needed thousands of extras, whereas Buxton is quite small in comparison," said Ray Butt. "Even so, I couldn't afford to fill it completely but still hired two hundred people for it. I also hired The Kent National Opera Company with all their scenery and orchestra, and that all cost an awful lot of money. But it was a very funny scene so it was worth it."

The delays in filming meant there was no time to show the episode in front of a studio audience in order to record a laughter track nor was there time to add music. The interior shots of the flat were filmed on a set built at Elstree studios and there was even a contingency plan at one stage to do the final scene at the flat live on Christmas Day. The episode was only just completed in time, with Ray Butt and Tony Dow finishing off editing in the early hours of Christmas Day. "I went to sleep on the floor of the edit room," Ray recalled.

The result was an entertaining episode with some fine moments, like the unforgettable shot when we see Rodney dressed up as a toff, but which has a slightly incomplete feel about it. It is generally conceded, though, that the dinner scene at Victoria's father's stately home wasn't up to the usual standard. Del, it seems, turns from being mischievous towards Rodney to almost nasty.

It's something Ray Butt takes the blame for. "I think that scene ruined Del's regard in the public eye," he said. "It was the one scene I wasn't happy with. I think that David went a bit over the top. That was my fault because I should have spotted it and brought him down. In retrospect I wasn't happy with it. I think Del turned too nasty and lost his warmth. Del's a villain, fine but, like Bilko, there's warmth there and you've got to maintain that."

John Sullivan was away in Paris on location with his other hit show *Just Good Friends* while the dinner scene was being filmed, something he later regretted. "I wish to God I'd been on *Only Fools* instead," he said. "That scene was written for laughs not drama, and I wanted David to be Del as a jolly drunk rather than a morose drunk, which is what he ended up looking like. Not having a studio audience didn't help matters either."

"You pays your money and takes your choice," said David Jason. "Perhaps that scene wasn't as good as it could have been but the episode itself was fine. Some people think it was a weak episode though but I just think of bits like Del turning up at the clay pigeon shoot with a pump-action shotgun that he's borrowed from Iggy Iggins, the bank robber. That was classic."

"I wanted to cut twenty minutes out," Gareth Gwenlan said in an interview in The *Only Fools and Horses* Appreciation Society's newsletter, *Hookie Street*. "Oh God, it went on and on and on. It was made under the most difficult of circumstances ever. John had great difficulty writing it. It was filmed in the middle of December in the most awful weather and we only had daylight for four hours. David and Nick were both ill with the flu. The tent scene was filmed in the middle of the night with lights to make it look like daylight. The fact that it was ever shown is a miracle."

Tony Dow, the episode's production manager and later the show's director, recalled how BBC1 Controller Michael Grade once again came to the programme's rescue. "David lost his voice, we had an electricians' strike, the weather was terrible and we got way behind," he said. "I remember phoning Gareth Gwenlan to tell him we were in a bit of trouble and that we'd need a couple more days of filming and that would cost quite a bit of extra money. I remember Gareth going 'Oh my God – I'll have to speak to the Controller.' Within half an hour Gareth came back and said that he'd spoken to Michael Grade who said: 'as far as I'm concerned *Only Fools and Horses* can have what the hell it likes' and that was the end of the story. *Only Fools* was to be his main Christmas show and his attitude was very supportive. Back then it was a big thing for the BBC to beat the opposition."

As if the actors weren't busy enough filming *A Royal Flush*, in October 1986 a request came through asking the three stars if they would appear at the *Royal Variety Show*, which was to be staged at the Theatre Royal, Drury Lane, on November 24th.

"That was horrendously difficult," recalled David Jason. "They asked us to do it and we thought we'd take something out of one of the episodes but they wanted something original. So John went away and came up with this wonderful piece of material that ran to about twenty-five minutes when it needed to be about three! So he went away and pared it all down. We thought it was very funny, but we weren't sure we'd get away with it." The story had the trio supposedly making a delivery of dodgy booze to a pal of Del's called Chunky Lewis, who ran a nightclub in London's West End. The plan for the Trotters was that they would take a wrong turning and end up walking on stage at the Palladium during the show.

The script had arrived in Salisbury, where they were filming and it was only really then that the cast realised just what they had taken on. David recalled: "We got the running order of the show and realised that everyone else who was appearing either had an act – like Bruce Forsyth does – or were from a West End musical and had singing or dancing routines. That meant that everyone was really well rehearsed and knew their stuff backwards – except for us.

"We were the only people to appear who had never tried their material in front of an audience before and it was going out live. That started to hit home. From then on, every night after we finished filming, for about a week beforehand, we would get back to our hotel and the three of us would rehearse it over and over again. And as it got nearer, we worried and we worried and we worried.

"We took out all sorts of insurance like learning each other's parts and learning it backwards, because if one of us forgot our lines no one could help us but ourselves because you couldn't have a prompt. We'd be out there on our own and if anybody dried up no one would be able to give us a cue. We were ready to help each other out if one of us went wrong but we were still very worried about it.

"Then we finally got in the car to go to Drury Lane and on the way we rehearsed it and then fell into silence. We all felt sick with nerves. We were told to wait at the theatre over the road because we weren't on till the second half. There were all these singers and dancers there, getting excited about the show and all we were feeling was very, very nervous. We fancied a drink but we couldn't have one because that would be fatal because we needed our wits about us."

Another worry was the line David had to deliver to the Royal Box, which would be occupied by the Queen Mother and the Duchess of York. "I'd said to John Sullivan: 'Christ, we'll get ourselves locked up in the tower for this!'" said David. John Sullivan recalled: "When I wrote about Chunky I didn't know the Duchess of York was going to be there. It was before she'd joined WeightWatchers and in those days she had a few pounds on her. I wasn't invited to the actual show so I was watching at home and thought: 'Oh God' when I saw she was there in the Royal Box. I thought: 'That's going to go down a bomb!' I just sat at home cringing."

"We didn't even know if anyone was going to laugh because, although we knew it was funny, we'd never tried it out on an audience," said David. "Comedy has this weird trick that it can play on you, in that the line you'd thought they'd laugh at they don't, and then they'd go mad about another one and catch you out. As soon as we walked on we got a huge round of applause, which was great and made us feel welcome, and then we got our first laugh and it gave us a bit of confidence, but really you are on a knife edge because you can't afford to fail.

"The Royal gag was very funny. Rodney looks up to the Royal box, while Del is looking elsewhere, and he sees the Royal family and starts scraping and bowing and I say: 'What's the matter with you?' and then Del looks up to this box and, dazzled by the lights, says: 'Chunky is that you?'" The line brought the house down – and provoked an instant reaction from the Queen Mum as David recalled: "I could actually see - and she started to do the Royal wave," he laughed. "I couldn't believe it. Everybody fell about. Bless her cotton socks; perhaps she was well on the gin and tonics by then, but for whatever reason she did it!"

After the show, along with all the other performers, the trio were presented to the Queen Mother – and it was Buster who received unusual Royal attention. "She spoke to David and Nick and then when she got to me she put her hand out to my beard and said: 'So it's real then!' and I just said: 'Yes Ma'am!' which was all I could think of saying at the time." Afterwards David and Nicholas had to be taken by car back to Salisbury for filming the next day but they got their driver to stop off at an off-licence on the way back to buy a bottle of Famous Grouse whisky. "And between London and Salisbury we did the whole bottle," recalled Nicholas. "It was a great way to let off steam!"

GETTING AWAY WITH IT

Nothing was ever cut out of *Only Fools and Horses* scripts due to lack of taste or because executives thought the language was too strong. "It never happened on *Fools*," said Ray Butt. "In fact the only time I ever had a problem with my head of department over one of John Sullivan's scripts was with the pilot episode of *Just Good Friends*. Vince was talking to Penny about having acupuncture to stop him smoking.

"He'd had to have this needle stuck in his ear and she said to him: 'Did you feel a prick?' and he said: 'Well I felt a bit foolish….' That line brought the house down. I was told to cut that line and I wouldn't. John went bananas when I told him what they had wanted to do and it stayed in. I had a terrible row with my boss about it but we won the day."

David Jason believes that in some ways *Only Fools and Horses* got away with more cheeky lines because some senior executives at the BBC didn't realise what they meant. He recalled: "I remember the first time John put 'You dipstick' in a script. I said: 'You can't do that' and he said: 'Why not?' and I said: 'You know what it means' and he said: 'Course I do' and I said: 'They'll stop us, they'll have that out' and he said: 'Leave it in and if they take it out, they take it out and we'll use something else.'

"So of course Ray and the rest of us all knew what it meant

who'd all been to universities thought: 'Ahh, that's funny. Yes, 'cos of course Rodney is long and thin.' They all thought that dipstick meant that he looks long and thin! The same thing happened with the word 'plonker'. Had they known then what it really meant then they would have cut it out of the script because at that time they were very sensitive about saying rude things on the box.

"John always shrouded bits like that and we were covered in that people who were old enough not to be offended would probably be the only ones who'd twig what he was really saying anyway. It's innocent but it's not innocent if you know what I mean. It's you that makes it dirty. It's all in people's minds!"

1987 Christmas Special

The Frog's Legacy was the 1987 Christmas special and it always stuck in Ray Butt's memory because not only was it his last episode on the show, but also because his father Bill died during the filming. "It was incredibly difficult," he recalled. "I got a phone call on the Friday evening as we wrapped, and I had to go and tell my mother and then the next morning we were filming a funeral scene where Rodney gets a job as a pallbearer."

The episode was being shot in Ipswich in East Anglia and by coincidence the company hired to provide the funeral cortege for the programme came from Colchester. "My father died in a hospice in Colchester and I said to the undertaker: 'By the way, I've got another job for you next Wednesday or Thursday' and he said: 'What more filming?' and I said: 'No, my old man died last night, can you bury him for me?'

"He didn't believe me at first and then he did, and he buried my dad for me. That was hard but not as hard as Lennard Pearce's death because I was so hyped up with work that my father's death didn't hit me for another six months." Shortly after filming *The Frog's Legacy* Ray Butt left the BBC for a new post with ITV. "I was offered a job at Central as Controller of Comedy which sounded interesting but ended up as a disaster. It was so small after the world I was used to working in.

"It was like playing for Liverpool then joining a team in Division Three – it was a different league. Although I was Head of Comedy, you're really head of nothing. Head of Pencils was more important!" Tony Dow took over as director, a choice that was very popular with Ray Butt. Tony had worked on the show on and off from the first series after joining as a trainee assistant floor manager.

"I always thought he had a lot of talent," said Ray. "That's why when I was leaving I backed him to take over as director because Gareth Gwenlan, who was then Head of Comedy, was a bit nervous because Tony wasn't that experienced. But I knew he could do it because he'd filmed bits for me unofficially and he had a great rapport with the actors. He also worked hard, knew the game very well and he was a very quick learner."

Tony Dow was joined by Gareth Gwenlan who took over as producer, while also remaining as Head of Comedy, and a new era for *Only Fools and Horses* was underway, building on the old strengths and adding a new element – longer episodes.

John Sullivan had always wanted to write longer episodes – and in fact often did. His episodes always over-ran and had to be cut back, with huge chunks ending up on the cutting room floor or torn out during rehearsals.

When he was producer, Ray Butt had gone to the then Controller of BBC1, Alan Hart and tried to persuade him to let it become a forty-five minute or preferably a fifty minute show. "But he turned the idea down, on the grounds that 'it would dilute the comedy,'" Ray recalled. "They should have gone to a fifty minute slot much earlier because we had to cut and throw a lot of good stuff away because of the time restriction because John always over-wrote. But John was a very astute writer and he managed to use some cut material again in other episodes."

John talked over his frustration at being restricted to writing just thirty minutes with David Jason, who was in full agreement. Between them they decided to launch a joint campaign to lengthen the show. David recalled: "We were throwing away really good material in order to get episodes to fit into half an hour. We were tearing more good material out and throwing it on the floor than most other sitcoms had in an entire episode. We would always cut what we thought was the weakest and what would tend to go would be very good jokes, good situations and the emotional stuff. All that would go because you couldn't cut into the actual narrative. So what you'd end up with is a piece of material that had been ripped and then sewn up and put back together and plastered over in order to get it into half an hour. This was getting more and more frustrating.

"We wanted to do them longer but all the hierarchy would say was: 'That's impossible because situation comedy is thirty minutes.' I'd say: 'Yes, but that is other writers, that is not John Sullivan.' They said that they could cut any sitcom into thirty minutes and that that was standard BBC format. I said: 'I know you can cut it to thirty minutes and I have seen some of your cutting and you end up with ******* rubbish.' It all started to get a bit heated. I got so frustrated I said to John afterwards: 'It's sacrilege - and all for the sake of people saying that you have to write to a set thirty minutes.'

"The problem with John at this time was that he was gaining so much strength with the characters and was enjoying them that when you asked him to write thirty minutes you'd end up with a forty minute script or more and then we'd have to cut it about. John and I went out for dinner one night and had a meeting and he was really getting upset because he could just see all this stuff being thrown away. Some of it he would retain and use again but a lot of it was just apposite to that particular episode and would be wasted. In the end we decided that we'd tell them that we wouldn't do any more unless we could do forty minutes. We agreed it – and we both meant it."

New producer Gareth Gwenlan, a pragmatic, astute man, wasn't against the proposal in principal. However he had a major problem in that studio time was already booked and the episodes had to be produced and finished in a week. Getting a half-hour episode made in a week with just one day in the studio was the standard form, although most directors and producers would have been grateful for more time. Filming a forty minute episode in that time scale was considered near impossible and Gareth Gwenlan told John Sullivan so. On top of that the cast had been contracted to appear in thirty minute shows and any increase in the episode running time would lead to a big increase in the series budget. Nevertheless Gareth went to see his boss Michael Grade, Controller of BBC1, and said he wanted to give Sullivan an extra five minutes for his episodes by. way of a compromise.

"Michael said that from the point of view of finding a transmission slot for a thirty-five minute programme, it wasn't too much of a problem," Gareth recalled. "There would be a problem with a show of that length for overseas sales but *Only Fools and Horses* doesn't sell, which in those days it didn't.

"Both John Sullivan and the series were held in very high regard and Michael said: 'Tell him to do thirty-five minutes.' So I told John he could have the extra five minutes and what happened? The first script came in and it was an hour long. I said: 'John.....' and he said: 'What about fifty....' I said: 'Listen, I'm sure the controller would be delighted with fifty minutes but we are in deep shit. We had got six Sundays in the studio to record them and no one has recorded a fifty minute show in one day.'"

A massive forty per cent increase in the show's budget had to be found and location filming, which always took place in one whole block for the series prior to the weekly studio recording, was extended so that each episode would have more film inserts, leaving less to be done in the studio. That was fine for the first three episodes of the series, which had large chunks already written for location filming but the last three episodes were almost totally studio based. "It was a seriously difficult thing to do and it nearly bloody killed all of us," Gareth recalled.

David Jason, partly responsible for the new heavy workload, laughed as he reflected on the hours he and his colleagues then had to put in. He said: "We really shot ourselves in the foot! Nick and

I nearly died. We had to work almost twenty-four hours a day. We stopped to sleep. I'd get up at 6am and try to learn my script, rehearse all day, come back and look at the next day's script and then go to bed early to be up, and so on. We were absolutely dead after we'd done the studio recording on the Sunday. After we'd done the last one someone piped up and said: 'You've proved that a fifty minute show can be done in seven days, so you'll be able to do it again next time.' I said: 'Over my dead body' and I nearly was a dead body. We said: 'Never again – unless we get more time' and when it came to doing the next series everything was redesigned and we had ten days to rehearse and film them in which was much more sensible."

"It was very hard work," recalled director Tony Dow. "We'd rehearse Tuesday to Friday, then pre-record some studio scenes on the Saturday and then film in front of a studio audience on the Sunday night. The Monday would be a day off for the actors but I'd be editing the episode for transmission the following Sunday."

The pace of it all did have some benefits though. "As we were recording on Sunday nights, the same night as the episode we'd shot the week before was screened, we were able to get almost instant feedback on the shows," said Tony. "The ratings were really high and the whole country was talking about the show and that helped keep everyone's energy levels up."

The other major change for the programme-makers at that time was the decision to move location filming to Bristol. "During the early part of the eighties filming in London was always difficult," said Gareth Gwenlan. "One by one, the markets became impossible to use and didn't want to know because filming was too disruptive for them.

"It also became increasingly impossible to film with Nick and David on the streets of London because they would just get mobbed. We knew we needed to move out to a provincial city and someone suggested Bristol. So Tony Dow, John Sullivan and I went down for a recce. Architecturally it had everything we needed in terms of the pubs, houses, a market and most importantly, we found the block of flats.

"We talked to the residents' association who were absolutely fantastic and, although it's not exactly the same as the original block in north Acton, London, that we used in the opening titles, it was just what we needed.

"It would be dangerous to film in north Acton now. I spent half a day there in 1996, filming a commercial (for Rover cars in New Zealand) with David and John Challis and we had to have the police with us all the time. The back of Acton is not a very pleasant area and you could never film there at night because things would probably get nicked.

"In Bristol it was very different. The police were very co-operative and the people were very nice and the only thing we had to do to make it look a little more like London was to take a couple of red London buses down to put in the background in various scenes."

WHY A THREE-WHEELED VAN?

John Sullivan gave Del a three-wheeled van to drive as a chink in his armour. "I had this smart, confident little guy with the gift of the gab who cared about his appearance a great deal and then had this silly vehicle," said John. "It's a real contradiction but it's all he can afford. Outwardly he tries to project this image that he's doing very well in life and he walks outside and there's the truth.

"I thought he'd need something practical to carry his gear round in so that ruled out something like a Capri. Reliants are cheap to run and you only need a motorcycle licence to drive one." And amazingly, even though the van is so key to the show and is instantly recognisable, John said: "It was kind of a last minute thought. I had to give him something to drive and it could have been an old transit van and I suddenly thought: 'I'll give him a three-wheeled van.'

"I got the New York – Paris – Peckham idea on the side of the van from a packet of Dunhill cigarettes except theirs says London – Paris – New York. Del would have seen it and been slightly in awe of it and therefore impressed and stuck it on his van."

1988 Christmas Special

Filming of **Dates** began promptly on the morning of Monday November 7th 1988. *Dates* was, of course, the 1988 Christmas special but was filmed as the first part of series six or F as it was known to the production team. "I decided to do *Dates* because I felt Del had to start meeting more mature women," said John Sullivan. "I couldn't have him continually hanging round discos chasing twenty-year-olds, so I brought Raquel in, although when I wrote it I hadn't planned to bring her back the following year. For me *Dates* was a try out for Del to have a more mature relationship because I knew that it had to come."

Of course the episode ended with the revelation that Raquel had been working as a kissogram – and Del reacted badly because his pride was hurt – although as soon as he'd said the cutting words to Raquel he regretted them.

One of the most famous scenes in the episode – Rodney driving the van over a hill very fast to impress nervous Nerys, the barmaid, nearly didn't happen. "Everyone was so worried about it," said John Sullivan. "The stunt people said that when the van landed the engine might come out and whoever is driving might end up with a lap full of engine. So they wouldn't let Nick drive it but it worked OK and the old van stood up to it brilliantly well and it was a great shot.

"*Dates* was one of the episodes I'm proudest of," continued John. "Because in pure construction terms it fits like a wonderful Mechano set and everything makes sense."

It was also the first episode Tony Dow directed, but his involvement with the show went way back to the first series. He'd been a theatre director and had never planned to work in television but ended up at the BBC as a trainee assistant floor manager. On his very first day at the BBC he worked on *Blue Peter* where, he said, he had to do the 'make' and then pass it to presenter Sarah Greene "And I messed it up completely," he recalled.

On his second day he was told to follow Mandie Fletcher, the AFM on a new programme called *Only Fools and Horses*. "I assumed it was something about animals," he said. "Ray Butt was ill at the time but when we finally met we got on like a house on fire and he asked for me to come back to work on the second series. Working on that series was a funny and joyous time." By 1985 and *To Hull and Back*, Tony had been promoted to production manager.

"When Ray Butt left to work at Central Television there was a queue round the block of people wanting to take over as director," said Tony Dow. "Completely unbeknownst to me, I think John Sullivan and David Jason had a conversation with Gareth Gwenlan, who was then Head of Comedy, to the effect that they wanted me to take over." Tony was sent on a director's training course – including learning how to studio director in the gallery which included training on *Top of the Pops* and *Blankety Blank* and was then duly installed as Ray Butt's successor.

"My very first shot as director of *Only Fools* was on a crane at Waterloo Station filming Del waiting for Raquel with a bunch of flowers. The words *Only Fools and Horses* opened so many doors so the whole station was under control for us and there were people holding the crowds back and I remember thinking: 'This isn't a bad job...'" Nor did Tony do a bad job on the episode, for it won a Bafta award.

Series Six

The first fifty minute episode *Yuppy Love* saw the first appearance of Gwyneth Strong as Cassandra and also featured Del adopting his new image for the first time. The film *Wall Street*, which starred Michael Douglas as ruthless stock market trader Gordon Gekko, had clearly had an impact on Del whose new style sees him wearing the standard City garb of striped shirt, bright braces with, of course, the obligatory filofax.

"Del was always a trend follower and of course he'd always get them wrong," said John Sullivan. "Yuppies were the big thing at the time so Del moved into that image. I also saw the film *Wall Street* and I knew that if Del had seen it then it would have had a big impact on his life and he'd be straight out the following day to buy a pair of red braces and a smart shirt. So we got rid of the camel hair coat and smartened up his image giving him a green mac, an aluminium briefcase and a mobile phone but kept the yellow van."

Rodney too is trying to better himself by attending evening classes, and it was at one of these that he met Cassandra. Of course, things rarely go smoothly for Rodney and he's humiliated when she finds his name written in his coat – kindly put in by Del as a joke. The episode featured one of the show's most famous moments when Del leant on a bar flap in a yuppy wine bar and hadn't noticed that the barman had opened the flap. The resultant fall humiliates Del, who'd been trying to impress two girls with his spiel about being a high-flying trader.

John Sullivan had seen someone do it for real at The George pub in Balham. He recalled: "I just saw it happen in front of me – and I thought: 'Thank you!'"

It looked so easy on screen but the scene took lots of planning. "John Sullivan was in a wine bar and he saw this bloke lean on the bar and it wasn't there because they'd lifted the flap up," David Jason recalled. "He just recovered himself and he looked round to see if anyone had seen. We both thought it was really funny and agreed Del should do it in a scene but I said: 'He's got to fall right over.'

"It took a long time to set up and we distracted the audience's attention with a cutaway of two girls so they didn't particularly notice the barman lifting up the flap. It was planted there but it wasn't made obvious. The actual fall was very difficult to do because if you fall like I did, it's a comic fall, not a real fall which is what makes it funny. The trouble is, though, when you do it your instinctive reaction is to try to break your fall with your hand and look where you are falling.

"It's hard to do because you have to ignore all the danger signals that your brain is giving you. But it was worth it because everyone loved it and it was one of those moments that people always talk about. Thank goodness we got it right first time so that I only had to do it once on camera and I landed on a small crash mat out of sight."

The scene wasn't in the original script as Roger Lloyd Pack wasn't available, but then his schedule changed and he was. So John Sullivan was able to write a new scene. "We had them in the wine bar and we had a bit of time because the script was a bit short," John said in an interview in *Hookie Street*. "I thought I'd bring that scene in from what I'd seen in Balham. It's become a sort of classic scene but it was written in ten minutes."

Rodney meanwhile makes headway with Cassandra but is too ashamed to admit that he lives in a lowly block of council flats like Nelson Mandela House on a rundown estate. Instead he convinces her that he lives in an upmarket suburb and when she gives him a lift he gets her to drop him off outside someone else's home. For John Sullivan it was a real life experience that inspired the scene.

Years before he met his wife, John was at a party in London and met a girl he quite fancied. At the end of the evening she offered him a lift home in her car, as she was passing through south London where he lived. "She was a friend of a friend and she lived in Ewell, a nice place just outside London, whereas I was living in a rough terraced street," he recalled. "Her dad was a stockbroker and she mentioned they had a swimming pool and by contrast I was going to take her back to the Bronx! I didn't want her to see where I lived because I was hoping to see her again and didn't want to put her off. I remembered a road near my old school called Clarence Avenue with some nice big detached houses and one there that particularly impressed me so I told her I lived there. We said goodnight and she drove off and then I had to walk two miles back to my real home. It started to rain very heavily and by the time I got home I was like a drowned rat. Not only that but I never saw her again, so it was all in vain anyway!"

Del's eagerness to make a few quid goes very wrong in ***Danger UXD*** when the Trotters discover that the faulty dolls Del has persuaded Denzil to give them are more the type for weirdos than children. The inspiration for the episode came from an incident at a party when a friend of John's had his room filled with dozens of inflatable dolls as a joke. "They looked so stupid," laughed John. "I had to put them in a story and I was also amused by the thought of: 'How the hell do you get rid of them all?'" The end of the episode sees the dolls exploding and this sequence was filmed on a disused part of Bristol Docks. Nicholas Lyndhurst recalled: "It was a bloody big bang and we all got showered with dirt."

Another explosion had been planned for an early episode that never reached the screen. Del was trying to sell a damaged radio which had lots of wires protruding out of it and left the van with the radio in the back, along with Rodney who was sleeping off a hangover outside a government building while he goes off in search of Boycie. A security guard spots the wires, thinks it is a car bomb and calls out the army bomb disposal squad who seal off the street and, using a robot device do a controlled explosion on the van, blowing it to pieces. Del was to have come back and found his van blown apart and no sign of Rodney except his boots. Later he discovered Rodney had changed into his trainers and gone off to get a pint before the security alert.

John recalled: "Ray Butt pointed out that if we blew up the van there was no way Del would go and buy another one that was identical and we'd lose the van that was giving everyone so many laughs, because by then it had become the Trotters' trademark, so we abandoned the idea."

The inflatable dolls used in *Danger UXD* led to a number of complaints to the BBC from viewers and early the following week, after the Sunday night transmission, David and Nicholas took a break from rehearsing the next episode to go on live daytime TV to respond to the criticism. One woman asked how she was supposed to explain what the dolls were to her seven-year-old daughter. "We were happy to go on and defend the episode," said Nicholas. "The dolls in the shows had been specially adapted by our special effects people so that they weren't that explicit."

The next episode ***Chain Gang*** is a classic ensemble story in which all the supporting cast got plenty to do. It also saw the team make a brief return to London for location filming. "It came about because I just wondered what would happen if someone had a heart attack just when they'd taken your money for a deal," said John Sullivan. "You couldn't grab it from them nor could you follow the ambulance because they'd dash through red lights. I just developed it from there and made it into a scam."

The Unlucky Winner Is... sees Rodney winning a trip abroad in an art competition. He's delighted until he remembers that he never actually entered one and it's only once he's in Spain that Del reveals that he sent his entry in but in the under fourteens category. Rodney is furious and not an enthusiastic member of the 'groovy gang' which all the winners are enrolled into. The classic moment in the episode comes when Rodney – all six foot two of him – is seen for the first time in his skateboard gear being chased round by a youngster with a crush on him. "Nick was great in that episode and immediately saw the great comedy in the skateboard scene," said director Tony Dow.

The Unlucky Winner Is... contains Gwyneth Strong's favourite *Only Fools* moment. She said: "Del gives Rodney and Cassandra a list of things to do to get ready to go to Spain and the last line is to Cassandra when he said: 'And there's just enough time to get your bikini line waxed.' I just found that so awful for someone to say that to you in a pub in front of everyone! I just kept laughing and then when we came to actually shoot the scene I thought I had it under control until David squeezed my knee under the table because he knew that would make me laugh – and it did. I nearly knocked the whole table over and we had to do it again!"

Michael Fenton Stevens, who played holiday rep Alan Perkins in the episode, has been in dozens of comedy series but still gets recognised from *Only Fools*. "In almost any pub I go to someone will come up to me and say: 'Sorry mate, but weren't you in *Only Fools and Horses*?' he said. "It was only a week's work but it's a real highlight of my career."

Michael recalled David Jason being a joker on set. He said: "One lunchtime I remember he went over to the table next to us where Imogen Stubbs, who had just been in a BBC adaptation of DH Lawrence's *The Rainbow*, was reading a script and he said: 'I don't want to embarrass you or anything but I just wanted to say I saw that *Rainbow* thing you did and I thought it was brilliant, really brilliant, you were fantastic in it.' She said: 'That's very kind of you, thank you very much' then he said: 'There's just one question I wanted to ask…what are Bungle and Zippy really like?' It was a very good line and everyone roared with laughter. David apologised for the joke and Imogen took it in very good part.

"The rehearsals were great fun," he continued. "At the start of the week David Jason said we had to make a paper plane for a contest later in the week. The crew came in on the Thursday to watch a run through and afterwards everybody threw their paper plane out of the window and the person whose plane went the furthest won a bottle of champagne. The person who held the record for the longest throw was Nick Lyndhurst. It was a very normal paper plane but it must have caught a thermal or something because it landed on a roof miles away!"

In the next episode *Sickness and Wealth* Del has stomach pains and goes to the doctor's. He discovers that his old male doctor has left and instead there is a new woman doctor at his local surgery whom he offends by stripping from the waist down when she asks him to strip to the waist. Poignantly, though when he's told he needs to go to hospital for tests, he lets his usual guard down and the viewer sees the vulnerable side of him when he tells Rodney that he needs him with him.

Del's illness is a mystery but he mistakenly thinks he's got AIDS. It turns out it's all down to too many curries and pina coladas but it gave John Sullivan the chance to show his ability to combine pathos with comedy. At the time AIDS awareness campaigns were running non-stop and there was a great deal of misinformation surrounding the virus being talked about in terms of how people could be infected. John Sullivan tackled this in that Del reckons he might have caught it because he once had a gay hairdresser, making the point but not in a preachy, politically correct way.

During filming Buster was once again the victim of a wind-up. "David or Nick phoned him to say there had been some massive changes to the script and that I was virtually writing it as we went along," John Sullivan recalled. "David came in to rehearsals with a plaster cast on his leg and the pretence was that he'd broken his leg. Everyone knew it was a wind-up except poor Buster and he'd been told not to say anything to David about his leg because he was sensitive about it. Poor old Buster was there rehearsing with David in his plaster cast and we were all trying to keep straight faces. David took it off during a coffee break and was then sitting there perfectly normally without it and Buster still didn't comment – because he'd been told not to!"

In *Little Problems* Rodney finally ties the knot and marries Cassandra. It was an episode that David Jason found very moving. "It was a very emotional one because we realised that Rodney had become a man and that was quite an eye-opener for Del and for me too because Nick and I had been together for years. It was the Simply Red song *Holding Back The Years* that got me and I shed a few tears for real when that started during rehearsals. By the time we came to film it though the tears were gone and my eyes were dry again."

Back in early 1988, leading film and stage actor Anthony Hopkins told Terry Wogan on his BBC1 chat show how much he loved *Only Fools and Horses* and how he'd love to appear in it. John Sullivan happened to be watching and decided to create a character for him in the hope he'd be available when it came to filming it. "Because we'd heard he was a great fan we got very excited about him coming in," said David. "He would have been brilliant. It's nice to know he likes the show. When you get everyone from the Royal Family, Anthony Hopkins to whoever, it's very gratifying that people have taken the show to their hearts and enjoyed it."

John Sullivan had mentioned the gangland hard-men, the Driscoll Brothers, before in scripts and decided to bring them into the show with the elder one, Danny, the ideal role for Anthony Hopkins. "Unfortunately when we got to film it he wasn't free. He was in America filming some movie called *The Silence of The Lambs* and after that we never heard of him again, did we?" John joked. "He could have come with us and become famous!"

Of course Anthony's performance in *The Silence of the Lambs* earned him a Best Actor Oscar and confirmed his place as one of the world's biggest stars. "By then I had the Driscolls in the script so we got another good actor, Roy Marsden, in to play the part instead and he was brilliant, as was Christopher Ryan who played his little brother Tony," added John.

Little Problems could have been the last episode of the series and it would have gone out on a terrific high. The fifty minute episodes had gained an average of 16.7 million viewers and everyone seemed to be talking about the series. John Sullivan was getting letters almost every day from desperate pub landlords who were going spare because their takings were falling on Sunday nights because so many people were staying in to watch the show. "They'd write and ask me not to make it so funny," he recalled. "And some of them decided that if you couldn't beat them then it was time to join them so they moved their televisions into their bars!"

THE FANS

Only Fools and Horses has always appealed to a complete cross section of people. It straddled the social and age divide in a way few other programmes were able to and repeats of old episodes are constantly bringing a new generation of fans to it. Famous fans include actor Sir Anthony Hopkins, pop stars Sir Paul McCartney and Tom Jones and entrepreneur Richard Branson.

Even members of the Royal Family are known to be fans of the programme, and Her Majesty Queen Elizabeth The Queen Mother was certainly familiar enough with the characters to join in the fun at the 1986 Royal Variety Show. Advance tapes of Christmas specials were regularly requested and sent to Buckingham Palace and, as Nicholas Lyndhurst once said: "I guess they must have liked them because they never gave them back!"

Only Fools and Horses has a thriving fan club run by Perry Aghajanoff, a publisher from Essex. Formed in 1993, The *Only Fools and Horses* Appreciation Society now has more than 8,500 members worldwide. It produces a glossy newsletter *Hookie Street*, has a thriving website - www.onlyfools.net - and holds an annual convention which is attended by members of the show's cast.

"I got into the series right from the off in 1981," said Perry, who has become good friends with some of the cast and even appeared as an extra in two different episodes. "One of the reasons I love *Only Fools* is because of the British mentality of loving a loser and Del is the eternal loser. The show is infinitely watchable and however many times you see the same episode it's still funny."

Perry has a vast collection of *Only Fools* memorabilia including a number of Trotter vans, some of which he bought for as little as £30. "I've got one-and-half actual vans from the show," he said. "The 'one' is the van used in *The Jolly Boys' Outing* and the 'half' is all that is left of the one you see in the title sequence, which is the back door and the two side panels." His collection also includes the whole Trotter flat, a hundred and forty costumes and almost all the major props used in the series. At one point he even owned the Trotters' Ethnic Tours bus and Inga, the boat used in *To Hull and Back*. "I'm slowly turning Essex into Peckham," he added.

1989 Christmas Special

On Monday May 1st 1989, a little over two months after the show went off air, production began on that year's Christmas special *The Jolly Boys' Outing*. In the episode, Del organises a day out to Margate for the regulars of the Nag's Head, but things don't go to plan.

One unforgettable moment in the story came when a car radio – no need to guess who supplied it – ignited the fuel tank in the coach and caused a massive explosion which blew up the vehicle. Normally vehicles for filming are supplied by specialist hire companies but none of them would have been too pleased to have their coach brought back on a lorry as a mass of burnt out metal. So the production team bought their own for a Del Trotter-style knockdown price of £2,000. The coach had to have passed its MOT and be safe for use on roads for the scenes of the group travelling to Margate.

For the explosion scene a BBC visual effects team got to work and placed tanks containing hundreds of gallons of petrol all the way along in the luggage compartments. Three cameras were used to film the shot so that it was covered from different angles and everyone in the cast and crew was moved back to a safe distance of about four hundred yards. Firefighters from the Kent Fire Brigade also stood by ready to extinguish the flames. "We knew that we could do the explosion two or three times if the flames were put out quickly," said producer Gareth Gwenlan. "If you look carefully on the tape you can see there are about six different shots of the explosion all cut together very quickly."

Gareth was closer because, along with director Tony Dow and

cameraman Alec Curtis, he was behind one of the cameras about a hundred yards from the coach and felt the blast. "I wasn't blown over but I was certainly blown back," he recalled. "Then the fire brigade went in, put it out and a while later we did it all again."

While filming it became apparent that the show was in the running to scoop a BBC award as a childrens' favourite show but the schedule was too tight for the cast to be given time off to attend. Later the team learned that the show had in fact won and a helicopter was sent to pick up David Jason, Nicholas Lyndhurst and Buster Merryfield and take them to the awards ceremony. "It was wonderful," recalled Buster. "The helicopter waited for us to finish filming and then flew back into London along the route of the Thames before landing at Westland Heliport, which meant I was able to fly over my old school in Battersea. I thought: 'If only my mum could see me now!'"

Nicholas had worked with the pilot before and decided to play a trick on Buster Merryfield. "I told him to come in and introduce himself to Buster and David and say to me: 'Have you done the pre-flight briefing, Nick?' David was in on the joke and I told Buster that I was going to do the passenger briefing because the pilot was busy. I went on about straps and things and explained that in the event of engine failure or needing to ditch, because of the rotor blades you have to keep your hands over your head and we ought to practice it. I said to pretend that the winnebego door is the helicopter door so he should open the door, shout: 'one thousand, two thousand, three thousand – check' and jump with your hands on your head and run away as fast as you can' and he did it and we got a lovely Polaroid of him doing it!"

Back in Ramsgate where the team were staying, John Sullivan spotted a shower cap in his hotel room, and, due to the close proximity of Dover and the number of French visitors who stayed there, it had the words "shower cap" also in French. The translation "bonnet de douche" seemed to be the sort of thing Del would say for a toast. At dinner that night he tried it out on the cast and crew. "I said: 'Well boys, we're filming tomorrow, so bonnet de douche to you all' and they all returned the toast with 'bonnet de douche'. When people went off to bed they said: 'Goodnight, bonnet de douche.'" John then added it to the script and a little bit of *Only Fools and Horses* mythology was born.

In an interview in the *Radio Times* to promote the episode John Sullivan reflected on how he now felt about writing the show. "The first series was difficult – I never really enjoy the beginning because you haven't had a chance to establish the characters in your mind – but now I know everything about Del: I know where he went to school, I even know what desk he sat at. And when I'm writing, I am forever pacing around the room, impersonating every role, to get the rhythm of the dialogue."

The episode was the most popular programme that Christmas. "The acting was ace, the plot was so neat," said the *Daily Mirror*. "But the really blissful moments... were the emotional ones." The *Sun* said: "Del Boy is No 1 for festive fun" and the TV reviewer in *Today* said it was "the only Christmas special worthy of the title."

FAMOUS FANS: SIR ANTHONY HOPKINS

Among the millions of fans of *Only Fools and Horses* is Oscar-winning actor Sir Anthony Hopkins. He said: "John Sullivan's scripts are way up there with the very best of them, like the work Galton and Simpson did for Tony Hancock. Like theirs, his characters are drawn from real life and very well observed. I always love those exchanges between Trigger and the guys. One of my favourite moments was in the final episode when they are in the Nag's Head talking about everyone having fifteen minutes of fame during a lifetime and Trig says: 'Like

Gandhi.' And Rodney says: 'Gandhi?' and Trig says: 'He made one great film and then you never saw him again.' Also the time Del and Rodney burst into the funeral dressed as Batman and Robin was just brilliant. The acting is absolutely first rate. The skill of the actors in the situations that are presented to them is spot on – it's as simple as that. David Jason and Nicholas Lyndhurst are superb actors. It is obvious that they work really well together. They play their scenes straight and they make us laugh because they are just so convincing. Their timing is superb and having lived in London for many years now I love cockney humour. As a young actor I certainly knew a couple of Del Boys in the Waterloo Road area! I used to hang around in the Windmill pub where you'd come across traders of all sorts – fishmongers, florists, barrow boys and spivs – all great characters to spend time with. The show is also such a great ensemble piece. It works like a well-oiled machine with all the other characters that appear played by an excellent array of supporting actors. I would have been delighted to have had a part in the programme, but I know my limitations and I'm not a Londoner so I don't think I'd have fitted in unless I'd played a Welshman. *Only Fools and Horses* is a classic – and will remain so. I can't offer any mystical insights into it, it's simply wonderful comedy."

1990 Christmas Special

The 1990 Christmas special *Rodney Come Home*, was filmed as the first episode of a new series, 'series G'. Following on from the end of *The Jolly Boys' Outing*, it saw John Sullivan concentrating on the faltering relationship between Rodney and Cassandra. "It was quite a downbeat episode but that was down to John moving the characters on a couple of gear changes," explained Gareth Gwenlan. "The episodes that followed were only possible because we'd done *Rodney Come Home*. John and I had long conversations about it because it wasn't a conventional episode but it was very pivotal to what happened afterwards."

It had been filmed in Bristol in October 1990 and by that stage Gareth Gwenlan had relinquished his post as Head of Comedy in order to spend more time making programmes as a producer. I was on set for filming in Bristol - and even, thanks to director Tony Dow, appeared in *Rodney Come Home* for about half a second as an extra - and wasn't surprised to see just how popular the cast were with passers-by. David Jason was happy to play along. I remember two builders walking past him wearing Halloween masks and gently jeering him. He instantly responded in ad-libbed Del-speak: "What's your problem, pal? We aren't 'arf glad you're wearing them masks." Other people nearby laughed. To them David was Del Boy and it's Del Boy they wanted to see – and David was brilliant with them. In between scenes, as lights and cameras were adjusted, he stayed in character and carried on in full swing as Del. They lined up for autographs and he obliged. I imagined David would probably rather not have been signing autographs. I expect he'd rather have been sitting down, going over his lines and drinking tea – but he didn't disappoint his fans.

Once the crowd had gone, as David walked back to the location catering truck to get some lunch and snatch a short break another eager autograph-hunting young girl ran after him waving a scrap of paper and calling: "Mr Jason... Mr Jason!" For a moment David kept walking, deep in thought. Then the youngster caught up with him and mumbled her request. "Go on then..." he said, a smile spreading across his face. "What's yer name...?"

He was in the same cheerful mood just over a month later when the studio recording took place at BBC Television Centre. He bounded on to the set to thunderous applause from the two-hundred-strong audience. He welcomed the audience as David Jason – and then switched into Del Boy mode. Wandering over to a young woman in the front row he asked with a grin: "Pick a number between one and ten." "Seven," she said. "Wrong," he said with a mischievous grin on his face. "Take your clothes off." The audience roared – and with that, it was on with the show.

It was the biggest Christmas Day show with 17.97 million viewers, followed closely by Steven Spielberg's hit film *ET* that got 17.50 million. ITV's best shot, a Ken Dodd special, didn't even make the top ten. The critics too seemed to like the domestic drama brought about by Rodney's tempestuous marriage to Cassandra and Del's rollercoaster relationship with Raquel.

Pam Francis, television critic of *Today* newspaper, said: "Rather than keep the Trotter brothers in a time warp, their creator John Sullivan has taken the risk of moving them on with the times. By doing so, and getting Rodders hitched he's been able to tackle relevant issues." The *Daily Mail* agreed. "John Sullivan clearly still loves the show and thanks to his fertile imagination it's far from running out of steam," wrote critic Marcus Berkmann. "He's kept the series alive but it's lost none of its energy and pace."

Series Seven

After the Christmas Day show, the next episode *The Sky's The Limit* went out just five days later and launched the new series. In it Boycie's new satellite dish gets stolen and Del buys it back for him – for a profit. Or so he thinks, until he actually discovers that he's got an air traffic control radar from the main runway at Gatwick Airport and that planes are now homing in on Nelson Mandela House.

"They say never work with children or animals and during the filming of that episode we had to do both," recalled John Challis. "We were filming at the house that plays Boycie and Marlene's mock Tudor home and Boycie was messing about with this huge satellite dish which he didn't really know how to operate. At the same time as trying to control it, Duke the dog was bounding about all over the lawn and we had the little lad who plays Tyler there in the pram dressed in a replica of what Marlene was wearing.

"The Great Dane playing Duke was actually quite lazy and didn't do that much bounding around and his trainer was trying desperately to get him to move rather than just lolling around. Then the sound people needed some slobbering noises from this dog so the guy with the boom microphone knelt down to record them and the dog saw the furry microphone cover and leapt on it and savaged it, which reduced everyone to hysterics."

David Jason cites the episode as an example of John Sullivan's originality. "Some of the things that John came up with were just so stunningly original, clever, brilliantly disguised comedy like where at the end you find out someone pinched the satellite dish from the end of the runway at Gatwick and all the aircraft were homing in on it. That's a brilliantly conceived joke which John held right back to the very end. Of course if you go out on a big laugh like that you leave people talking about it – and people enjoy the aftertaste."

The Chance of A Lunchtime sees Raquel realising there is more to life than clearing up after the Trotters at Nelson Mandela House and deciding to go back to acting. "That episode saw a turning point for Raquel because she got an audition to join a theatre company and then she got offered a part in a tour but she had to turn it down because she'd discovered that she was pregnant," said Tessa Peake-Jones.

Stage Fright guest starred Philip Pope as singing dustman Tony Angelino, who we later discover, in a hilarious scene where the cast can almost be seen laughing for real, can't pronounce his Rs and therefore has to sing *Cwying* and the *Gween Gween Gwass of Home*. Philip is a multi-talented performer. In addition to acting roles in shows like *Blackadder, Drop The Dead Donkey* and *Underworld* he's also a brilliant musician and one of the country's top programme theme tune writers with dozens of credits to his name – not to mention the infamous *Chicken Song* from *Spitting Image*.

Tessa Peake-Jones spoke to director Tony Dow shortly after getting the script for the episode and seeing that she'd have to sing as Raquel. "But I don't really sing," she explained. "And Tony said: 'Well she's not meant to be good!' and I thought: 'Oh thanks!' I had sung and danced to get my Equity card but I'd never put myself forward as a professional singer.

"It was a bit nerve wracking in the night-club where we filmed it because a lot of the supporting artists that were there were club acts themselves. I was very aware of singing *Crying* rather badly in front of an audience who were sitting there being paid to look fairly bored and who were rather bored. They'd seen everything shot loads of times so I was very aware of their critical eyes but I just had to get on with it. I started very nervously and hit none of the right notes but

I think I got better as the day went on. I did hit a couple of bum notes though, which Tony had to cut away when it came to editing. He disguised them by cutting to Del and Rodney at the bar and turning my singing down and their voices up. I was just too out of tune and Tony said: 'There are a couple of times I just can't hide it!'"

Class of '62 sees the return and final appearance of Jim Broadbent as Roy Slater, who viewers discover has just been released from prison, where he's been serving his sentence for diamond smuggling revealed in *To Hull and Back*. More surprising was the revelation that Slater was in fact Raquel's much referred to but never identified ex-husband. "I'd never met Jim before," said Tessa Peake-Jones. "He was great fun though and I know that the others felt that it was like another old boy and member of the team back. There was a school reunion in the story and it was a bit like a school reunion for the boys too!"

"It was a fabulous episode and it was brilliant to get Jim Broadbent back for it," said Tony Dow. "He's a great actor and he was superb as Slater."

In *He Ain't Heavy, He's My Uncle* Uncle Albert is trying to woo Marlene's mum against competition from his friend Knock-Knock. Meanwhile Del decides that, with a baby due, it is time that the Trotters become a two-car family and he buys a brightly-coloured, clapped-out Capri Ghia (which Rodney promptly dubs the 'prattmobile'). I was on set for the scene where the car was unveiled for the first time at garages near the flats in Duckmoor Road, Bristol, which doubled as Nelson Mandela House. Bristol City Football Club was very close and birds on the floodlights were making such a racket and interrupting filming that some of the crew let off fireworks to scare them away.

The episode also saw the team return to filming in London for scenes shot all over the City of London and nearby Docklands, when Albert goes missing and Del and Rodney try to track him down. "That was no problem to shoot because the City is deserted at weekends," said Gareth Gwenlan. The soundtrack for the scene was Paul and Linda McCartney's 1971 single, *Uncle Albert*, which had been a number one hit in the United States. John Sullivan remembered it and it fitted in perfectly with the mood of the episode. There were issues over getting the rights to use the track but Paul McCartney personally intervened and made it available. Buster Merryfield particularly found filming parts of the episode very emotional. "I found it very moving filming the scene where Albert had returned to the place where he'd lived as a boy," he said. "I could easily have cried. Not many people can write scripts like John Sullivan."

The hospital scenes in ***Three Men, A Woman and A Baby*** were filmed at a recently-closed ward at West Middlesex Hospital at Hillingdon, which has also been used for filming births in *Waiting For God* and *Roger, Roger*. The ward below though was still open and that made finding a newborn baby to play Del and Raquel's child Damien very easy.

"When we were ready to film we went down and said: 'Hands up who's had a baby in the last hour who's prepared to lend it to the BBC?' recalled Gareth Gwenlan. "I think the mum was thrilled that her baby was going to appear on the telly."

Tessa Peake-Jones asked a midwife for advice because she hadn't any children at that time. "I didn't have a bloomin' clue at the time how you did it," she laughed. "So she sat David, Nick, Buster and myself down in a room and showed us a video of a woman giving birth. We'd all just had a cooked breakfast and we all felt sick at the end of it because it went into very graphic detail.

"I remember at one point looking at the others. There was Buster, this man in his seventies, with his mouth just wide open in amazement watching this baby coming out, David was going: 'Oh my God' and obviously being put off for life, Nick was speechless and I'm sure wanted to vomit and I was just thinking: 'I can't do that!' The woman looked in such pain and terror and was making horrible noises. That lasted half an hour and then I went into the ward and sat on the bed and did what the woman did in the film – well almost. I knew John didn't want me to hold back so I put in lots of screams.

"I was tired at the end of the day but it was just acting and it was less than a year later that I gave birth to my own daughter Mollie for real. I didn't scream half as much because I didn't have the breath to do that but like Raquel I did have a male midwife called Paul who was lovely."

Inspiration for many of the hilarious lines during the birth sequence came from John Sullivan's own experiences when his wife Sharon gave birth to their children. In the script Raquel said to Del: "Don't you ever come near me again, Trotter" and John said: "Sharon had said that to me and then she asked to hold my hand and she dug her nails in and I said: 'Ahh' and she said: 'Now you know what it bloody well feels like!' so I used that too."

A month after the 1991 series ended David Jason scooped a Bafta Best Light Entertainment Award for his performance, after unbelievably missing out previously despite being nominated five times. At the glittering awards ceremony – the British equivalent to the American Oscars – David generously paid tribute to John Sullivan saying: "He gives me the ammunition and I fire the gun."

"I was very pleased," said David. "I'd been nominated every year and was always being pipped at the post. I started getting used to it and then in the end my tenacity paid off!" Over the years he's collected a staggering list of more than twenty awards – two Sonys, three Baftas, three British comedy awards, three from the Royal Television Society and so on. David quipped: "I'm thinking of building an extra room for them."

THE SECRET GULF WAR SPECIAL

During the 1991 Gulf War a special fifteen-minute episode of *Only Fools and Horses* was shot at RAF Strike Command at High Wycombe. A special Trotter van was decked out in brown and yellow desert camouflage complete with a machine gun mounted on the roof with Peckham scrawled out and Kuwait written in. "I wrote the script," said John Sullivan. "Gareth Gwenlan directed it and the van was sent out to the boys in the Gulf with the message: 'Don't worry – the secret weapon is coming. The Iraqis will start running when they see this!'"

It featured David, Nicholas and Buster and everyone gave up their time for free for the one-day shoot. "It was great fun and after we finished filming they laid on a buffet for us," recalled John. There was no time to edit the material filmed and it was immediately dispatched to the Gulf to entertain British forces. "It went out just as we filmed it – mistakes and all," added John. The film was done like a home movie straight to camera.

It begins with Rodney scrawling 'Kuwait' onto the van then Del says: "This is Derek Trotter talking to you from a secret location somewhere in southern England." Explaining that the specially adapted Trotter van was a secret weapon, he says: "This is the Concorde of three wheeled vans."

At the end, Del turns serious and, after a shot of the wives and children at the base who were watching the filming, said: "We're all very proud of what you've done. We know you've worked hard and we can't wait for you to come back here safe and sound so that you can buy us all a pint. Well done and God bless you." Then Rodney chipped in: "And don't worry about the wives and girlfriends. We'll look after them for you. They're safe in our hands."

Del takes to the sky

Rodney and Cassandra tie the knot

FAMILIAR FACES

Boycie and Marlene in Miami

Tony Angelino, the singing dustman

The Trotters become
a two car family

Down the Nag's Head

**FILMING MIAMI TWICE
PART ONE -
THE AMERICAN
DREAM**

The actual watch
(well the prop at least...)

A ticket to a
studio recording

★ONLY FOOLS AND HORSES.★

WRITTEN BY JOHN SULLIVAN
Starring DAVID JASON NICHOLAS LYNDHURST BUSTER MERRYFIELD

John Sullivan meets up with
his teacher Jim Trowers

Doing a runner in Monte Carlo

KEEP OUT

Bonjour...

THE FINAL EPISODES

Joan's grave

Studio recordings

With Jonathan Ross

John Sullivan, Tony Dow and the team
during The Green Green Grass rehearsals

The Green Green Grass

Del and his pa[...]

Freddie and Jelly[...]

Del and Rodney's
Mum Joan

Baby Rodney's washing
drying on the balcony

David Jason visits the set

1991 Christmas Specials

In October 1991 filming began in Miami, Florida, on the second of a £2 million two-part *Miami Twice* story called *Oh To Be In England.* Before he had left his post as Head of Comedy, Gareth Gwenlan had talked to Jonathan Powell, who had taken over as Controller of BBC1, about taking the programme to America for an extra special Christmas episode. "The show could do no wrong by that time and he agreed we could do it," said Gareth.

The idea was that in the first episode, *The American Dream*, which also saw Damien's christening, Del would use Rodney's pension refund – or Maxwell money as he topically called it - to buy two tickets to Florida so that he could hide from someone he'd stitched up over a wine deal with some dodgy Romanian Riesling.

The final moments of the first episode saw the brothers flying out of Gatwick Airport and featured a guest appearance by Virgin boss Richard Branson. "Richard is a nice man but he can't act to save his life," Gareth laughed. "For the first ten minutes of filming he couldn't keep a straight face and then he had to take it seriously because he was holding up his own plane which was waiting to go to Los Angeles. In order to get him to say his line convincingly we had to shoot it quite a few times."

In the story Del and Rodney run into trouble when Del is spotted by a Mafia gang who realise he's a doppelganger for the beleaguered head of the family, Don Occhetti, which meant David Jason having to film twice as many scenes as normal for the dual role. The actual filming in Miami for *Oh To Be In England* was no fun for the cast or the crew. "Foreign filming is always problematic because it costs a lot of money and I believe you are running a risk editorially when you take a series out of its normal environment," said Gareth Gwenlan. "I'm not sure it totally paid off. Although it's a very good two-parter, it's not *Only Fools and Horses.*"

Gareth had flown to Miami knowing that filming the show would not be a picnic but he hadn't expected it to be quite the nightmare that it turned into. Before filming had begun, he and Tony Dow had visited Miami and talked in detail about the project with the Florida Film Board, who assured them that they would have no problems with the unions and that they could bring over their heads of departments and then hire local technicians with no difficulties.

"We had to have a crew that was made up of sixty percent of local workers, which was fine because we didn't want to have to take loads of people over from the UK," said Gareth. "So we ended up taking the heads of make-up, costume and design and the cameraman and sound recordist. Everyone else we employed there."

Problems arose when they needed to hire vehicles for props and costumes and for make-up and changing rooms. Having been assured by the Film Board that they could just hire vans that had owner-drivers who would drive them around, Gareth and his team soon found that they had crossed the all-powerful Teamsters' [drivers] Union. "We started shooting, then on the third day I got a call from production manager Sue Longstaff saying that we had problems with the Teamsters. This guy had just come down and said that they were going to start picketing our set. I was literally summoned to go down and see the head of the Teamsters' Union in Miami and, I swear to God, had it not been so serious, I would have thought I was in a bad American B movie.

"I was shown into this very sombre, dark wood panelled office with heavy leather furniture where I found this great fat, balding guy sitting at his desk. He had a real James Cagney-at-his-worst accent and he said: 'So what are you doing in my town?' I explained how much money we were spending in the city and that we were employing some sixty local technicians and he said: 'Yeah, but you ain't employing any of my members?' I said that we weren't because we had owner-driver vehicles and we were told that was fine.

"He said: 'Well I'm here's to tell you that it ain't fine. I want twelve of my drivers on that set tomorrow, otherwise I shut you down.' I know it sounds like something out of a film but it's absolutely true. I thought: 'Do I laugh or do I take this seriously?' I was worried because we'd spent or committed a lot of our budget and if everything went wrong then that would go down the drain.

"Eventually I said: 'Well, if you are saying we have to do this then I'll have to shut the unit down and I'll have to go back to England' and he said: 'I'll drive yous to the airport.' I said: 'I'll talk to you again tomorrow,' then I went back to the office."

"Gareth was ashen when he came back," John Sullivan recalled. "He was as grey as his hair. His cigar light had obviously gone out a long time before. He said to me: 'I've never been so frightened in all my life.' This guy terrified him."

"I phoned this useless Florida Film Board and they said that I was going to have to come to a compromise," said Gareth. "I said: 'Why? You told me I could do this, you tell him to sod off.' They said they couldn't do that and then it just dawned on me how much the union system out there is still in the Dark Ages. As expected, the following day the union picketed us and completely shut production down because none of our American crew would cross the picket line."

At 7am the following morning Gareth had another meeting with the Union boss and they came to a compromise. The unit would employ three Teamsters' Union drivers. "So after that these three guys would arrive in the morning, do nothing all day and then go home," said Gareth. "As you can imagine I was far from happy about it but there was little else I could do.

"Everyone was under huge pressure anyway because it was costing so much to be out there that there was no way we could overrun and stay longer. We were working fourteen-hour days, six days a week and we did not have time to enjoy ourselves. The bar at our hotel wasn't open, so on Saturday nights when we had Sundays off we'd all chip $20 into a kitty and Robin Stubbs, our costume designer, would go off and buy big bottles of gin, scotch and vodka. Then we'd all sit round in the bar and chat and just drink to oblivion!"

The unit had no work for the Teamsters' drivers so one of them was assigned as a chauffeur for John Sullivan, instead of him running up big taxi bills. "He was a stocky guy of about five foot eleven, in his early forties and he was a very nice, polite man," said John. "We got on quite well and one day I was talking to him about petrol being measured in gallons not litres. Suddenly this mild-mannered man started effing and blinding and I was quite shaken. It was a real Jekyll and Hyde thing.

"By the time he dropped me off, he was back to his old gentle self. I had my family over with me and just before I flew home this American woman on the set asked me how I was getting to the airport. I said that this guy Charlie was going to be taking us. She asked me if I knew that Charlie had just come out of prison after sixteen years after serving time for armed robbery, murder and something else. And this guy was going to be taking my family and me to the airport.

"When he dropped us off he was polite as hell. He came across as a really nice man and I gave him a ridiculously big tip because I thought if they had any problems on the set I might have to come back and Charlie would be waiting for me. It was like I gave him a protection money bung. I thought I ought to keep on the right side of him. He'd once asked me where I lived in England and I'd said it was a quiet little village with twelve shops and two hundred horses and one policeman on a bike. He said: 'It sounds like my kind of town' and it was only later I realised what he meant!"

John Challis and Sue Holderness had an easier time. "We went out there for ten days but only did about four days' work," John recalled. "So we had a sort of holiday which was great because I'd never been there before." It wasn't all fun and games filming scenes in the Everglade swamps on airboats, though, as John recalled: "We were being driven by a guy called Wayne who had a confederate flag and a cowboy hat and fancied himself as a bit of a rebel. He was a complete lunatic and after we'd filmed our bit, he sank one of the other boats by going too fast and swamping it, with the wash from his boat. Fortunately there was no one on it because if there had been they might have been eaten by alligators, which wouldn't be a very nice way to go!"

Sue Holderness nearly didn't make it back to England. She had decided to take a camcorder to film a memento of the production and on one occasion was taping Nicholas Lyndhurst and David Jason, who were filming a scene in the Everglades where an alligator crept up behind them and they'd leap up and run off. "I was filming this with my camcorder," Sue recalled. "And I'm hopeless with it and I lost this alligator out of my view finder and I was trying to find it again. When I finally took the camera away from my eyes, the alligator had headed straight for me. I hadn't seen it coming because I'd been looking through the camera trying to spot this creature. Luckily the trainer, who had great presence of mind and strength, grabbed hold of this alligator's tail and it stopped about six inches from my feet. I was so close to having my legs bitten off. It was very scary – but could have been a lot worse."

Nicholas and David filmed the scene sitting on a log with the six-foot alligator less than eight feet behind them. "Some people think we shot it behind a glass screen but we didn't, we were genuinely just a few feet away from some big old jaws," said Nicholas. "We knew it was close because we could hear it breathing but when it came to start filming it wouldn't do anything. It just sat there and then when they needed it to react and move a bit, they got a ranger with a long stick to jab it in its private parts and of course then it snarled! But just in case it reacted too violently and went for us precautions, were taken.

"We had a guy off to my left with a rifle pointing at the alligator's head and then between us, just to the side of the camera, was a ranger with a .44 magnum pointing just past us, again at its head. I said: 'Quite honestly I'd rather have the gator than a gun five feet away waving at my head.' I knew it wasn't pointing right at me but it wasn't far away!"

The script also called for Del to fall into a swamp at one point although when he wrote it John Sullivan had no idea that the scene would be shot in the real Everglades. "We were pushed for time and David ended up filming it in alligator infested water," John said. "It was one of the bravest things I've ever seen because we had no idea what was underneath the surface and splashing in like he did would alert every alligator around. That took some guts."

John and director Tony Dow had gone deep into the Everglades on a filming recce. "I remember zooming through miles of high reeds on an airboat," John recalled. "I looked at Tony and he was covered in these maggots – and so was I – and as you hit them they burst. We eventually came out of the reeds and were on a very calm lake and we saw a bit of land and Tony said: 'What's that?' and Tom, the bloke driving the boat, said: 'That's Snake Island' and Tony goes: 'Can we go and look at it?' I thought: 'No – it's called ******* Snake Island – not Cuddly Wuddly Bunny Island!' So we went over there and he pulled up and he said: 'When we go on here I want you to follow me – do everything I do.' He then put his hand on a tree to jump onto the island and cried: 'Ahhhhhhhh' and I thought we had to do the same! But it was fire ants all up this tree and he was in agony with it. We got on the island and everywhere you walked through, the undergrowth was rustling. At one point I ducked under a spider's web and it apparently was the biggest tarantula Tom had ever seen. I said to Tom: 'Are there alligators on here?' and he said that it was alligator infested but mainly at night. 'At the moment they are all out hunting.' I said: 'Well what if one of them had a headache and was still laying around here...' I could not wait to get off that place, I can tell you."

Afterwards Tom took the pair to meet the chief of the Seminole Native American people. "We had to square it with him before we could film," John said. "He was OK and obviously a deal was going to be struck and they were going to get a bit of dosh out of it. Before we left he said: 'Would you like any trinkets, something to take home to your family?' Tom whispered that we should take something as a sign of respect. So I said: 'Thank you, can I take those beads for my daughter...' and as I said it he brought out a swipe machine for our credit cards. This was an ancient Indian chief who'd told us all this stuff about respecting the spirits and all that stuff..."

He then offered John and Tony alligator meat with fried bread. "It was about six in the evening by now and Tony went: 'No thank you, because we had breakfast,'" John said. "I was glad we said no because afterwards Tom said it wasn't really fried bread as we knew it - it was bread dipped in alligator fat and then sloshed in a pan and not done crispy...."

Back in the UK with filming over, David Jason found out that at Christmas he would be competing against himself for ratings with *Miami Twice* up against his other hit *The Darling Buds of May* on ITV. The *News of the World* reported that rival television executives were taking the unusual step of making arrangements so that the two programmes didn't clash in the schedules. Vernon Lawrence, then entertainment chief at Yorkshire TV, makers of *The Darling Buds of May*, declared: "It would be suicidal to screen both at the same time." The *Daily Express* later reported that the deal was brokered by David Jason personally. "I was very fortunate to have been asked to do Christmas specials of two very popular shows," he told the paper. "So I asked if Mr ITV and Mr BBC could speak to each other so that I, or the British public, was not put in an embarrassing position; could they make sure that the two specials were not going out against each other."

The first part of *Miami Twice* scooped the 1991 Christmas Eve TV top spot and power company National Grid announced that viewers switching on kettles after the show caused a seven hundred megawatt power surge. Unusually the critics had mixed views of the show. The *Sun*, as usual, offered solid support with TV Editor Andy Coulson calling the two-parter "a double delight." He went on: "Only fools would have missed the hysterical moment when Del Boy, complete with shades and Bermuda shorts, disappeared off towards Cuba on an out of control jet-ski."

Garry Bushell, writing in the *Daily Star* said the show started: "Slower than Trigger on Mastermind" but went on to say that: "Minor moans aside, the Trotters have been brightening up the festivities for a decade." *The Independent* said: "Instead of exploring the potential embarrassments and excitements of Del Boy deploying his entrepreneurial skills in the Sun Belt it lapsed into a preposterous and long-winded thriller yarn."

Part one of the show was watched by 17.7 million viewers but part two slipped to 14.88 million although it was still the number one show in the Christmas Day ratings, beating the multi-million pound film *Batman*. Unusually though, the show was beaten to the overall Christmas ratings top spot by BBC1's *Auntie's Bloomers*, fronted by Terry Wogan, which got 18.24 million viewers. *The Darling Buds of May,* in which David Jason starred as Pop Larkin, attracted 16.44 million viewers but was narrowly beaten to the ITV top spot by *Coronation Street.* The New Year however brought bad news for fans with the *Sun* reporting on January 3rd in a story headlined "Game Is Up For Del Boy" that the show may have reached the end of the road. David Jason, the article said, was busy on other projects, and John Sullivan, then busy writing his sitcom *Sitting Pretty* and his wartime comedy drama *Over Here*, confirmed there were no plans for another full series at that time and that remained the case. David Jason was certainly going to be busy over the next few years as in November 1991, while filming of *Only Fools* was taking place in Florida, ITV announced that it had signed up David Jason to star as a detective in a new series called *A Touch of Frost*. The success of that series and the demand for more episodes would go on to have an impact on David's availability in future years. However, despite rumours that Del would be killed off in a Mafia shoot-out in *Miami Twice*, the Trotters were far from finished.

From the 1991 Christmas specials onwards, John was given an executive producer credit for his work, reflecting the fact that his involvement in his programmes was far more than writer. "I was always involved with every aspect of my shows, from casting to editing and I used to give up an awful lot of time, sometimes going through tapes until 3 or 4am. I may have been at the BBC editing until midnight, when as far as writing was concerned I'd finished at 4pm. So I'd be doing an extra eight hours just for the love of the thing and because I wanted it to be right so I thought it was fair enough that they drop me a couple of quid here and there."

John decided to set up his own independent production company so that he could have more control over the finished production – and his reward for doing that would be a share of profits. BBC Executive Jim Moir, then Head of Light Entertainment, rang John's agent Roger Hancock and said he didn't want John to go down that route, partly because it might mean the company also working for ITV. Instead John was offered a deal giving him more control and independence for his productions but still working in-house at the BBC, and in addition he'd become an executive producer on his shows. John took the deal. "Now I don't just write the scripts, I'm with the show from the blank page to the final scenes," he explained at the time. "I write or choose a lot of the music but at least I get paid something for all those extra hours now."

POSTCARD FROM DEL BOY

In 1991 John Sullivan and I jointly wrote a postcard from Del in Miami back to the rest of the Trotters as a piece of publicity for the Christmas special. Here it is:

To: Raquel, Damien and Albert
368 Nelson Mandela House
Dockside Estate , Peckham,
London, England

Dear All,

Having a triffic time here in the old US of A. Me and Rodney have found ourselves a nice little Miami El Taverna for a glass or two of the old Californian vino. The Barman here can't make Pina Coladas like Mike at the Nag's Head - thank God!

Rodney's been wearing his shades and looking a right plonker I can tell you and he looks a total dipstick in his Hawaii shorts. He's being very careful not to get sunburnt - he's using blocking cream number 85 and looks like someone who's had a nasty accident with a barrel of lard. I, by contrast look like a proper Englishman abroad in me Fred Perry T-shirt and white suit - a right John Donson lookalike, me.

Yesterday we went out on one of them glass bottom boats. Tell Albert we saw a lot of his old ships. Me and Rodders did fink about hiring ourselves a posh limo - but then we found out that the yanks drive on the wrong side of the flippin road. I told Rodney: You have enough trouble driving properly in Peckham. You ain't driving over here. No way Pedro!

We haven't seen anyone famous yet - but I'm hoping to get to see that Dave Trump bloke as I reckon I've got a few fings we could do a deal over.

I did try and ring you all on me mobile dog and bone but it doesn't seem to be working. P'raps the cable has broken under the Atlantic.

Anyway, have a nice day, as they keep saying over here. See you soon.

Kisses to Raquel and Damien.
Bonnet De Douche!

Del Boy

(P.S. Albert – keep off my brandy)

1992 Christmas Special

On Wednesday November 25th 1992, filming began on a Christmas special *Mother Nature's Son* and even before the episode had been finished, bookmakers William Hill were giving odds of 13-8 on it coming first in the Christmas ratings with *Coronation Street* close behind at 9-4. Anyone who backed *Only Fools and Horses* would have been quids in when the show topped the Christmas ratings, scooping a colossal 20.13 million viewers, the highest ever at that time. The figure was more than double the nine million which *The Darling Buds of May* attracted and more than three million ahead of its nearest rival, an episode of *Birds of A Feather*.

Unusually the episode was filmed not in Bristol but in Brighton, East Sussex. That was because a key part of the story saw the Trotters spending a weekend at the stunning Victorian Grand Hotel on the seafront, most famous for the 1984 bombing when the IRA tried to assassinate Prime Minister Margaret Thatcher. The story also required the Trotters to clear up Grandad's old allotment so when Gareth Gwenlan spotted the ideal location on the Moulsecoomb Estate, Lower Bevendean, in Brighton while filming a series of the BBC comedy *Waiting For God,* it made sense to shoot everything in the one area. Other locations were found, like the White Admiral Pub, also in Lower Bevendean, which doubled as the exterior of the Nag's Head and Swaine's Farm Shop in nearby Henfield appeared as Rodney's friend Myles' shop. The poshest location was, of course, the Presidential Suite at the Grand Hotel and the total bill for filming there came to £2,500.

Director Tony Dow has good memories of filming the episode in Brighton. "We wanted to do a shot of the yellow van driving down the motorway so we went to the police who were brilliant," he said. "They backed up all the traffic on the big main road into Brighton and let us film and then let the traffic go. It was another example of the words *Only Fools and Horses* opening doors.

"I also recall spending two days filming the allotment scene and the first day was glorious sunshine and the day after it just rained – so if you look carefully at the sequence you can see that the weather changes."

WINNING AWARDS

Only Fools and Horses won a stack of awards over the years including: Television Situation Comedy of the Year – Television and Radio Industries Club (TRIC) 1984, Bafta Best Comedy Series 1986 and 1988, Funniest Television Programme – 1989 SOS Award, Television Situation Comedy of the Year - TRIC, 1997, Best Situation Comedy Award and Best Comedy Drama Award 1997, Royal Television Society, Best Comedy, Bafta, 1997 – and that's not counting individual awards to writer John Sullivan and actor David Jason.

1993 Christmas Special

Loyalty to the series has always been strong in Del's fictional stomping ground of south London and in December 1993 a Peckham man was so sure that he was on to a winner with it that he staked £2,000 that that year's Christmas special *Fatal Extraction* would be the most watched Christmas Day show. Sadly, his hunch didn't pay off and his 2/1 on bet went down the drain when the show was marginally pipped to the ratings number one place. It was beaten by a special Victor Meldrew story *One Foot In The Algarve*, written by David Renwick, who, like John Sullivan, had begun his comedy writing career on *The Two Ronnies,* which attracted 20 million viewers to *Only Fools'* 19.59 million.

Nevertheless *Fatal Extraction* was a cracking episode and saw Del running into trouble when he asked out a blonde dental receptionist called Beverly, played by actress Mel Martin. Perhaps the most notable scene, though, was the riot sequence outside Nelson Mandela House, with the twist that many of the hundred people involved – both police and rioters - were wearing Del Boy's latest line in ski masks. The actors hired to play rioters for the filming were all students from the famous Old Vic drama school in Bristol, among them Aled Jones, the ex-choirboy singer, who was studying there at the time.

The riot scenes were filmed under strict controls to make sure no one got hurt. However one extra who played a policeman complained later to a newspaper that the students had got carried away and had been too rough, a claim which producer Gareth Gwenlan dismisses.

"We did the first rehearsal and it was supposed to be a riot for Christ's sake and I'd seen bigger upsets at the Women's Institute," laughed Gareth. "So we said to the drama students: 'We don't want anyone being silly or getting hurt but we do want it to look a bit more realistic.' That's what happened and no one got hurt." And Gareth should know. After all, he was literally right in the thick of the action as a riot policeman on horseback. Gareth, who is still a member of the actors' union Equity from his days as an actor, played the cop who broke up the riot temporarily to let Del, Raquel and Damien through in Del's 'tasteful' Capri Ghia, by announcing over the megaphone: "Hold it, hold it, hold it - it's Del Boy."

"We couldn't find an actor who could ride," he said. "So I did it and I was keeping a firm eye on what was going on and they were having a bit of a go but nobody was injured at all. And we were well covered if anything had gone wrong because we had first aid there, ambulances, the police – even a helicopter! The whole thing was done very carefully. The students were bloody marvellous. They were being real but within the bounds of being safe and no one was even bruised."

After *Fatal Extraction* was transmitted Gareth Gwenlan assumed that it was likely to have been the last episode. David Jason was then under an eighteen-month contract with Yorkshire Television to make episodes of his hugely successful police drama *A Touch of Frost*, in which he played downbeat Detective Inspector Jack Frost. Nicholas Lyndhurst meanwhile became busy with his new series *Goodnight Sweetheart*, in which he plays TV repairman turned shopkeeper Gary Sparrow, who found himself able to switch between the present day and the 1940s and began living a double life with women in both time zones.

Neither Gareth nor John Sullivan though wanted to leave the show alone without having rounded it off in a manner befitting Britain's favourite comedy series. Gareth recalled: "Eventually I said to John: 'It would be a shame if we just let it bleed away.

Shouldn't we try to do just one final one?' He said he would be very happy to. We then had to find a time when both Nick and David were free at the same time and that had proved very difficult over years as their careers had developed and they'd become increasingly busy."

FAMOUS FANS: AL MURRAY

Only Fools and Horses was very successful because it was so unpretentious; it set out to be funny and warm, and was just those things. The casting was impeccable, the relationships were realistic, but its emphasis was always on being funny. It did the most difficult thing for a comedy of sitting firmly in the mainstream without being pap - not to put too fine a point on it. John Sullivan had a great ear for how his characters spoke, and his portrayal of their endless struggle to get rich and never quite succeed (until luck came their way in the end) was perhaps a subtle dig at the Thatcherite age; Del and Rodney were the last people cut out to be go getters, yet their loyalty to one another was their real fortune. It was also the last hugely successful comedy show with a live audience, and for that it now seems very old fashioned. *Only Fools'* audience grew because it was repeated pretty often - certainly for me the first couple of series form a sort of backdrop to my television viewing in the eighties - proving really that familiarity rather than novelty is something that makes comedy work. And because the characters were perhaps familiar types to everyone, and dealing with the familiar struggle of making ends meet, the show became hugely popular.

1996 Christmas Specials

In the spring of 1996 producer Gareth Gwenlan was busy working on the pilot episode of John Sullivan's new comedy drama *Roger, Roger*, based around the drivers working at Cresta Cabs mini-cab firm, when he learned that David Jason would have a two month gap in his schedule in the autumn. He seized his moment and arranged for David, John Sullivan, director Tony Dow and himself to go out for dinner at upmarket restaurant The Greenhouse in London's Mayfair. Nicholas Lyndhurst was busy filming elsewhere and couldn't attend but Gareth already knew his view.

The four men ate, drank and talked about the show and John Sullivan outlined a few ideas he had for rounding off the series. Several hours and a number of decent bottles of wine later they agreed to make one last feature length episode.

"The fact of the matter was I'd been very busy and I didn't think it needed rounding off, but I knew John more than anybody just wanted to tie it all up and he wanted the Trotters to become millionaires," said David. "That had always been his ambition and plan. There was talk of making a series but I couldn't because of my other commitments. Then at the end of the dinner John said to me: 'What do you think?' And I just said: 'Yeah, come on, let's go for it!'

"John was so pleased and subsequently so was I because it brought back all the fun and memories and I missed it. I missed it greatly – the camaraderie and the fun and the good friendly atmosphere and laughs at rehearsals. It was a bit like a drug – it was wonderful and I missed that."

The following morning Gareth Gwenlan got straight on the phone to David's agent Meg Poole to confirm that he wanted to book him for two months. He discovered that she knew all about it as David had called her even earlier to tell her what he'd agreed to do. He'd cleared his time even before the mundane details like money had been discussed.

Gareth's second call was to his boss Geoffrey Perkins, the new Head of Comedy at BBC Television just to check that they did actually want a final *Only Fools and Horses* story for Christmas 1996. Of course they did, came Geoffrey's immediate response. John Sullivan, delighted and excited to be writing for Del and Rodney again, temporarily put aside his other projects and got down to work sketching out his storylines.

After a week he realised he was having trouble so he called Gareth Gwenlan. "I can't do it in one episode," he told him. "I can see a two or maybe even a three-parter coming on." Gareth's immediate response was to wonder whether they could film three cracking episodes of *Only Fools and Horses* in the two months without rushing it and jeopardising the results. Not only that but he'd need to get an increase in his budget and check that his cast were happy with the extra work. "I needn't have worried," he said. "Because, by the time the scripts came through, I'm sure they would have done six episodes had we had the time." By July matters had been settled and it was decided to make three fifty minute episodes of the show, later extended to an hour each, to be filmed between October and early December, which would round off the series.

Word got out and the *Daily Mirror* announced the good news with the headline: "Lovely Jubbly... Del's back on the telly." Details also emerged of the sacrifices both Nicholas Lyndhurst and David Jason had made so that the shows could be made. Nicholas had postponed a new series of *Goodnight Sweetheart* and David had turned down a lucrative offer from Yorkshire Television to film an extra episode of *A Touch of Frost*.

David Jason recalled reading the script for **Heroes and Villains**, the first of the trilogy, for the first time. "I remember sitting there and getting to the Batman and Robin scene and just having to close the script and having a couple of minutes of laughter and thinking: 'I can't believe this! What do they do now?' It was one of those many times where you just wanted to keep reading to find out how he was going to end it," he said.

John Sullivan described the read-through of the three scripts which took place before filming as "a bit odd" and explained to me at the time: "When we came to the last one and David said the last lines there was silence. There was no laughing and then everyone got up and made coffee. Everyone realised they would be the last lines we'd ever hear. I think when we actually come to do it it'll be funny but also sad for all of us."

Location filming for the three episodes began in Bristol on the morning of Thursday October 3rd 1996 and began with scenes with Del and Rodney and Dr Singh outside Nelson Mandela House. Later filming would briefly move back to London for the scenes in Rodney's apocalyptic futuristic dream at the beginning of *Heroes and Villains*, which will remain among the most classic moments of the series. Del and Raquel are in their dotage, Rodney is a messenger boy, Cassandra a maid, Albert has been preserved for posterity and Damien is now the boss of the world-powerful global TIT Co barking orders to US President Keanu Reeves and announcing that 'War is Good.' The scenes were shot at the Royal Horticultural Hall in London and filming began at 6pm and went on right through the night until 8am the following morning. Damien was played by Tessa Peake-Jones' real life partner, actor Douglas Hodge, who is best known for his roles in the TV series *Middlemarch* and *Capital City*.

"Tony Dow rang up and asked if Doug would like to do it and he was delighted because he's a huge fan of the programme and he thought it would be a great laugh to be in it," said Tessa Peake-

Jones. "We didn't have any lines together and if we had it would have been pretty weird. It was a bit odd seeing him as part of the team although he knew everyone anyway. He practised his David Jason impersonations at home the week before we filmed it, trying to be Derek Trotter and I thought he was great except that he has blue eyes and Damien has dark brown ones, so Doug had to wear brown contact lenses."

Filming the memorable Batman and Robin scene in *Heroes and Villains* required David Jason and Nicholas Lyndhurst to make complete fools of themselves. "You have to have a tremendous sense of fun and self-deprecation and you can't take yourself too seriously and do things like that," grinned David. "You've got to be a bit daft in the head to do it. When I got the script I read it for a while, then I had to stop. I closed the page and laughed out loud. I had to put it down. I could see in my mind what John had written and it was priceless." Filming it, in the early hours of a cold November morning, was another matter. David recalled: "Nick and I had to film it about six times because we couldn't do it for laughing. I'd be looking at him in all his gear and he'd be trying to say serious lines and I just found it very funny. He'd say: 'What are you laughing at?' and I'd say: 'Well you've got to see you from where I see you.'"

The production team went to great lengths to make sure the press didn't get pictures of David and Nicholas as Batman and Robin and spoil the surprise. They kept their costumes covered up until the last minute and when a camera lens was spotted the unit electricians dazzled it with powerful film lights. Finally one persistent photographer was encouraged to leave the area by a security guard with an impeccably trained Rottweiler.

"I kept David and Nick dressed as Batman and Robin in their caravan until the very last minute. We used two stand-ins for focusing and setting up and then got them to run to the actual spot where we were filming, shoot it and then immediately got them back out of sight. We were desperate that no one should get pictures of them as Batman and Robin because we didn't want to spoil the surprise for people watching on Christmas Day – and we managed it. We were there all night but the actual filming of David and Nick only took about two minutes."

One photographer though did get pictures of David, Nicholas and Buster filming scenes from the final episode with the boys' new cars. Seeing the Rolls Royce made some papers leap to the wrong conclusion that the Trotters win the lottery. Although they would have preferred nothing had leaked, Gareth Gwenlan decided not to knock down the story in the hope that the papers would then stop digging for the real storyline. "We didn't feed the lottery idea to them," he said. "They said: 'Is it this?' and we said: 'Could be'. We didn't deny it nor did we agree with it but we said it in such a way that made them feel that they were on to something. They printed it and it worked for us because after that everyone else gave up trying to find out what the plot was."

After location filming was completed the focus moved to London where the three episodes were to be recorded at BBC Television Centre in front of studio audiences over three nights from Thursday November 14th, with the final episode to be filmed on Friday December 6th.

One of the most poignant scenes ever in the series came in **Modern Men** when Del engineers a lift breakdown in order to get Rodney talking about Cassandra's recent miscarriage. "I wanted to go for the tears because I thought it would be realistic," said Nicholas Lyndhurst. "We only recorded the scene once because it worked right first time and that was the one that was used."

"There was a particularly wonderful moment in that episode," said director Tony Dow, "It's when Rodney goes into see Cassandra after she has lost their baby and Del says he wants Rodney to go in and be strong for her which is very moving. Then they go in and Del starts to sob. Rodney's reaction to that is priceless. We had to shoot that bit so many times because the crew were hysterical. They just couldn't stop laughing. We almost couldn't get through it. We had to shoot it loads of times."

"Awful" is the word Nicholas used to describe rehearsals for the studio recording of the final episode *Time On Our Hands.* "We were at the BBC rehearsal rooms at a tower block in north Acton, which is somewhere where I grew up really and I just couldn't imagine that this was going to be our last time there doing *Only Fools and Horses*," said Nicholas.

"Rehearsals were very hard," agreed David Jason. "When I'd read the script at home it took me ages because every time I tried to read it it made me cry. I knew I couldn't do that in rehearsals and I needed to have more control, although everyone seemed to have tears in their eyes."

The atmosphere in Studio Six was subdued as preparations for the final recording of *Only Fools and Horses* went ahead. In the dressing rooms emotions were already running high. Feelings of nervousness are commonplace before a performance in front of a live audience, although for the last episode it was to be filled almost exclusively by fans and friends and relatives of the cast, but this time it was different. This was to be the last episode and very much the end of an era for so many people.

A little before 6.45pm the studio audience began arriving and filling up the seats. At 7.15pm the warm-up man Bobby Bragg came on and did his usual routine of being cheeky about the cast and crew and generally trying to make the audience feel at ease. That night his job was not a hard one. Everyone in the studio was delighted to be there and knew they were seeing television history in the making. He introduced the cast and a clearly moved David Jason said a few words to the audience before bounding off to prepare for his first scene.

Cameras moved into position. The familiar theme tune rang out for the last time in a BBC studio and the lights came up on the set. The final recording was under way. A little over an hour later it was almost over. The recording had gone well. The audience had been in hysterics when Del, then Rodney fainted at Sothebys and then had been almost crying with laughter as the Trotter boys screamed with excitement as they sat in the van when the auction was over and they'd become multi-millionaires.

As the actors filmed the final Nag's Head scene when all their friends and pub regulars clapped and cheered them, the props team and scene-shifters cleared out the flat set of everything except the carpets and Del's cocktail bar in preparation for the last studio scene. For Nicholas Lyndhurst it was the final reminder that the show was at an end – and it wasn't a pleasant feeling. "The flat was all lit up with full studio lighting and seeing it stopped me in my tracks," he said. "It was really horrid. It was like seeing an old friend and thinking: 'What have they done to you?' It was a shell. It didn't look like a flat any more – it looked like what it was – just a studio set. It was three walls propped up. It was very sad.

"The final scene of Del, Rodney and Albert walking off into the sunset had already been shot some weeks before in Bristol, so the last scene in the flat was our last scene ever. As we did it I was fighting so hard to try to stop tears that my voicebox just dried up completely. My last line was: 'We're not in business any more mate' and I had trouble getting it out because I was so choked up and I ended up sounding like a woman."

"I cried before I made my entrance," admitted Buster Merryfield. "Then I wiped the tears away and went on. I was so moved and I really felt the lines I was saying." David Jason too spent the whole night struggling with his emotions. "Doing the final scene was so sad. It was the realisation that you'd actually done the last scene and said goodbye to them forever. I had to fight very hard all night to keep control," he said. "And when it was all over and the final credits went up I shed more than a tear or two."

As the credits rolled the audience thundered their applause and then did something that no one can remember happening before in a studio recording of any show. They took to their feet and gave a standing ovation which lasted many minutes. "I'd never seen that before and nor had anyone else," said David Jason. "It was very moving and it seemed to go on forever. It rounded off one of the most unusual nights I've ever had and I'll never forget it."

As the cheering died away and the studio audience trooped out still chattering excitedly about what they'd seen, the crew began clearing the studio ready for the following morning's edition of the kids' show *Live and Kicking*. The set was taken down and put into storage. The contents of the flat were boxed up and sent to the various warehouses from where they had been hired and the costumes were taken away and hung up for the final time.

The action for the cast and crew moved upstairs to the Reception Suite on the sixth floor of Television Centre, where BBC Television boss Alan Yentob threw a party and thanked everyone for their efforts. Familiar faces from the show's history like Ray Butt, Martin Shardlow and Jim Broadbent had come up specially.

However work wasn't over for John Sullivan, Gareth Gwenlan or Tony Dow. They still had to edit the show and get it ready for transmission three weeks later. "When we were editing we knew we had something special," Gareth recalled. "But then again John and I sat down on Christmas Eve doing a final sound edit. Everyone had been saying it was going to be the greatest thing ever, Ladbrokes were offering odds on it being the most watched show at Christmas and the Beeb had gone overboard saying: 'This is the BBC's Christmas present to the nation.'

"I turned to John and I said: 'What happens if they don't like it?' and he said: 'I've been thinking about that' and I said: 'It's a possibility isn't it?' We've all done shows in the past where you've been convinced that they are going to be OK and they've bombed. I said: 'The only time that I'm going to know is after about half an hour in when it is going out tomorrow when I'm sitting at home with friends and family.'" Half an hour into transmission the following day Gareth picked up the phone and called John Sullivan. As he expected he got the answerphone so he left a message. "John, I'm telling you, it's OK!" he said.

It certainly was. *Heroes and Villains* chalked up a staggering 21.3 million viewers, exactly the same figure achieved by *Modern Men*. *Time On Our Hands* though really took the biscuit and was watched by 24.3 million people, becoming the most watched television programme in British history, bar none. It was more of a send-off than anyone on the production could have dreamed of and for the next few days the programme dominated tabloid newspapers. The *Sun* kicked off after the transmission of part one with a front page splash: "Del-Namic Duo" announcing the huge ratings success. And after the last episode went out the *Daily Mirror*, using a picture of Rodney and Del's emotional lift scene, ran the headlines "Luvvly Blubbly" and "Del of A Way to Go".

THAT WATCH - THE TRUE STORY

Only Fools and Horses might be fiction but the story of the missing antique watch that enabled the Trotters to become millionaires is absolutely true. If someone finds John Harrison's missing H6 watch then they would be seriously, as Del might put it, quids in. The pocket-watch, the fabled H6 made by English inventor John Harrison, really is lost and anyone who found it would be in line for a Del Boy style payout which could easily reach the £6.2 million Del and Rodney got for it in the show. "It's a real possibility that it's out there somewhere so I'd advise people to have a root around for it," said watch expert Jonathan Betts of the National Maritime Museum at Greenwich.

"I don't like putting exact values on things but it would certainly be worth millions. The *Only Fools and Horses* team said to me: 'If it sold for £6 million would you be surprised?' and I said: 'No, I can imagine the bidding getting very silly if two collectors at an auction really wanted it.' It's totally unique. I'd be incredibly excited if it was found and be totally gobsmacked. I'd jump on the next plane to anywhere in the world to see it if it turned up somewhere. Someone who found it, who like Del Boy, could prove they owned it would be an extremely wealthy person. It would be like them winning the lottery."

Back in the early eighteenth century sea captains found it almost impossible to plot their position out of sight of land until Pontefract-born horologist John Harrison invented the first accurate marine timekeeper to tell seafarers exactly where they were on the globe. His invention won him a £20,000 prize - a fortune in those days and equivalent to about £2 million in today's money - and he went on to make five more watches. The whereabouts is known of five of them but his last one - the lesser watch as he called it - disappeared. The designs for it are kept at the National Maritime Museum but the watch itself has never been found and people have been searching for it for over three hundred years. In *Time On Our Hands* Del's father-in-law James spotted it amongst the junk in the Trotter's garage. It had been there for sixteen years since Del bought it with a load of junk after a house clearance and left it there thinking it was a Victorian egg timer. When it was sold at auction in the show it went for £6.2 million, making Del and Rodney instant millionaires.

The *Only Fools and Horses* production team went to great lengths to make sure the story in the show was believable. They approached the National Maritime Museum asking for help finding something that the Trotters could realistically find which would make them millionaires.

"It was all very mysterious and they kept the nature of the

programme very secret at that time but their brief was to find an object that was extremely valuable but was known to exist but which had been lost and could possibly be re-found," explained Mr Betts, who is the museum's curator of Horology, the study of time-keeping and time-telling. "They said it had to be worth millions rather than thousands because it had to be something that would give Del Boy a real fortune. They were really determined to find something that actually could be found."

They rejected one suggestion, a jewelled brooch that Nelson had worn in his hat which would be worth millions, because it had belonged to the National Maritime Museum but had been stolen. "So if Del Boy had found it, it would have had to be returned to us," said Mr Betts. "And he wouldn't have been able to keep the cash. Then they asked me if I could think of anything and it was then that I suggested the missing Harrison watch. I was very impressed by how they used the information in the programme. They'd obviously listened carefully to what we told them.

"Harrison dedicated his whole life to building these watches which was a task at the time nobody believed would be possible, because all the watches from then were hopelessly inaccurate. But he believed it would be possible to make a portable timekeeper that was accurate enough and he proved that it was. He made his first - H1 - in 1730 and for the next forty-five years he dedicated his life to improving and developing it and his fourth one was the one that solved the problem and won him the enormous prize of £20,000 and gained him worldwide fame. He had to make a fifth to prove it was possible to make others and to get his money, and he records that he made another smaller watch but nobody knows what has happened to that although we've got drawings of it. We've got the first four watches here at the museum and the fifth is with the Worshipful Company of Clockmakers in London."

DEFENDING DEL BOY

In the aftermath of the success of the 1996 trilogy, Chris Woodhead, the Government's Chief Inspector of Schools, launched an attack on the morals of the show and concluded that: "If Del Boy and Rodney are the only role models available to the young then we have a problem."

John Sullivan was persuaded to hit back and in an article for the *Sunday Times* he defended his creations. He pointed out that Del had brought up his younger brother after they lost both parents, cared for and fed his ageing grandfather and later his old Uncle Albert and strove to make sure he could always provide for them.

He admitted that some of Del's 'business arrangements' may not have fared well in a court of law but said that compared with the activities of some politicians and captains of industry, Del was squeaky clean. Rodney, he said, was a decent, law-abiding young man and the first to warn against anything unsavoury and Albert had spent his life fighting Nazism and his only fault was that he constantly reminds everyone of the fact.

He asked if Mr Woodhead believed that youngsters were so stupid that they would copy everything they saw on screen or stage. Did Shakespeare's *Romeo and Juliet* induce young people to commit suicide, he wondered, or did Charles Dickens endorse pickpocketing as a fun career in *Oliver Twist*.

"Throughout the series," he concluded. "I have tried to emphasise the basic decency of the Trotters. They are not violent, they don't take drugs and they don't drink and drive.

They respect the old and the very young. More importantly, they have strong family values, loyalty and love and the ability to laugh at themselves. If more people followed their example, Britain might be a happier place."

COMIC RELIEF

The press got a little excited in the spring of 1997 when they got wind of news that *Only Fools and Horses* was to feature amongst the line-up for that year's *Comic Relief* show on Friday March 14th. In reality there was no full episode of the show as many had hoped, but instead a short sketch in the Trotters' flat. It had been recorded the previous November during filming of the 1996 trilogy and featured David Jason and Nicholas Lyndhurst as Del and Rodney talking about poverty in the developing world. Because they were so busy with other filming, autocue was used for the first time, which meant they spoke straight to camera for much of the time.

TYING UP LOOSE ENDS

John Sullivan's attention to detail is second to none. In *Time On Our Hands* Rodney finds the receipt confirming that the Harrison watch legally belongs to him and Del. Way back in the first scene of the first episode Del castigates Rodney for keeping receipts and records in case the tax man comes snooping. Of course, amongst the pile of receipts Rodney is leafing through is the one for the watch with the neat twist that they would have been millionaires back in 1981 if they'd known they were sitting on a priceless antique watch!

2001 Christmas Special

By the end of January 1997 the clamour for more episodes of *Only Fools and Horses* had reached fever pitch. Everyone involved with the show had so much fun on the last three episodes that no one was prepared to keep saying that it was really over for good. The show's stars kept the fans hoping and said they'd be willing to do one more. "I think we could do it," said David Jason. "Mind you, Del and Albert will have identical Zimmer frames before too long." Nicholas Lyndhurst was certain John Sullivan could engineer a great script. "If I know two characters who could lose £6 million it's Del and Rodney," he said. "I'd love to do more."

By early 1999 there was talk of a special episode to celebrate the new millennium. In February, at a press launch for *A Touch of Frost*, David Jason reportedly said that he and Nicholas Lyndhurst had been keen to do a millennium special but couldn't get any interest from the BBC. This inevitably led to criticism of the BBC in the press, with the *Sun* leading the charge. And in an article headlined "Give Us Del", *Only Fools and Horses* Appreciation Society vice-president Keith Bishop was quoted as saying: "The BBC have gone barmy. Our petition asks them to change their minds. A millennium special is worth the licence fee alone."

The group gathered a three thousand signature petition to be given to BBC bosses and there was even talk of fans marching on (well, driving round, I suppose) BBC TV Centre in a fleet of yellow Trotter vans. The truth as to why there wasn't a millennium special was a bit more complicated. It was usually down to David Jason's lack of availability due to him being busy filming *A Touch of Frost* and his other work for ITV. "I would have been delighted to write it but no one is available," John told me at the time. "It took long enough to get the guys together to do the last trilogy – I'd be more than delighted to write another one if David and Nick were free to do it – and if the BBC could work out everyone's schedules."

"There was a pressure after we'd done the last three to do one for the millennium," said Gareth Gwenlan. "John had the ideas but then we had a great deal of difficulty in getting Mr Jason free from Yorkshire, who were quite anxious to not have him come back to us obviously, so we missed that deadline."

However, the demand for more episodes didn't go away. The final decision on whether to bring the show back rested with John Sullivan. "We said to John: 'If you've got stories to tell then we will do them.' David and Nick and the BBC comedy department had enough confidence in John to know that if he said yes to that then that was it, " said Gareth Gwenlan.

So by February 2001 schedules had been cleared and John Sullivan began writing three more episodes – all to be filmed at the same time. The new episodes were officially announced by BBC Director of Entertainment Alan Yentob: "It's been a long wait, but the best things are always worth waiting for."

In writing the first script John had to overcome the fact that two key members of the cast, Buster Merryfield and Kenneth MacDonald, had died since the previous episodes had been filmed. He decided that Albert would die during the episode and we discovered this in a poignant scene where Cassandra answers a phone call from the son of Albert's erstwhile lady friend, Elsie Partridge. John was always a master of blending pathos with comedy, and Albert's funeral was beautifully written and moving, but with a marvellous comic twist at the end when we discovered the Trotters are at the wrong funeral.

Mike Fisher had, we learned, been caught up in the Trotters' financial woes and had tried to recoup his losses by fiddling his

Nag's Head accounts and ripping off the brewery. This landed him a spell in prison and in the story, Sid (Roy Heather) was now managing the pub until Mike's release.

The three episodes were ambitious in scope and consequently a logistical nightmare for Gareth Gwenlan, director Tony Dow and their teams with locations as varied as Monte Carlo, Normandy, Paris, a Portsmouth to Cherbourg car ferry and Weston-Super-Mare in Somerset. Filming was scheduled to begin in the millionaires' playground Monte Carlo in October, but a month beforehand the shocking terrorist attacks on the World Trade Center and the Pentagon in the United States led to a worldwide increase in security at airports. This had an impact on production. "The airport security people couldn't guarantee that the unprocessed film wouldn't be damaged by their x-ray scanners," recalled Gareth. "We couldn't get it processed in France in less than about twenty-one days, which was too late for us because we needed to know that we'd got our shots OK before we flew home from Monte Carlo and we were only there for four days.

"So for the first time on a BBC comedy we shot in high definition – which is video and means you can watch it back to check the shots as soon as you like. Don't forget this was more than a decade ago and very few shows were shot in HD then. This was all my idea but it came back to bite me because just as we were about to start filming Tony Dow's wife was taken ill and I was left directing the first Monte Carlo scenes. Working in high definition now holds no fear for me, but back then it was pretty new. But it all worked out and it looked fantastic because HD gives such great results."

It was the first time some of the actors and production team had been together properly for some years and it didn't take long for everyone to get back in the swing of things. "As always with *Only Fools*, the moment we got together the time just rolls away and it was like we'd seen each other the week before," said Gareth Gwenlan.

"In spite of the fact we were resurrecting something we had

huge confidence in, everyone was feeling the strain. It was obvious with David that he was a few years older than he had been and it wasn't really until we played in front of the first studio audience that he got his full energy level back because some of those scenes on film are very good, but they are leisurely. But the moment he faced his first audience, suddenly he moved up three gears and became the old Del Boy."

At the start of *If They Could See Us Now* we see flashbacks of the Trotters, five years on from becoming millionaires, living the high life and enjoying a stay in the millionaires' paradise of Monte Carlo in Monaco (although there had also been talk at various stages of filming in either Barbados or South Africa).

Most of the filming in Monte Carlo took place at the Hotel de Paris which is just about the poshest hotel in the principality. "The hotel and its staff were really helpful," said Gareth. "Nothing really fazed them – but then they are used to film crews."

The production was told that they couldn't film in the main casino nearby. "But that didn't matter that much because we didn't really want to do another casino scene and anyway, the disappointment about the casino was that you expect it to be all 007 and black tie and ninety percent of customers in there were in shorts, vests and had tattoos!" said Gareth.

Designer David Hitchcock and one of his team members went to Monte Carlo while the rest of his team were in Western-Super-Mare preparing the set for Uncle Albert's funeral scene. In addition to the props already on a required list, David took along a few in his hand luggage which he thought might come in handy including some of Del's cocktail umbrellas, which was a good decision as they were unexpectedly required. "One prop I didn't take that we suddenly needed was a cigar for Del but that was quite easy to come by," he said.

Ever mindful of *Only Fools'* appeal to the tabloids, the production team were keen to ensure that any British press photographers after a scoop were thwarted so that nothing was given away early that could spoil the story for viewers. "We knew the red top press were desperate to get some pictures so we had security to make sure no one got near," said Gareth. "I was having coffee one morning when I was told a suspicious car had been spotted parked in the square opposite the hotel containing three guys in suits who looked like press.

"I thought: 'Well, I haven't seen any journalists in suits for a while but there you go...' but we went over and spoke to them and it turned out they were Prince Rainier's personal doctor and bodyguards. He was having lunch in the hotel and wherever he goes they are always within calling distance. We apologised for troubling them and went back to filming!"

Filming moved from Monte Carlo a few weeks later to the less exotic setting of Weston-Super-Mare where Albert's funeral scene was shot. During a break in filming on a Saturday morning David Jason and Nicholas Lyndhurst spoke to a small group of reporters, including myself, at a press conference held in the Town Hall. David revealed that he had never expected to be play Del again. "But it is great to be back – and the adventure can start again!" he said.

"It is a very pleasant experience to be back. There was a lot of pressure from the general public for us to come back, so after much deliberation we said: 'Why not?' John Sullivan was all for it and he's the man with the creative ideas so we said: 'Great!' Playing Del again is like putting on a pair of old shoes. And when we came to start filming it was like we'd never been away."

"There was always a thought in the back of our minds that we might do some more episodes one day," said Nicholas. "And I'm very pleased that we are. Not a day would go by when someone didn't say to me: 'You must do some more!'"

To make sure Del was fresh in his mind, David watched some old episodes with extra attention. "Some episodes are very timeless," he said. "They seem to hold up so well and are still of today, mainly due to the extremely clever writing."

Both men admitted that before filming began they wondered if the old magic would still be there after five years – but their concerns disappeared as soon as they read the script together. "Touch wood – we're still doing it," David smiled. "By page two of the script the old spark had returned," added Nicholas. "Playing Rodney again is like welcoming back an old friend." David agreed.

David said he hoped it would bring some much-needed Christmas cheer – particularly after September 11th. "It's great to be able to make people laugh and we need it in this day and age," he said. "I'd like to hope that people could sit there on Christmas Day and watch it and have a good laugh and escape the problems of the world for a while – and we're delighted to be able to bring a smile to people."

David also spoke of the loss of Buster Merryfield and Ken MacDonald. "When all the team are together you do miss them very much," he said. "It does seriously change the balance of the show. Certainly Ken was a tremendous funster and never stopped laughing and playing practical jokes. He is sorely missed."

Not far into the episode we discovered the awful truth about the Trotters' finances – a stockmarket crash has wiped out their millions and they are, as Del might put it, brassic. The episode ended with Del trying to put the family's finances back on track by appearing on television game show *Goldrush*. There were plans to film a scene for the episode in which Del would be seen appearing on ITV's top gameshow *Who Wants To Be A Millionaire* but ITV refused to allow it. Reports in the press said in exchange for letting the BBC film the scene, ITV wanted to be able to repeat the episode on its channel.

John Sullivan told the *Daily Telegraph*: "Like the British and the German armies playing football together on Christmas Day in World War One it would have been fantastic to put the ratings war to one side for one day." The *Sun* labelled television bosses who failed to come up with an agreement "Plonkers".

"We'd been talking to the production company Celador who

make *Who Wants To Be A Millionaire* and they were fine with the idea," recalled Gareth Gwenlan. "They had no problem with it at all. Everyone was enthusiastic about it and then ITV suddenly said to them: 'No – you're not going to be appearing on the BBC in a show that's going to go out over Christmas' and pulled the plug on it."

It was just a fortnight before the sequence was to be shot. John Sullivan rewrote the scene and invented a fictional gameshow called *Goldrush*. The scene was filmed at Pinewood Studios on a modified version of *The Weakest Link* set. "We got Jonathan Ross along as the host and he was great," added Gareth. "Despite his vast experience, he was terrified, though, as he held David in such awe. First of all he was shaking and then he couldn't stop laughing. But he loved it and he was very good – the perfect show host. The sequence worked out really well – and in many ways it was better as I'm always suspicious about mixing fact and fiction. Chris Tarrant was disappointed though as he was really looking forward to it."

John Sullivan was asked by the *Radio Times* if he was worried about the show outstaying its welcome. "You secretly worry," he admitted. "When we came back with the trilogy we thought, 'Are we taking this too far?' But if the letters from the public are anything to go by, they make us feel that we are welcome back."

The episode was screened on Christmas Day 2001 and was the most watched Christmas show, with 21.34 million people tuning in, but newspaper critics were unusually harsh about the episode. Charlie Catchpole, TV critic of the *Daily Express*, summed up their collective view by saying: "Come on, admit it. *Only Fools and Horses* wasn't that good, was it." Ally Ross of the *News of the World* was even harsher. Under the headline "Trotter load of rubbish" he wrote: "Like *Friends* after series four, *Ab Fab* after three episodes and *My Family* after one episode, many will think Christmas 2001 was the moment *Only Fools and Horses* lost the plot."

But Tony Purnell of the *Mirror* was kinder. "Del Boy and co returned in *Only Fools and Horses* after an absence of five years, but was it worth the wait? The answer is a resounding yes." Fiona Whitty, writing in the *Sun*, said: "I'd worried Del Boy might not be able to carry on delivering the fun that made this Britain's best-loved sitcom ever. But the chuckles soon started rolling in. Del and co have matured rather than gone stale." She added: "But best of all was when Rodney appeared dressed as Russell Crowe in *Gladiator* to spice up his sex life." In 2009 the episode was confirmed as the decade's most watched television programme.

SEEING DOUBLE

Christmas 2001 saw David Jason starring in another John Sullivan series, *Micawber*, inspired by the character from Charles Dickens' novel *David Copperfield*, and made for ITV. The four-part series followed the fame and misfortune of Wilkins Micawber, Dickens' most extravagant, optimistic and loveable character before his encounter with David Copperfield.

The drama also introduced an array of colourful characters, rogues and cads created by John Sullivan in the style of Dickens. "Micawber has been a great role to bring to life," said David. "The locations are spectacular, the cast has been tremendous and it is wonderful to work on a new project with John Sullivan." David had been determined that schedules on the rival channels wouldn't make viewers have to choose between the two shows. So he had it written into his contract that neither show could be scheduled against the other by the broadcasting rivals. "It would be very unfair to everybody to do that, particularly the audience," he said. "So I got it put in writing that they wouldn't put them head to head."

2002 Christmas Special

In *Strangers On The Shore* 2002 Del and Rodney headed off to France as representatives of Uncle Albert for a reunion of the crew of one of his ships, which sank off the French coast in 1942. "Travelling abroad for anyone always presents some sort of problem, but this is the Trotters we're dealing with here," John Sullivan told me. "So even a simple emotional act of scattering their Uncle's ashes over the side of a cross channel ferry doesn't go to plan – and this is only a hundred yards outside Dover at the start of the trip. Del is determined to prove what a Francophile he is so he goes equipped with a phrase book and a beret and we're then presented with the frightening prospect of two English idiots driving across France in a three-wheeled van. As you'd expect they meet and make more problems than you can chuck a stick at, but the real grief begins after their safe return when we discover that their journey has caused something approaching a diplomatic incident."

John explained why the Trotters had become poor again in *If They Could See Us Now*. "Rich isn't funny," he said. "The Trotters are Peckham people and that's when they are at their funniest, which is why I brought them back to Nelson Mandela House."

P&O Ferries swapped its ships around so that its newest and smartest ferry the *Pride of Bilbao* could be used for filming and afterwards it dropped the cast and crew off in Cherbourg, France. Producer Gareth Gwenlan filmed the scene of Del and Rodney scattering Uncle Albert's ashes at sea from a helicopter. Filming from the helicopter went remarkably smoothly. "We were in radio contact obviously," said Gareth. "And we had a hugely experienced helicopter pilot who was brilliant. The ship's crew and passengers were also incredibly helpful. The captain made an announcement asking passengers not to go out and wave at the helicopter – and they were very good and didn't!

"There was a helicopter pad on the ship and there was an idea to land on the ferry so that I could re-join my team and not have to go on another ferry. But the BBC person in charge of health and safety, the production manager, said no. And that was Gail – my wife!"

Filming in France went very smoothly. After looking at lots of small villages in Normandy, the production team chose Gatteville-le-Phare and designer David Hitchcock turned an unused building into a café. It overlooked a small square with a war memorial which the loyal Mayor allowed to be used for filming, with some additional decoration. Permission was also given for signage to be added to nearby buildings. One major plot in the episode was the revelation from Albert's old shipmate George (James Ellis) that Albert had been quite a ladies' man – and Del and Rodney then suddenly see a lot of bearded men around the village and are left wondering: just how much of a Lothario was their Uncle and could they have beaucoup de French cousins?

"We used some English and some French extras to play the bearded men and we cast them carefully so they did look a bit like Uncle Albert," recalled Gareth Gwenlan. "A couple were real but most of the beards were actually fake, added on by our wardrobe department – and they looked very good. I've no idea what the local people thought of us, but the shoot went very well and was trouble free, as were ninety-eight percent of the location trips we did on *Only Fools* – with the clear exception of Miami, which was horrendous." The episode was screened on Christmas Day 2002.

Sara Nathan in the *Sun* said that on Christmas Day "*Only Fools and Horses* saved the day from all the free-range turkeys roaming across the schedules. Another gem from the gifted pen of John

Sullivan saw Del Boy and Rodney back where they belong in Peckham and trying to rebuild the lost family fortune." The episode was watched by 17.4 million viewers and, once again, topped the Christmas ratings.

DAMIEN TROTTER'S DIARY
(or rather Benjamin Smith's!)

In 2002 I interviewed the then twelve-year-old Benjamin Smith, who played Damien Trotter, about his experiences on *Only Fools* for a filming diary magazine article. Here it is:

Thursday February 21st 2002
Woke up quite early and really excited about seeing all the cast members again. We all met for a read through of the script at a church hall in west London. Read the whole script - and everyone was laughing at the jokes because it was the first time we'd actually done it all together.

Friday February 22nd
More rehearsals - and they are great fun. Normally I'd be doing English, Maths and Science today - and I didn't mind missing them at all! My friends at school are really nice about me being in *Only Fools*. One boy once even asked me to sign an autograph on one of his schoolbooks! Later I went shopping to Gap Kids with the costume designer to choose Damien's clothes.

Monday March 4th
Back at the church hall. This time there is lots of tape on the floor to mark where the furniture will be at the Trotters' home. It's funny when something happens like a phone is supposed to ring. Usually it is for Del Boy, so David will be going: 'Ring-ring, ring-ring' or if he opens a door he'll stamp on the floor to

make a sound. The first time I ever saw someone like David doing things like that I really laughed. One time Boycie is supposed to have had some of one of Del's dodgy curries and wakes up in the night in bed. All of a sudden we heard a very strange noise and everyone looked around. It was David Jason making funny fart noises with a big grin on his face.

Tuesday March 5th

The church hall looks different today with some of the props all over the place. From now on, because we have to use the actual props that we will be filming with, we're not allowed to use our scripts anymore. Fortunately I find it really easy to learn my lines. I don't like having to learn spellings at school but learning my lines for an *Only Fools* script is much more fun.

Saturday March 9th

My Mum and I travel down to Bristol on a train to film scenes for the second episode. It's too busy to film in London most of the time so they use Bristol as Peckham. We check in to the Marriott Hotel and Mum and me shared a room. I'm allowed to have room service - but I didn't touch the minibar because I'm not allowed to. I'm not sure Damien would be quite as good!

Sunday March 10th

It's an early start today to film scenes in a hospital. People think filming is really exciting but it can be really slow and boring. There is lots of waiting around. Sometimes things go wrong like there is a noise from a car or something nearby and we have to start all over again. If I'm not needed for a scene I love watching David and Nick filming because they are so different when they are acting than how they are in real life. When someone does forget a line it all goes quiet while we try to work out whose line it was – but its always done with a smile and a laugh.

Monday March 18th

Here we are again – filming in Bristol. If we are filming somewhere for a long time then we have caravans to wait in while other people are filming but if we are only going to be filming for a short time then we just wait around somewhere and chat. I always have long chats with Paul Barber who plays Denzil because we are into the same sort of music. We both like listening to rap and no one else really does.

Wednesday March 20th

I get recognised today which is a bit of an odd experience. Obviously I look like Damien but I'm not like him because he's very rude to his Mum and Dad and in the Christmas episode last year he even had to talk like an Ali G gangster rapper. He is just too rude and I wouldn't want to be like him. Damien would probably spend his money on clothes but I've invested most of the money I get from *Only Fools and Horses* in an ISA and I can't get my hands on it until I'm eighteen.

Tuesday March 26th

Had a funny day in rehearsals today at the church hall. Paul Barber kept forgetting a line in a scene in the Nag's Head. In the end they wrote it down on the table so he could drink his pint and read it. I got recognised in Asda today. This family pointed at me and said: "Damien!"

Wednesday March 27th

Today we're rehearsing at the BBC in the actual studio which I always enjoy. Sometimes when something goes wrong David and Nick start speaking French and I haven't got a clue what they are saying. They are really good at it but even though I've done French at school, I don't understand what they are saying. Del Boy comes out with his silly French expressions but in real life David's French is really good and so is Nick's. Rodney is supposed to be scared of Damien and so Nick and I have to do scenes where we stare at each other and give each other dirty looks. I like doing that because it makes the audience laugh.

Thursday March 28th

Today is the day when we record the first of the two new episodes in the studio. During the day we practice our lines in the studio then at 5.30pm I go back to my dressing room. Paul Barber has kindly bought me a fantastic minidisc player as a present. Just before the show starts I go for a walk round the BBC with Paul and have a look at all the other dressing room doors. Gary Lineker is in tonight and we bumped into him. He was really nice. We're called onto the set at 7.30pm and we are introduced by the warm-up man. That's the nerve-wracking bit because we do the recording in front of a real audience and that can be a bit scary. Nick and I had to do a scene where we were playing a game on the Playstation. When we rehearsed it we were playing the real game – Nick was pretty good but I kept winning.

Saturday March 30th

Tonight will be the recording the second and last episode, which is sad. It all goes well and then we head back into the studio. It's a bit quiet tonight because a whole party of people haven't made it as their coach broke down. It's quite emotional doing the last bit and I admit I did have tears in my eyes because I've known everyone for so long and I knew I might never see them all again. After filming we went to the BBC bar for a drink and then we all said goodbye. Gwyneth Strong bought me a really nice book and Tessa Peake-Jones gave me a rocket that you put baking soda and vinegar in and it fires up into the sky. It's brilliant and I got everyone to sign it so I've got a record of the great time I've had doing *Only Fools and Horses*... and of course I'll have the videos of the episodes as a reminder of those happy days with Del Boy and co.

2003 Christmas Special

Twelve years after Del and Raquel became parents, it was the turn of Rodney and his wife Cassandra to discover the joys of parenthood in *Sleepless In Peckham*. But far from being relaxed about the prospect of becoming a dad for the first time, Rodney was terrified because their continuing financial worries meant the whole family was soon likely to be turned out onto the street and their home sold to pay off a big debt to the taxman.

Meanwhile Trigger had become spellbound by science fiction and was captivated by programmes such as *The X-Files*, which led to some very unusual moments from him – but then he'd always been a little odd. John Sullivan saw the episode as showing the Trotters coming back to their roots. "It's very much Del as we've really always known him," he said. "He's always trying to turn a penny into a pound.

"All his efforts to pay off his creditors – in this case the Inland Revenue – have failed," said John. "His bankruptcy is coming home to roost and they are also being pursued by various lawyers, one of whom is particularly tenacious, and they are forced to face the music.

"Some minor mysteries about the Trotters' past are also cleared up in the episode, like why there are no pictures of their late mother, Joan, round the flat, whom Rodney has never seen a photo of. The past then steps right into the present – and it is wearing hobnail boots – but it is not all bad news for the Trotters. A member of their family comes to their aid from an unexpected source and the future finally looks bright."

"The Trotters are brassic and aren't happy," Nicholas Lyndhurst told me when we met at his agent's office in west London to talk about the episode. "But as usual they have got some hair-brained money-making schemes on the go which could save them. Rodney is terrified because he knows he's got no prospect of being able to look after the baby financially. This is an emotional episode for Rodney. He has much to learn and some of it comes as a great shock."

With Rodney in a flap about money before the baby is even born and driving Cassandra nuts with constant fussing, it was already clear that he was going to be a nervous parent, which was something Nicholas could sympathise with. He admitted feeling terrified, because of his new responsibilities, for a while after his wife Lucy gave birth to their son Archie three years previously. He said that before he became a dad, his experience of children was limited. "All of my friends had their children long before me and they were always saying pick him or her up," he said. "I was quite frightened though – I was quite convinced I was going to drop the child or the head was going to come off but now I'm a father I realise that they are remarkably resilient."

For filming, producers hired a five-day-old baby to play Cassandra and Rodney's daughter. "I've now had a lot of practice but I was a little nervous holding it because it's still someone else's very newborn baby," he said. But he said being a real dad helped with filming. "If I hadn't done it for real a few years ago then I might not have understood the complete emotional joy of becoming a father and hopefully I've been able to put some of that across," he said. "And after about an hour, once it had sunk in that I was a father, I became really quite scared because I realised: 'It's down to me now', obviously with Lucy as well, but it's the biggest responsibility I'd ever been handed." Despite the old acting adage of never working with children or animals, Nicholas had no complaints about his tiny new co-star. "The baby was very well behaved and I don't think we even got a gurgle out of it," he smiled. Nicholas said he thought Rodney would make a good dad and said he hoped the child would inherit his gentler outlook rather than brother Del's brash personality. "So that means Rodney will try to keep his child well away from Del's son Damien!" he added.

After the final studio recording finished there was a sense among the cast and crew that this time it really was the end of *Only Fools*. "Doing the last three episodes had been a very considered affair and we realised we had done what we set out to do, which was not spoil the brand in any way and add to it rather than detract from it. We felt that's what we'd done," said Gareth Gwenlan.

John Sullivan was already writing the prequel which was to become *Rock & Chips* and it really did seem that *Sleepless In Peckham* would be the end of *Only Fools*, although Nicholas Lyndhurst said that as long as John wanted to keep writing the show and the public wanted to see it, he'd be happy to appear in it – and he expected the Trotters to always be scraping by. "John Sullivan is right when he says rich isn't funny," Nicholas told me. "When the Trotters became millionaires it was great to see the characters getting what everyone thought they deserved. But I think everyone knew in their heart of hearts that it wasn't going to last and that they were such idiots that they were going to find a way of losing all that money."

Critics were again somewhat harsh about the episode with Ally Ross in the *Sun* calling it "limp" but nevertheless it was still the most watched programme on Christmas Day, with an audience of 16.37 million people (fifty-eight per cent of the people watching television at that time).

Reflecting on it now, Gareth Gwenlan said: "It was very much a piece for Nick and David and they had some wonderful studio scenes in front of an audience." But he admitted that bringing the Trotters back for the last three episodes was always a big risk. "We were on a hiding to nothing basically," admitted Gareth Gwenlan. "Because for everyone who said please bring it back, there was someone else who said don't bring it back. But the last three episodes did get a good audience and they still stood up very well – indeed they got a better audience than ninety percent of the other comedies that were being done at the time."

Postscript

It was more than possible that we might have seen the return of *Only Fools and Horses* in 2011. There had been plans afoot to bring the Trotters back for a Christmas special to tie-in with Del's sixty-fifth birthday and the show's thirtieth anniversary.

David Jason and Nicholas Lyndhurst had agreed to the plan and the plot was to have centred around Rodney arranging a party for Del, Trigger, Boycie and Denzil. Just before the party Del was to have disappeared with no one knowing where he'd gone to.

"John Sullivan was very keen to do it," said Gareth Gwenlan. "He could have written a funny sixty minute, sixty-fifth birthday party episode for *Only Fools and Horses* in a couple of spare afternoons, such was his knowledge of the characters. There was a huge appetite from the Beeb who were falling over themselves to have it and we had everyone on side to do it. Now, inevitably, those plans have gone, because of the loss of John."

PART 4
Pastures New: *The Green Green Grass*

The idea for a spin-off from *Only Fools and Horses* wasn't a new thing. Back in 1986, when David Jason hinted he might not want to do any more episodes of *Only Fools and Horses*, John Sullivan planned to write a series for Nicholas Lyndhurst called *Hot Rod*.

But in the summer of 2004, six months after the screening of the final episode of *Only Fools and Horses*, the BBC commissioned a pilot episode of *The Green Green Grass*. The new show focused on Boycie and Marlene, with the plot centring on their flight from London, away from the much feared Driscoll brothers.

The idea had come about after the wife of John Challis, who played Boycie, arranged a sixtieth birthday party for him. Many of their friends, including John Sullivan and David Jason, travelled from London to their home in Shropshire for it. "Afterwards I remember John saying to me that he had something he wanted to talk to me about," said John Challis. "He'd had the germ of an idea about the show while he was there, having seen the area where we lived and met lots of people, and he'd gone away and developed it."

John Challis couldn't have been more pleased about the spin-off. "You bet I'm pleased," he said at the time of the commissioning of the pilot episode. "I love playing Boycie. Sue Holderness and I get on really well so it's been just great to work together again and develop the characters even more than we could in *Only Fools and Horses*. We had a lot of fun filming and John's scripts are terrific. I'm just delighted about it!

"It's very flattering that people, especially John Sullivan, think we are worth it. Boycie is great fun to play and I'm looking forward to playing him again – it is a real privilege to play a character that people enjoy so much."

John Sullivan explained the premise of the show to me like this: "Boycie has been very successful with his second-hand car business and he decides to sell his car-lot and the family home and move out into the country. He's fed up with London and the rat-race and has decided that he wants to become a gentleman farmer, although Marlene isn't quite as enthusiastic. He makes a packet from the sale of the car-lot so they buy a three-hundred-year-old farmhouse in Shropshire, together with eight-hundred acres of farmland. Both Boycie and Marlene have always had aspirations to social climb so they are very keen to join the country set and make an impression. Boycie doesn't really have a clue about farming – he brings his car trader mentality to farming and obviously makes a lot of mistakes in the process."

John had been delighted to be writing for two of his favourite characters again. "When we used to do thirty minute episodes of *Only Fools and Horses* I'd always be really frustrated having to throw so much extra material away," he told me. "I never had room to develop the other characters like Boycie and Trigger because they had to be peripheral to the Trotters and that was even the case when we did longer episodes. So the characters of Boycie and Marlene were ripe for development and it has been great for me to look at their lives in much more depth. They have a bittersweet relationship where it seems that they can say anything to the other one and no offence is taken. There's a real bond between them."

A pilot episode was filmed in November 2004 with the first scenes, supposedly in Boycie and Marlene's London home, being shot at a large house on the outskirts of Ludlow, Shropshire. Shooting went well and a successful day was rounded off with drinks in the bar of The Feathers hotel. The following morning John Sullivan gave me a lift in his new 4x4 to the next location – Boycie and Marlene's country home, Winterdown Farm – set at John Challis' real-life home, twelfth century Wigmore Abbey.

As I watched the episode being shot it seemed clear to me that it was highly likely that the show would be commissioned into a full series. The combination of John's terrific writing, two great lead characters, already favourites with viewers of *Only Fools*, plus a great line-up of supporting characters including newcomer Jack Doolan as Tyler, Boycie and Marlene's son, to me made it a cert for a full series.

A few months later, in April 2005, came the news everyone on the production had been hoping for – a full commission. "I'm very pleased," John told me. "I love writing for the characters of Boycie and Marlene and always have done, so it is great to be able to write for them at length."

It was great news, too, for lead actors John Challis and Sue Holderness. In an interview to publicise the first series, John reflected on how it had all begun. "There had been a lot of talk about whether we should see Marlene, because previously she'd been a bit of a 'er indoors' character who was talked about but didn't appear," said John Challis. "But Marlene's reputation had gone before her and there had been references to 'all the lads remembering Marlene' – with the implication that she had quite a reputation with men."

In 1984, when John Sullivan decided to bring Marlene into the show, John Challis was slightly nervous at the prospect of suddenly having a screen wife. "It's quite a big thing suddenly having someone playing your missus – and you just hope that you get on with each other," he explained. "Fortunately we did. Sue and I hadn't met before but I had heard of her through her work. By a stroke of luck we got on well straight away and we've been chums ever since."

But the pair didn't become close friends straight away. "We weren't immediately on the phone to each other – that's grown over the years – but I always looked forward to her coming to do episodes," he said. "We sparked off each other well and the writer John Sullivan picked up on that. He started to write more scenes for the two of us, which was terrific."

In 1991 they headed to Miami to film an *Only Fools and Horses* special but a union dispute delayed filming and they ended up having a week-long paid holiday. "We were thrown together while David Jason and Nicholas Lyndhurst were out filming other scenes," says John. "So we had a kind of holiday together and that cemented our friendship. We went to Coconut Grove, rocked around Miami, went out in boats and zoomed around the Everglades. We met lots of extraordinary characters out there."

The couple have been firm friends since then and have often gone on tour in plays together as a double act – and because of that, it is often assumed that they are married in real life. Well, they are – but to other people. Sue is married to theatre boss Mark Piper and John is married to Carol, a former model. But it is easy to see why people make the mistake of thinking John and Sue are married. "If we are on tour in a play then we might sometimes go shopping together and then people just assume we're married," John said.

John and Sue got on so well that they used to stay at each other's homes. When they filmed *The Green Green Grass* on location at John and Carol's abbey in Shropshire, Sue stayed with them, and then when the studio recordings took place in Teddington, John stayed at Sue and Mark's home in Windsor. "It's very handy and works really well," John said. "We all eat together and Sue and I can go through the lines again after rehearsals and that makes things easier when it comes to filming.

"Sue is a terrific woman and a great actress. She's great with people and has a natural friendliness and ability to involve people. As an actress she makes me laugh and over the years we've developed a shorthand which means working together is just a joy."

By the time they came to film the first series of *The Green Green*

Grass John had been playing Boycie for nearly twenty-five years but he said he never tired of the character – despite his apparent meanness and harshness towards Marlene. "Boycie is a great character to play because he's so pompous," he said. "He's got aspirations and would like to climb the social scale and he thinks he's quite superior. His relationship with Marlene is bittersweet and they do say some awful things to each other, but there's actually a real bond between them and deep down, he thinks the world of her."

Sue Holderness likened working with John Challis to being married again. "We know each other really well now – and we especially got to know each other when we went on theatre tours, often playing a couple in a play. We really like working together," she said. "And the longer you work with someone the easier it gets because you pick up real shorthand about how the other person does things. So it is like a terrible old marriage, but without having all the anxiety of actually having to be married and pay bills. It's lovely and very comfortable. John and I get on really well and in real-life he is nothing at all like Boycie because, although Boycie has got a soft side deep down, John is a soft touch, really."

The fact that they aren't actually married does come as quite a shock to some people. "We've met a lot of people who are very disappointed when they learn that we aren't actually married in real life," she said. "I remember one woman coming up to us in Tesco somewhere up north. Eventually she asked if we were actually married to each other, and when we said we weren't, she said: 'Oh, you should be!'"

John and Sue were joined in the series by a strong line-up of co-stars including Jack Doolan as their recalcitrant son Tyler, David Ross (who had worked with John Sullivan in *Roger, Roger*) as farm manager Elgin Sparrowhawk, Ivan Kaye as herdsman Bryan, Ella Kenion as housekeeper Mrs Cakeworthy, Peter Heppelthwaite as ploughman Jed and Alan David as neighbouring farmer Llewellyn. They were joined for various episodes by Roy Marsden and

Christopher Ryan as Danny and Tony Driscoll, June Whitfield as Marlene's mum Dora, Paula Wilcox (who went on to appear in *Rock & Chips* as Del's Gran) as Marlene's sister Petunia, *Cheers* actor George Wendt as Cliff Cooper and even boxer Ricky Hatton appeared in one episode. The only other members of the *Only Fools and Horses* cast to appear were Paul Barber (Denzil) and Roy Heather (Sid) who appeared in the first episode.

The Green Green Grass ran for four series before it was axed by the BBC in May 2009. "We've had four good series and made thirty-two episodes," John Sullivan said at the time. "We'd hoped to have done one more series but that's the way it goes. We've had a lot of fun making the show and obviously we are disappointed not to be doing any more."

THE TRIGGER AND DENZIL SHOW

After the success of *The Green Green Grass* many people suggested that John Sullivan look at the possibility of doing something with Trigger. "For a time I actually toyed with the idea of teaming him up with Denzil for a thirty minute pilot," said John. "The problem with a character such as Trigger is that I've always used him very conservatively, rather like a goal-poacher, who walks into a scene, usually takes the biggest laugh, and then walks off not to be seen for another fifteen minutes. The fear is that the moment you extend Trigger into the wider form he begins to lose his uniqueness and surprise. So I decided not to go any further with the idea."

The Early Years: *Rock & Chips*

The idea for exploring the Trotter family history had been in John Sullivan's head for many years. When *Only Fools and Horses* was at its height, he mentioned at an awards ceremony back in 1997 that he was planning to write a novel covering Del's early years. The following morning offers from publishers were made to his agent, as well as expressions of interest from the BBC in doing it for television. But over the years, other television writing projects like *Roger, Roger* and the next *Only Fools* trilogy took priority and the idea to do the Trotters' early years as a book went by the wayside. "It fell through a crack in the floorboards," said John.

Then, in 2003, John began planning the prequel – now definitely as a television production rather than a book – and it gained the working title *Once Upon A Time In Peckham*. The idea was to start in 1960, with Del a teenager, but the central focus was to be Joan Trotter, who had always been such a strong but unseen presence in *Only Fools and Horses*. Although the BBC had immediately showed interest in the project, back then it was not definitely going to have been a BBC programme as other players had also shown an interest. "There's been a lot of interest from television companies in general plus a few film companies," John told me.

However, by 2006, with *The Green Green Grass* doing well and into a third series, the prequel again got pushed down the agenda. On top of that, John wasn't sure about how much appetite there was for more of the Trotters, albeit their early days. Understandably, the critical mauling the last three episodes of *Only Fools* had received (despite more than healthy ratings) had made him wary. "The press leapt on it and kicked it to pieces," he told me. "So after that I thought I couldn't keep doing the *Only Fools* thing. So I'm waiting for the right time."

That right time was August 2008 when, over a drink, the BBC's new Head of Comedy Mark Freeland suggested to John that he resurrect the prequel idea. "When Mark said it, I thought: 'He's right, what a good idea,' and I couldn't wait to get started on it." The following July the BBC finally commissioned a ninety minute pilot episode of the show, then called *Sex, Drugs & Rock 'n' Chips*. John was over the moon. "I am delighted we're doing it," he said at the time. "I first mentioned wanting to write about the Trotter's early years more than ten years ago because I always wanted us to meet Del and Rodney's Mum, Joan Trotter, and see how Del and Rodney started out. Meeting Joan has been wonderful because I've had her so much in my imagination."

John set out what was needed in an actor to play the young Del. "The actor who'll play Del will be playing a sixteen year old, so he'll need to look sixteen, even if he is actually eighteen or nineteen, which might be better as he might have a bit more experience," John said. "He's obviously got to be believable as Del Boy when he was sixteen – it's going to be a cracking role for some young actor and I imagine we will cast a complete unknown in the role. The same will go for the actors we will find to play young Trigger, Boycie and Denzil."

One name not in the frame to play young Del was David Jason. "David is an incredibly talented actor but playing a sixteen year old I think is even beyond his immense powers!" John joked. "But it would be a real hoot if we could get him in there somewhere." John already had storylines for future episodes mapped – and even had notes about Joan's life from 1980 when he was writing the first episode of *Only Fools*. However, he admitted that he didn't find the writing of the pilot episode an easy task. "Because of the nature of the thing all the good stuff happens a bit later," he said. "So the first episode is the hardest one to write because you are introducing characters, the area and the time and I've got to come up with a story for it."

As the show had looked likely to be commissioned since the end of 2008, casting directors had already been given a heads up that the BBC were looking for a range of different actors to make up the cast including, crucially, for the parts of Del and Joan. Dozens of young actors auditioned for the part of Del, most of them unknown. "I think we saw about fifty potential Dels," said John Sullivan.

Eventually James Buckley, who had already found fame as foul-mouthed Jay in the Channel Four comedy *The Inbetweeners*, was cast. It proved to be a fine choice. And some of the actors who originally auditioned for the role of Del were hired for other parts in the show. "I'd seen James in *The Inbetweeners* and I thought he was very, very good in that," said John. "He came in and he was excellent. He knew Del and knew the series totally. He was instantly Del. He didn't attempt to mimic David Jason but he just had that energy that Del has always had. He was optimistic and dynamic, even as a sixteen-year-old. He was perfect for the part."

"When David came down to the set we were all chatting away about *Only Fools* in the make-up caravan and the young actors were correcting us - and they were right. They knew more about it than we did – and I wrote it and David acted in it!"

Nicholas Lyndhurst, always incredibly loyal to John Sullivan, had already agreed to play gangster Freddie Robdal, so the next piece in the jigsaw to be arranged was the right actress to play Joanie Trotter. It was no easy task – and a whole host of actresses – many of them very well known – were seen for the part. It was essential to get it right.

"The real search was for Joan, because she was so vital," said John Sullivan. "Then I got sent a DVD of Kellie Bright reading the part. I watched her for three or four minutes and I knew we'd found Joan. We carried on looking, although I didn't want to, to be honest, because I was happy that we'd found Kellie. But we did see an awful lot more other actresses – some of them very, very well-known actresses – but we finally got down to a top five and asked them in to read with Nick [Lyndhurst] at TV Centre. Kellie was the first one in and, as far as I was concerned – and I found out later as far as everyone in the room was concerned – she had the part.

"Joan had to be a proud woman, a woman who was different to the other women of that period. I remember the women of my own street who were kind of grey and colourless because they'd had such a hard life. These people had been through the war – in the case of Joan she'd been an evacuee. But Joan was different. She wanted colour in her life. She had a hard life with her husband, who wasn't the nicest man in the world.

"She was also a hard-working woman with two jobs, but she wanted fun. She was a part-time usherette and she lived for romantic films, read slushy romantic novels and played love songs on the record player. She was a woman in a loveless life and she sought love. When Freddie met her he detected this, and maybe took advantage of her, but he didn't, really. It was a romance.

"Joan and Del loved each other without question. They adored each other. He was the best son in the world to her. Del's whole way of being came from Joan, not from Reg. When Joan went out, she knew that men found her attractive. It was the only attention she got until Fred came along and changed everything. She had a heart of gold and was generous and good to her friends, particularly her best friend Reenie Turpin, played by Emma Cooke, who is wonderful.

"Her life was interrupted, but in many ways, improved when she met Fred. He was a serial safe cracker and a villain – even worse than Reg in many ways – but he brought fun to her life. He made her laugh a lot."

In addition to James, Kellie and Nick, an equally strong supporting cast added weight to the show. Phil Daniels was cast as

Grandad – Ted Trotter – after impressing at his audition. "Phil came in and he became Grandad's shape and almost had the beginning of Grandad's croaky voice," said John. "I believed at that moment – even before the hat went on – that he could be Grandad back in 1960. He was perfect."

Shaun Dingwall was cast as workshy Reg Trotter because John believed he instantly got the essence of the character. "We don't know a lot about Reg – he only appeared for about fifteen minutes in one episode of *Only Fools* [*Thicker Than Water*], when he was played by Peter Woodthorpe. Peter played him as a man who thought he had charisma and buoyancy, even though he was lazy – a real sponger.

"Even though Reg was a hard man and wasn't nice to his wife, Shaun played him more like how Peter had played him years ago, with a smile and a twinkle. But at the same time we know there's something horrible underneath it, whereas others who'd auditioned had played him with menace."

Robert Daws, who had starred in John Sullivan's series *Roger, Roger* joined the cast as lecherous cinema manager Ernie Rayner. Emma Cooke played Joan's best friend Reenie Turpin, Paul Putner was cast as 'Jelly' Kelly, and *Only Fools* and *The Green Green Grass* warm up man, Bobby Bragg, played Don, the Nag's Head's landlord.

Six young actors made up Del's group of mates (and Slater!): Stephen Lloyd (Boycie), Lewis Osborne (Trigger), Ashley Gerlach (Denzil), Lee Long (Jumbo Mills), Jonathan Readwin (Albie Littlewood) and Calum MacNab (Roy Slater).

Filming for the first episode took place at Pinewood Studios where the show's set designer David Hitchcock had built a replica of the Trotter's two-up, two-down terraced family home in Orchard Road, Peckham.

"The house and the street were very much based around where I lived," John said. "The best room – the front room – and the living room, scullery and the outside toilet were exactly the same as where I lived. There was an Ascot heater in the kitchen which provided hot water for washing or bathing. Then there were a couple of bedrooms upstairs and an outside loo. These houses were dockers' cottages. My family lived down there, right by the docks in Tooley Street, so I knew that area very well."

Next to the house set was the set for the Trotters' brand new and yet to be occupied flat in Walter Raleigh House – later, of course, to be renamed Nelson Mandela House. John and I sat in there and he explained in detail how he had had the Trotters' back story in his head since 1981 and had been planning the prequel since 1997.

"Even when we were first casting *Only Fools* back in 1981 I wanted to make sure that Del and Rodney looked different. Del and Rodney are the only people in London who believe they are brothers," he said. "I have always been keen to look at the early years of the Trotter family. Joan Trotter was the strongest person in *Only Fools and Horses* even though she was never seen, as she died in 1964."

Ahead of the broadcast of the first episode of *Rock & Chips* John told me: "The story of Joan and Reg had been there before I even wrote the first episode of *Only Fools* back in 1980. I had to have the back story before I could start the story we know – because of all the back references to the mother. I had to know all that kind of history and everything that went on and every reference that was made to her will be seen if we ever go further than this first episode – because at this moment it is just a one-off. So we're kind of taking the *Star Wars* road, going back to the very beginning after more than twenty years."

John was keen to make clear that the new show was very different to *Only Fools and Horses*. "Anybody who switches on thinking they are going to see the usual *Only Fools* format but with Del in short trousers will be disappointed," he said. "This is more of a drama comedy. It's quite gritty and there is a little bit of colourful language. Basically, it's one for all the family, except the kids. It's a very different animal altogether and people should be prepared to be surprised."

The story started on February 4th 1960. Harold Macmillan was Prime Minister and the Swinging Sixties had yet to start. The Trotter family lived in a small terraced house in Orchard Road, Peckham, and life wasn't easy. Derek, who was sixteen, lived at home with his workshy Dad, Reg, and Mum, Joan. Rodney had yet to be born.

Derek hadn't officially finished school yet but spent his time hanging around with his schoolmates Boycie, Trigger, Denzil, Jumbo Mills and Roy Slater. But he was already showing early signs of being an entrepreneur, buying stuff from foreign sailors at the local docks and telling friends: "I guarantee you, one day I'm gonna be a millionaire."

Money was tight in the Trotter household and hardworking Joan had two jobs to make ends meet, whereas bone-idle Reg, who was quick with his fists, usually made Joan pay for the drinks at their local, the Nag's Head. Vivacious head-turner Joan was stuck in a loveless marriage. The only good things in her life were Derek, on whom she doted, and who clearly adored her back, and her job as an usherette at the Ritz cinema where she could lose herself in the glamour of black and white films.

Then Freddie Robdal, a debonair safe-breaker and art connoisseur reappeared in the area following a ten-year stretch in Dartmoor Prison. He spotted Joan and was instantly smitten – and set about pursuing her. "Freddie is the sort of man who just takes whatever he wants but in a charming way," explained Nicholas Lyndhurst. "It doesn't matter if it is a valuable painting or someone else's wife – if he wants it, he'll go for it. He's a gentleman villain but he has a very still menace about him. You really, really wouldn't want to cross him. That would be a very big mistake."

Freddie was a million miles away from dopey Rodney Trotter. "He's suave and sophisticated," said Nicholas, who relished playing him. "It was an absolute blast," he said. "John Sullivan had been talking about doing an *Only Fools* prequel for about ten years but I didn't realise it would include me.

"The years went by and you'd hear rumours and I'd see John and he'd say he was still planning it. Then we did an episode in which Rodney gets a picture of the first ever Jolly Boys' Outing blown up and there is Freddie Robdal looking basically like Rodney Trotter with a moustache. It was then I realised that John wanted me to play Rodney's father. We had lunch, the script arrived and I was completely hooked by the third page."

John Sullivan was full of praise for Nicholas: "It was a very different role for him, because he played this rather controlling gangster who we got the impression could be quite a vicious man. Nick played him brilliantly."

It was quite an understatement to say that James Buckley was pleased to be cast as young Del. "I really wanted to be in it," he told me. "I grew up with *Only Fools and Horses* which is very much part of people's lives and the Trotters do feel like part of your family. There's no one who doesn't like *Only Fools and Horses*.

"But this show isn't *Only Fools*. It is completely different, but I think people are interested in seeing what the early days were like for the Trotters and how they became they people we got to know later. It's a love story really. We all find out what we knew anyway – that Rodney had a different father to Del and we discover why that happened."

James said he didn't set out to do an impersonation of David Jason's Del Boy. "I watched every episode and studied David's performances. I've tried to put a tiny bit of David's Del mannerisms into the young Del. I took it very seriously and I was worried about playing Del though because the show is so important to so many people. It would have been really irresponsible and disrespectful if I hadn't taken it seriously."

He got the seal of approval when David visited the set. "I went into a trailer one lunchtime and John Sullivan introduced me to Sir David. I said: 'Hello, are you keeping tabs on me?' and he said: 'Yes, I've got a few notes for you young man!' He was lovely and a real gent."

Joan Trotter was one of television's most talked about characters, even though she never appeared on screen. Barely an episode of *Only Fools* went by without Del mentioning his much-loved dead Mum. She died when Del was a teenager and his brother Rodney was aged just four – yet she had a huge impact on Del, who was forever quoting things she'd said 'on her deathbed' and made her out to be a kind of cross between Mother Teresa and Brigitte Bardot.

"I really wanted the part and couldn't quite believe it when I got it," said Kellie Bright, who played Joan. "I grew up watching *Only Fools and Horses*. It was a big part of my childhood and was loved by everyone. I honestly don't know anyone, of any class, of any age, from any walk of life, who didn't love *Only Fools* – and that is mainly down to the very clever writing of John Sullivan, who manages to combine comedy with so much heart.

"I felt very lucky to play Joan because she was such a big, but unseen, presence in *Only Fools and Horses*. Del mentioned her all the time and there were scenes by her grave. She was very much there, but not there. In *Only Fools* we learned just how important Joan was to Del, and then in *Rock & Chips* we got to see just why he loved her so much. Joan had Del very young and they kind of grew up together."

Kellie said Del was the apple of his mother's eye. "Del was everything to her, there are no two ways about that," said Kellie. "She adored her boy and was very proud of him. He was the one thing in her life that she felt she'd got right. She was in an unhappy marriage with husband Reg and she wasn't where she wanted to be in life. She was a dreamer but at the same time, she made the best of what she had. Then Freddie walked into the unhappy scenario and he and Joan began an affair.

"It was a mutual thing between Joan and Freddie," said Kellie. "There was a real spark between them. It was a love story and it wasn't sleazy. For the first time in her life, Joan had fallen in love." She also fell pregnant and at the end of the first episode, Rodney is born.

The episode was screened on January 24th 2010. It was dropped into the schdules very late and only hours before the programme listings were issued by the BBC the name was changed from *Sex, Drugs & Rock 'n' Chips* to *Rock & Chips*. I remember exchanging texts with John Sullivan late that same evening after realising that due to the name change his company, Shazam Productions, didn't own the *Rock & Chips* internet domains, something we rectified just before the new show title became public knowledge.

Newspaper reviews of were mixed. Andrew Billen in the *Times* liked it, saying it was "a comedy-drama of charm and subtlety that did its writer John Sullivan nothing but credit", but the *Guardian*, *Telegraph* and *Mirror* were harsh. Nevertheless, it was a hit with viewers; ratings were an impressive 8.42 million, beating ITV's long-running drama *Wild At Heart*.

In May 2010 the BBC finally commissioned two more episodes of *Rock & Chips,* less than John Sullivan wanted, but two more nonetheless. Production moved from Pinewood Studios to BBC Elstree - where *Holby City* and *EastEnders* are filmed – and shooting began in October. There were additions to the cast, including Mel Smith as DI Thomas and Paula Wilcox, who'd played Marlene's sister in *The Green Green Grass*, as Ted's estranged wife, Violet.

In the story it was now Christmas 1960 and baby Rodney (played by twins Oliver and Harry Newman) was eight weeks old. Reg had no idea that the baby wasn't his. "He's not suspicious even though he can't remember making love with Joan for the last year and a half," John Sullivan told me when I visited the set in November. "Although Joan has managed to convince him that he came home drunk from a Millwall match and it happened then, so he's happy with that excuse."

The Trotters were rehoused by the council when Joan fell pregnant and they needed more space. "They are now living in Sir Walter Raleigh house, which, in 1963 or 1964 becomes Nelson Mandela house," John said. "They've got central heating and hot water and obviously a bathroom inside so life has improved immensely for them, although the lifts break down a lot.

"Fred is on remand for the Margate job – but gets out on bail. Joan wants to end the relationship with him, but does she really? Del is now becoming more entrepreneurial. He's organised a New Year's Eve party on the estate with paid tickets. So he's become a 1960s Peter Stringfellow and they've got a big radiogram up on stage as the only music they can provide. He's got a garage full of American records which he's selling so he's doing quite well and the sales of those are helping the family finances. Reg has been forced to take a job by the Labour Exchange but got sacked very quickly."

The second episode of *Rock & Chips, Five Gold Rings,* was screened on December 29th 2010 and was watched by 5.83 million people. Again, reviews were mixed. "It all feels a bit like trying to recreate a childhood holiday by going back to the same place, and finding it's not as you remembered," Sam Rollaston wrote in the *Guardian*.

By the time of the third, and what would sadly become the final episode, *The Frog and The Pussycat*, it is 1961. Rodney was a year old and Freddie was languishing in prison accused of a jewellery robbery – but not for long. Del, meanwhile, was continuing to work his dubious charms on the girls of Peckham – and got a date with nice middle class girl called Barbara whose father had a thriving funeral business and a well-appointed home in Peckham posh-spot, King's Avenue. Things were going extremely well until Del got trapped in the kitchen with Barbara's inebriated mother.

Joan was still plagued by the less than welcome attentions of her boss, Eddie Raynor. Every day she dreamt of a new life with

Freddie, but she knew she needed to see Del settled first. She'd been working as a cleaner for Freddie for six months and still didn't know how to turn on his vacuum cleaner as their time was spent in far more romantic pursuits. *The Frog And The Pussycat* was screened on BBC1 on Thursday April 28th 2011, six days after John Sullivan's death. It was watched by 3.37 million viewers and at least one review for the episode was kinder: "It may not be remembered as the late great John Sullivan's finest work, but *Rock & Chips* still wipes the floor with most of the dross drama we have to put up with," said Kevin O'Sullivan in the *Sunday Mirror*. "Packed with great one-liners, BBC1's *Only Fools and Horses* prequel is what feel-good telly is all about."

John Sullivan was passionate about *Rock & Chips* and although not autobiographical, it was clear that he was enjoying recalling his early years while writing it. He loved the period in which it was set and picked all the music. There was plenty from his youth in it and at least two of the things that happened to Del in *The Frog and The Pussycat* had happened to John. One was mistakenly thinking a slice of lemon on his fish was there by mistake and the other was finding out that flattering the mother of a new girlfriend in order to win her approval was a very bad idea.

"John's long-term plan was for more *Rock & Chips,* which was getting into its stride," said Gareth Gwenlan. "He was totally passionate about it and, having worked with him for the best part of thirty years, I believe he was writing at the top of his ability. It was funny, moving, a great story and the characters were fantastic. It was the back story he'd always had in his mind ever since he first wrote *Only Fools and Horses*."

Now, with John Sullivan no longer with us, we'll never know exactly what Joan Trotter actually said on her death bed. But as *Only Fools and Horses* Appreciation Society President Perry Aghajanoff said: "We will just have to believe Del Boy on that one..."

PART 5
Episode Guide

REGULAR CAST AND KEY PRODUCTION TEAM

David Jason - Del Trotter: All series
Nicholas Lyndhurst - Rodney Trotter: All series
Lennard Pearce - Grandad Trotter: Series 1-3
Buster Merryfield - Uncle Albert: Series 4 - 1997

Writer - John Sullivan
Producers - Ray Butt (1981-87); Gareth Gwenlan (1988-2003)
Directors - Martin Shardlow (1981), Bernard Thompson
(*Christmas Crackers*); Ray Butt (1982, 1983, *Video Nasty, Who
Wants to be a Millionaire?, To Hull and Back, The Royal Flush,
The Frog's Legacy*; Susan Belbin (1985); Mandie Fletcher (1986);
Tony Dow (1988-2003); Gareth Gwenlan (*Miami Twice* (part 1) –
The American Dream)

Episode Guide

SERIES ONE

Episode 1: Big Brother

After flogging one legged turkeys from the back of a three wheeled van, Del is confident he's onto a winner at last with Trigger's consignment of Old English vinyl briefcases. At the same time his brother Rodney is thinking of abandoning the high flying world of trading for a real job.

Cast: *Joyce the barmaid* (Peta Bernard) *Trigger* (Roger Lloyd Pack)
First broadcast: Tuesday September 8th 1981 at 8.30pm
Viewing figures: 9.2 million • *Duration:* 30 minutes • *Music:* None

Episode 2: Go West Young Man

Del enters the second-hand car market with a lethal vehicle that quite literally goes like a bomb. After a night on the town the boys are on their way home in a borrowed sports car when they run into the buyer of Del's old banger.

Cast: *Boycie* (John Challis) *Aussie Man* (Nick Stringer) *Waiter* (Barry Wilmore) *Nicky* (Jo-Anne Good) *Michelle* (Caroline Ellis)
First broadcast: Tuesday September 15th 1981 at 8.30pm
Viewing figures: 6.1 million • *Duration:* 30 minutes • *Music:* Ain't No Stopping Us Now

Episode 3: Cash and Curry

Del is swooping in on the deal of a lifetime - which could keep them all in pilau rice forever. All he has to do is get hold of £2,000 to buy a priceless Indian relic. The trouble is he hasn't reckoned on a touch of gang warfare.

Cast: *Mr Ram* (Renu Setna) *Vimmal Malik* (Amhed Khalil) *Indian Restaurant manager* (Babar Bhatti).
First broadcast: Tuesday September 22nd 1981 at 8.30pm
Viewing figures: 7.3 million • *Duration:* 30 minutes • *Music:* Money performed by Pink Floyd

Episode 4: The Second Time Around

When Del's old flame and Achilles heel, Pauline Harris returns from America, the flames of passion are quickly rekindled. Pauline moves in with the Peckham trio, but Rodney and Grandad are on hand to make sure

the course of true love runs anything but smooth and to save Del.
Cast: Trigger (Roger Lloyd Pack) *Joyce the barmaid* (Peta Bernard) *Pauline* (Jill Baker) *Auntie Rose* (Beryl Cooke)
First broadcast: Tuesday September 29th 1981 at 8.30pm
Viewing figures: 7.8 million • **Duration:** 30 minutes • **Music:** None

Episode 5: A Slow Bus To Chingford

What a great deal - a night-watchman in exchange for the use of an open topped touring bus! So begins Trotter's Ethnic Tours of Chingford and Croydon. No one turns up, but Grandad displays the family genius for making money.
Cast: Janice (Gaynor Ward)
First broadcast: Tuesday October 6th 1981 at 8.30pm
Viewing figures: 7 million • **Duration:** 30 minutes • **Music:** Layback peformed by Rock Spectrum

Episode 6: The Russians Are Coming

Another lucky deal makes Del the proud owner of three tons of lead. The information sheet reveals it is a self assembly nuclear fallout shelter. Del is persuaded that the real value lies not only in the metal but in the protection the shelter offers - just in case World War Three breaks out.
Cast: Eric the policeman (Derek Newark)
First broadcast: Tuesday October 13th 1981 at 8.30pm
Viewing figures: 8.8 million • **Duration:** 30 minutes • **Music:** None

Episode 7: Christmas Crackers

The season of good cheer is upon the family but Del and Rodney are dreading the gastronomic experience of Christmas lunch, as cooked by Grandad. In desperation they decide to go to the Monte Carlo Club in search of a "sacre blue chef" after Grandad goes to his old folks' do.
Cast: Earl (Desmond McNamara) *Anita* (Nora Connolly)
First broadcast: Monday December 28th 1981 at 9.55pm
Viewing figures: 7.5 million • **Duration:** 35 minutes • **Music:** Three Times A Lady performed by Brotherhood of Man, Daddy's Home performed by Cliff Richard, Shakin' All Over performed by Cliff Richard, Wordy Rappinghood performed by Tom Tom Club, Christmas Wrapping performed by The Waitresses, Bright Eyes performed by Brotherhood of Man

SERIES TWO

Episode 1: The Long Legs Of The Law

Rodney has the Trotter household in a panic when he announces that his hot date is a woman in uniform - a police uniform! He invites her back to the flat for a drink, then discovers to his horror that even the drink has been illegally procured.

Cast: Sid (Roy Heather) *Sandra* (Kate Saunders)
First broadcast: Thursday October 21st 1982 at 8.30pm
Viewing figures: 7.7 million • *Duration:* 30 minutes • *Music:* None

Episode 2: Ashes To Ashes

Trigger's Grandmother has died, so the Trotter family offer their support by agreeing to sell off some of her old possessions, including a pair of precious urns. But the trouble starts when they notice that the urns contain the ashes of Trig's grandfather. Del's idea of a final resting place is outrageous.

Cast: Trigger (Roger Lloyd Pack) *River policeman* (John D. Collins) *Council cleansing lorry driver* (Terry Duggan)
First broadcast: Thursday October 28th 1982 at 8.30pm
Viewing figures: 9.8 million • *Duration:* 30 minutes • *Music:* None

Episode 3: A Losing Streak

Del can't even win a few pounds with a flip of his double-headed coin. But when Boycie challenges him, not to mention his pride, to a winner-takes-all poker match, he wagers everything he owns to stay in the game. It's crook against crook in this match of the century.

Cast: Trigger (Roger Lloyd Pack) *Boycie* (John Challis) *Pub customer* (Michael G. Jones)
First broadcast: Thursday November 4th 1982 at 8.30pm
Viewing figures: 7.5 million • *Duration:* 30 minutes • *Music:* None

Episode 4: No Greater Love...

Rodney has lost his heart to a not-so-young woman and with her on his arm he thinks he's man enough to stand up to her violent jailbird husband who is about to be released. But Del is ready to ship them both to the far ends of the earth.

Cast: Irene (Gaye Brown) *Julie the barmaid* (Julie La Rousse) *Marcus* (Steve Fletcher) *Ahmed* (Raj Patel) *Leroy* (David Rhule) *Tommy Mackay*

(David Daker) *Zoe* (Lisa Price)
First broadcast: Thursday November 11th 1982 at 8.30pm
Viewing figures: 8.6 million • *Duration:* 30 minutes • *Music:* None

Episode 5: The Yellow Peril

Del has done his good deeds for the day. He's arranged for Rodney to paint the kitchen of a Chinese takeaway, and then decides to do a little paint job of his own... sprucing up their mother's tombstone. But how could he know that the stolen paint was luminous?
Cast: Mr Chin the Chinese takeaway owner (Rex Wei) *Trigger* (Roger Lloyd Pack)
First broadcast: Thursday November 18th 1982 at 8.30pm
Viewing figures: 8.2 million • *Duration:* 30 minutes • *Music:* None

Episode 6: It Never Rains...

It's holiday time as the Trotters head for Spain but while Del and Rodney are soaking up the sun, Grandad is hiding away in the hotel room in a peculiar sort of mood. At first the boys dismiss his behaviour as a reaction to too much squid. But bit by bit, the real cause is revealed...
Cast: Alex the travel agent (Jim McManus) *French girl* (Anne Bruzac) *English girl* (Jillianne Foot) *Englishman* (Michael Attwell) *Spanish guard* (Anthony Jackson) *Barmaid* (Julie La Rousse)
First broadcast: Thursday November 25th 1982 at 8.30pm
Viewing figures: 9.5 million • *Duration:* 30 minutes • *Music:* In The Summertime performed by Mungo Jerry

Episode 7: A Touch Of Glass

Del rubs shoulders with the high and haughty only to find that they are giving him the cold one. It's only when he presents some of his recently 'acquired' porcelain do they find him useful... as a chandelier cleaner!
Cast: Lady Ridgemere (Elizabeth Benson) *Wallace the butler* (Donald Bisset) *Lord Ridgemere* (Geoffrey Toone)
First broadcast: Thursday December 2nd 1982 at 8.30pm
Viewing figures: 10.2 million • *Duration:* 30 minutes • *Music:* None

Christmas Special: The Funny Side Of Christmas: Christmas Trees

Del's latest line, telescopic Christmas trees, aren't selling well. So he tells Rodney to take one and deliver it to the local church. However Del's gesture isn't quite as benevolent as it first appears and Rodney is furious when he finds his brother selling them as "The only Christmas tree used and recommended by the Church of England itself."

Cast: *Vicar* (John Pennington) *Sid* (Roy Heather)
First broadcast: Monday December 27th 1982 at 8.05pm
Viewing figures: 7.2 million • **Duration:** 8 minutes • **Music:** None

CHRISTMAS SPECIAL 1982
Diamonds Are For Heather

There's nothing like a heart-wrenching tune played late in the evening to kindle a romance between strangers. Del catches the eye of the lovely Heather after a moving rendition of Old Shep at a Spanish Night at the Nag's Head and suddenly it's love. It looks like she might just become the future Mrs Trotter. That is, until her husband shows up!

Cast: *Enrico* (John Moreno) *Heather* (Rosalind Lloyd) *Brian* (Roger Brierley) *Waiter in the Indian restaurant* (Dev Sagoo)
First broadcast: Thursday December 30th 1982 at 7.55pm
Viewing figures: 9.3 million • **Duration:** 30 minutes • **Music:** Zoom performed by Fat Larry's Band

SERIES THREE
Episode 1: Homesick

Lugging the shopping up those twelve flights of stairs is proving too much for Grandad. The doctor recommends a new council bungalow for the Trotter dynasty. Over to Rodney, the new chairman of the Housing Committee.

Cast: *Baz* (Ron Pember) *Trigger* (Roger Lloyd Pack) *1st old lady* (Gilly Flower) *2nd old lady* (Renee Roberts) *Doctor* (John Bryans) *Miss Mackenzie* (Sandra Payne) *Small boy* (Miles Rinaldi)
First broadcast: Thursday November 10th 1983 at 8.30pm
Viewing figures: 9.4 million • **Duration:** 30 minutes • **Music:** None

Episode 2: Healthy Competition

Rodney's decided to go it alone and leave Peckham's own multinational conglomerate - Trotters Independent Traders. By the end of the week he's already cornered the market in used lawn mower engines and with Mickey Pearce as his Financial Director, the sky's the limit...

Cast: *Auctioneer* (Glynn Sweet) *Mickey* (Patrick Murray) *Harry the foreman* (Rex Robinson) *Indian Waiter* (Dev Sagoo) *Young Towser* (Mike Carnell)
First broadcast: Thursday November 17th 1983 at 8.30pm
Viewing figures: 9.7 million • **Duration:** 30 minutes • **Music:** Theme from Jaws by John Williams

Episode 3: Friday The 14th
Del, Rodney and Grandad are bound for Cornwall to Boycie's weekend cottage and a spot of salmon poaching. It should be a relaxing weekend if they can forget about the mad-axe-salmon-fisherman-killer who's just escaped from the local institute, that is...
Cast: *Policeman on moorland road* (Ray Mort) *Gamekeeper Tom Witton* (Bill Ward) *Chief of security/madman* (Christopher Malcolm) *Police Sergeant* (Michael Stainton)
First broadcast: Thursday November 24th 1983 at 8.30pm
Viewing figures: 9.7 million • **Duration:** 30 minutes • **Music:** None

Episode 4: Yesterday Never Comes
Del's into art dealing in a big way, especially when it involves a "posh tart" like the glamorous Miranda. Has she really been wooed by his tequila sunsets or are her motives rather more mercenary...
Cast: *Mrs Murphy* (Lucita Lijertwood) *Miranda Davenport* (Juliet Hammond) *Harry the furniture restorer* (Robert Vahey) *Auctioneer* (Garard Green)
First broadcast: Thursday December 1st 1983 at 8.30pm
Viewing figures: 10.6 million • **Duration:** 30 minutes • **Music:** None

Episode 5: May The Force Be With You
A ripple of panic runs through the Nag's Head. Del's old school enemy, Slater is back in town, hell bent on revenge and now brandishing a police warrant card.
Cast: *Trigger* (Roger Lloyd Pack) *Detective Inspector Roy Slater* (Jim Broadbent) *Boycie* (John Challis) *P.C. Hoskins* (Christopher Mitchell) *Karen the Barmaid* (Michele Winstanley)
First broadcast: Thursday December 8th 1983 at 8.30pm
Viewing figures: 10.7 million • **Duration:** 30 minutes • **Music:** None

Episode 6: Wanted

Watch out! The Peckham Pouncer's about! Alias Rodney Trotter...? Surely there must be some mistake? Try telling that to Rodders, London's most wanted criminal....

Cast: *Mickey* (Patrick Murray) *Blossom* (Toni Palmer) *Trigger* (Roger Lloyd Pack) *Boycie* (John Challis) *Karen the barmaid* (Michele Winstanley)

First broadcast: Thursday December 15th 1983 at 8.30pm

Viewing figures: 11.2 million • **Duration:** 30 minutes • **Music:** Funky Moog performed by Disco Happening

Episode 7: Who's A Pretty Boy?

Del decides he can make a fast buck by persuading his old friend Denzil to let him, Grandad and Rodney decorate his flat in preference to Brendan, the Irish painter. Denzil's wife is far from keen on the idea and leaves clear instructions for them to stay out of her kitchen. They don't, of course, and mistakes will always happen with the Trotters around. But what are they going to do about Corinne's canary...?

Cast: *Brendan* (David Jackson) *Karen the barmaid* (Michele Winstanley) *Denzil* (Paul Barber) *Corinne* (Eva Mottley) *Louis the pet shop owner* (Anthony Morton) *Mike Fisher, Nag's Head landlord* (Kenneth MacDonald)

First broadcast: Thursday December 22nd 1983 at 8.30pm

Viewing figures: 11.9 million • **Duration:** 30 minutes • **Music:** High Fly performed by Contemporary Orchestra

CHRISTMAS SPECIAL 1983

Thicker Than Water

It might be the season of goodwill to all men, but to Del that doesn't extend to Rodney and his long-lost father Reg when he comes back to the fold after eighteen years - especially when Reg Trotter starts casting doubt on Del's parentage.

Cast: *Reg Trotter* (Peter Woodthorpe) *Karen the barmaid* (Michele Winstanley)

First broadcast: Sunday December 25th 1983 at 9.35pm

Viewing figures: 10.8 million • **Duration:** 30 minutes • **Music:** From the film *Sleepless Nights*

LICENSED TO DRILL

In this educational episode Del starts telling Rodney and Grandad all about oil. After insisting that they all watch a documentary about oil exploration, Del fails to explain why he is suddenly so interested in the product. The next morning Rodney wakes up to discover a stranger in the flat from whom Del has just bought an oil rig for £400...

Cast: Oil man (Iain Blair) • *Duration:* 19 minutes

SERIES FOUR

Episode 1: Happy Returns

Rodney is in love with Debbie from the newsagents. Could this mean the end of his dirty magazine fetish? Trouble is, she's only nineteen and nineteen-and-a-half years ago Del was pretty friendly with her mum June...

Cast: June (Diane Langton) *Trigger* (Roger Lloyd Pack) *Mickey* (Patrick Murray) *Debbie* (Oona Kirsch) *Maureen* (Nula Conwell) *Old lady in newsagents* (Lala Lloyd) *Jason* (Ben Davis)

First broadcast: Thursday February 21st 1985 at 8.00pm

Viewing figures: 15.2 million • *Duration:* 30 minutes • *Music:* None

Episode 2: Strained Relations

Grandad's funeral brings relations from as far away as north London, including Uncle Albert whose intentions leave Del feeling "like a turkey who's just caught Bernard Matthews grinning at him."

Cast: Trigger (Roger Lloyd Pack) *Boycie* (John Challis) *Mike* (Kenneth MacDonald) *Vicar* (John Pennington) *Cousin Jean* (Maureen Sweeney) *Cousin Stan* (Mike Kemp) *Old Lady* (Lala Lloyd) *Maureen* (Nula Conwell)

First broadcast: Thursday February 28th 1985 at 8.00pm

Viewing figures: 14.9 million • *Duration:* 30 minutes • *Music:* None

Episode 3: Hole In One

Rodney's none-too-shrewd investment in suntan oil during "the worst winter in two million years" demands emergency measures and Uncle Albert decides that it is time to display his only talent - that of falling down holes without any real injury.

Cast: Solly (Colin Jeavons) *Mike* (Kenneth MacDonald) *Judge* (Dennis Ramsden) *Mr Gerrard* (Andrew Tourell) *Mr Fraser* (James Woolley) *Maureen* (Nula Conwell) *Cockney man* (Michael Roberts) *Clerk* (Les Rawlings)

First broadcast: Thursday March 7th 1985 at 8.00pm
Viewing figures: 13.4 million • *Duration:* 30 minutes • *Music:* None

Episode 4: It's Only Rock And Roll

Instead of the Albert 'all Rodney's pop group were heading for 'sod all' until Del discovers their commercial potential. As usual, it doesn't quite work out as they'd like...

Cast: Policeman (Geoffrey Leesley) *Mental Mickey* (Daniel Peacock) *Charlie* (Marcus Francis) *Stew* (David Thewlis) *D.J.* (Mike Read)

First broadcast: Thursday March 14th 1985 at 8.00pm

Viewing figures: 13.6 million • *Duration:* 30 minutes • *Music:* Diane performed by The Bachelors, Toot the Shoot performed by Shakatak, Drivin' Hard, Boys will be Boys performed by Daniel Peacock - written by John Sullivan

Episode 5: Sleeping Dogs Lie

Del is onto a great new money making scheme: looking after Boycie and Marlene's new puppy, Duke for a steal at £60 a week should be a doddle, a bit of the old Pedigree Chum and they should be away. Then Dukie falls victim to salmonella poisoning.

Cast: Boycie (John Challis) *Marlene* (Sue Holderness) *Dog owner* (Linda Barr) *Receptionist* (Debbi Blyth) *Vet* (John D. Collins) *Doctor* (Brian Jameson)

First broadcast: Thursday March 21st 1985 at 8.00pm

Viewing figures: 18.7 million • *Duration:* 30 minutes • *Music:* None

Episode 6: Watching The Girls Go By

Rodders is desperate to find a woman for a party at the Nag's Head. Nothing new? This time he's got a bet on with Mickey and Del's gonna make sure he wins...

Cast: Trigger (Roger Lloyd Pack) *Mike* (Kenneth MacDonald) *Maureen* (Nula Conwell) *Mickey* (Patrick Murray) *Yvonne* (Carolyn Allen)

First broadcast: Thursday March 28th 1985 at 8.00pm

Viewing figures: 14.4 million • *Duration:* 30 minutes • *Music:* None

Episode 7: As One Door Closes

When the bottom falls out of louvre doors, times get hard for the Trotters. But nature will find a way as Del and Rodders go butterfly collecting...

Cast: Denzil (Paul Barber)
First broadcast: Thursday April 4th 1985 at 8.00pm
Viewing figures: 14.2 million • *Duration:* 30 minutes • *Music:* None

CHRISTMAS SPECIAL 1985
To Hull And Back
Del is reluctant to get involved with Boycie and Abdul's diamond smuggling scheme until he's offered £15,000 for his trouble. He then ropes Rodney and Uncle Albert into the enterprise that will either leave them rich or in jail. They end up taking to the high seas in a dodgy old boat and sailing over to Holland with old sea dog Albert at the helm. They get back to England exhausted only to find that Del's adversary Chief Inspector Slater seems to be onto them in a big way.

Cast: *Smuggler* (Jane Thompson) *Mike* (Kenneth MacDonald) *Vicky* (Kim Clifford) *Teddy* (Johnny Wade) *Ruby* (Annie Leake) *Boycie* (John Challis) *Abdul* (Tony Anholt) *Trigger* (Roger Lloyd Pack) *Denzil* (Paul Barber) *Slater* (Jim Broadbent) *Hoskins* (Christopher Mitchell) *Sid* (Roy Heather) Colin (Mark Burdis) PC Parker (Jeff Stevenson) Bridge attendant (Alan Hulse) *Lil* (Rachel Bell) *Boatman* (Joe Belcher) *Gas rigger* (David Fleeshman) *Van Kleefe* (Philip Bond) *Hussein* (Lorence Ferdinand)
First broadcast: Wednesday December 25th 1985 at 7.30pm
Viewing figures: 16.9 million • *Duration:* 90 minutes • *Music:* None

SERIES FIVE
Episode 1: From Prussia With Love
When a German damsel turns up in the Nag's Head she's definitely in distress - and nine months pregnant at that. Rodney's all beer and sympathy but Del's got an idea - could this be the answer to Boycie and Marlene's dreams of a child and a golden opportunity to make a few bob along the way?

Cast: *Boycie* (John Challis) *Marlene* (Sue Holderness) *Mike* (Kenneth MacDonald) *Anna the German Girl* (Erika Hoffman) *Maureen* (Nula Conwell) *Baby* (Michael Peters)
First broadcast: Sunday August 31st 1986 at 8.35pm
Viewing figures: 12.1 million • *Duration:* 30 minutes • *Music:* I Didn't Mean To Turn You On performed by Robert Palmer, Lady In Red performed by Chris de Burgh

Episode 2: The Miracle Of Peckham

Del reckons he's discovered a miracle. The statue of the Virgin Mary at the local church has been spotted weeping. Del soon has the cream of the world's media paying to film the event - and, of course, it's nothing to do with a leaky church roof....

Cast: *Father O'Keith* (P.G. Stephens) *Biffo* (John Pierce Jones) *Australian reporter* (Peter Wickham) *American reporter* (Carol Cleveland) *Man in the church* (James Richardson)

First broadcast: Sunday September 7th 1986 at 8.35pm

Viewing figures: 14.2 million • **Duration:** 30 minutes • **Music:** None

Episode 3: The Longest Night

A robber makes a raid on the local supermarket just as Del and family are out doing their weekly shopping. What's worse - Del sold him a duff watch down the market and it's that that's got them into trouble in the first place.

Cast: *Mr Peterson the store manager* (Max Harvey) *Lennox* (Vas Blackwood) *Woman in Kiosk* (Jeanne Mockford) *Check-out girl* (Catherine Clarke) *Tom, security officer* (John Bardon)

First broadcast: Sunday September 14th 1986 at 8.35pm

Viewing figures: 16.7 million • **Duration:** 30 minutes • **Music:** None

Episode 4: Tea For Three

Look out! Del's tampered with the sunbed controls and Rodney's seeing red - literally! His face is done to a turn. He'll hardly wow Trigger's lovely niece, Lisa, with his handsome good looks now which leaves the way pretty clear for Del himself. But revenge should certainly be sweet when he volunteers Del for a spot of hang-gliding...

Cast: *Trigger* (Roger Lloyd Pack) *Mike* (Kenneth MacDonald) *Lisa* (Gerry Cowper) *Andy* (Mark Colleano) *Pianist* (Fred Tomlinson) *Singer* (Joan Baxter) *Drummer* (Derek Price) *Stuntman/Double* (Ken Barker) *Stuntman* (Graham Walker)

First broadcast: Sunday September 21st 1986 at 8.35pm

Viewing figures: 16.5 million • **Duration:** 30 minutes • **Music:** I Who Have Nothing performed by Joan Baxter • **Filming locations include:** Hang-gliding scenes were shot at Butser Hill, near Petersfield, Hampshire.

Episode 5: Video Nasty

Rodney has gained a grant from the council to make a community film and

Del soon sees its earning potential. Mickey Pearce on the other hand sees the chance to make a far more dodgy type of movie.

Cast: Trigger (Roger Lloyd Pack) *Mike* (Kenneth MacDonald) *Boycie* (John Challis) *Marlene* (Sue Holderness) *Mickey* (Patrick Murray) *Amanda* (Dawn Perllman) *Vicar* (Rex Robinson) *Chinese take-away owner* (Chua Kahjoo)

First broadcast: Sunday September 28th 1986 at 8.35pm

Viewing figures: 17.5 million • *Duration:* 30 minutes • *Music:* West End Girls performed by The Pet Shop Boys, Red Sky performed by Status Quo, Avalon performed by Brian Ferry and Roxy Music

Episode 6: Who Wants To Be A Millionaire?

Del's old pal Jumbo Mills is back in town with tales of his booming business in Australia. What's more he wants Del to go back down under with him as his partner in the enterprise. Could Del really leave Peckham for good?

Cast: Mike (Kenneth MacDonald) *Boycie* (John Challis) *Jumbo Mills* (Nick Stringer)

First broadcast: Sunday October 5th 1986 at 8.35pm

Viewing figures: 18.8 million • *Duration:* 30 minutes • *Music:* None

CHRISTMAS SPECIAL 1986

A Royal Flush

Del decides a visit to the opera is the perfect opportunity for Rodders to impress his new "friend", the daughter of the Duke of Malbury. However, munching a packet of crisps through the duet and whistling along to the aria, is more Peckham Astoria than Covent Garden. So when she invites him to a shooting weekend, he hardly needs Del to arrive with a borrowed sawn-off shot gun.

Cast: Man in market (Paul McDowell) *Vicky* (Sarah Duncan) *Trigger* (Roger Lloyd Pack) *Policeman* (Andy Readman) *Sid* (Roy Heather) *Dosser* (Robert Vahey) *Eric* (Geoffrey Wilkinson) *Ticket Collector* (Alan Cody) *Programme Seller* (Christina Michaels) *June* (Diane Langton) *Man at opera* (Robin Hereford) *Lady at opera* (Richenda Carey) *St. Johns ambulance man* (Gordon Salkilld) *Mr Dow* (Roger Davidson) *Henry* (Jack Headley) *Charles* (Peter Tuddenham) *Patterson* (Arnold Peters) *Carter* (Ifor Gwynne-Davies) *Mrs Miles* (Kate Williams) *Lady at dinner* (Daphne Goddard) *Giles* (Stephen Riddle)

First broadcast: Thursday December 25th 1986 at 7.05pm

Viewing figures: 18.8 million • *Duration:* 80 minutes • *Music:* Ask performed by The Smiths, Sometimes performed by Erasure, Handel's Overture for the Royal Fireworks, extracts from Bizet's Carmen performed by Kent Opera. • *Filming locations include*: Scenes at The Duke of Malebury's stately home were shot at Clarendon Park, Wiltshire; however neither the house, nor the grounds are open to the public.

CHRISTMAS SPECIAL 1987
The Frog's Legacy
At the wedding of Trigger's niece his Aunt Reenie tells Del and Rodney about their mum's old friend Freddie The Frog. Rodney wants to know why this charming villain left his ill-gotten gains to the Trotters and why everyone notes his resemblance to him. Del is more interested in what happened to his hoard of gold bullion.

Cast: Boycie (John Challis) *Trigger* (Roger Lloyd Pack) *Mr Jahan* (Adam Hussein) *Vicar* (Angus Mackay) *Auntie Reen* (Joan Sims) *Mike* (Kenneth MacDonald) *Marlene* (Sue Holderness) *Andy* (Mark Colleano) *Lisa* (Gerry Cowper) *Man in market* (Duncan Faber) *Woman in market* (Angela Moran)
First broadcast: Friday December 25th 1987 at 6.25pm
Viewing figures: 14.5 million • *Duration:* 60 minutes • *Music:* Never Gonna Give You Up performed by Rick Astley, FLM performed by Mel and Kim, Faith, Wake Me Up Before You Go performed by George Michael, So Macho performed by Sinitta, Smoke Gets In Your Eyes performed by Brian Ferry

CHRISTMAS SPECIAL 1988
Dates
When Del sees the sort of girl Trigger meets through a new computer dating agency he decides it's worth giving it a try and through them he meets budding actress Raquel. Rodney meanwhile is out to impress Nag's Head barmaid Nerys by acting tough. Del's romance is progressing smoothly and all is well until Albert's birthday bash is interrupted by a couple in naval uniform.

Cast: Boycie (John Challis) *Mike* (Kenneth MacDonald) *Trigger* (Roger Lloyd Pack) *Marlene* (Sue Holderness) *Raquel* (Tessa Peake-Jones) *Mickey* (Patrick Murray) *Jevon* (Steven Woodcock) *Chris* (Tony Marshall) *Nerys* (Andrée Bernard) *Technomatch agent* (Christopher Stanton) *Sonia* (Jean Warren) *Charles* (Nicholas Courtney) *Policeman* (Paul Beringer)

Policewoman (Margaret Norris) *Sid* (Roy Heather) *Naval Officer* (Martin Cochrane) *Mrs Sansom* (Jean Challis) *Stunt arranger* (Colin Skeaping) *Stunt performers* (Graeme Crowther, Nick Gillard, Paul Heasman, Alan Stuart, Tip Tipping, Chris Webb, Tina Maskell)
First broadcast: Sunday December 25th 1988 at 5.05pm
Viewing figures: 16.6 million • *Duration:* 80 minutes •
Music: Nothing Can Come Between Us performed by Clean Heart, Haunt Me, performed by Sade, Smokey Blues performed by Aswad, Sad Songs performed by The Christians, Burning Bridges performed by Status Quo • *Filming locations include:* Del and Raquel met under the clock at Waterloo Station, London. The Trotter van was seen being chased by yobs and 'flying' over the bridge with the aid of a ramp at Talbot Road, Isleworth.

SERIES SIX

Episode 1: Yuppy Love

Eighties fever is spreading fast! Del's on the up and up into the exciting world of red braces and yuppy sorts. Armed with his filofax and briefcase he's ready to take on the city - well Peckham, anyway. Meanwhile Rodney's on the pull, with a classy new girlfriend called Cassandra. But what will she think of Nelson Mandela House?
Cast: Trigger (Roger Lloyd Pack) *Cassandra* (Gwyneth Strong) *Mickey* (Patrick Murray) *Jevon* (Steven Woodcock) *Emma* (Francesca Brill) *Marsha* (Laura Jackson) *Dale* (Diana Katis) *Snobby girl* (Hazel McBride) *Barman* (William Thomas) *Girl in disco* (Tracey Clarke)
First broadcast: Sunday January 8th 1989 at 7.15pm
Viewing figures: 13.9 million • *Duration:* 50 minutes • *Music:* Love Goes Up And Down performed by Errol Brown, Enchanted Lady performed by The Passadenas, Lady In Red performed by Chris de Burgh

Episode 2: Danger UXD

Just faking a signature on a delivery note means that Del can take possession of fifty dolls for absolutely nothing. The only problem is that "Lusty Linda" and "Erotic Estelle" are not exactly what he had in mind and would seem more appropriate to Dirty Barry's dubious trade rather than the local toyshop.....
Cast: Cassandra (Gwyneth Strong) *Mike* (Kenneth MacDonald) *Denzil* (Paul Barber) *Barry* (Walter Sparrow) *Boycie* (John Challis) *Trigger*

(Roger Lloyd Pack) *Waiter* (Paul Cooper) *Adrian* (Michael Shallard) *Chinese take-away owner* (Takashi Kawahara) *TV presenter* (David Warwick) *Clayton* (Tommy Buson)
First broadcast: Sunday January 15th 1989 at 7.15pm
Viewing figures: 16.1 million • *Duration:* 50 minutes • *Music:* Come Out To Play performed by UB40, Stop performed by Erasure, Tribute (Right on) performed by The Passadenas, Fisherman's Blues performed by Waterboys, Is You Is Or Is You Isn't My Baby, Jack You're Dead performed by Joe Jackson

Episode 3: Chain Gang
Faced with the opportunity of buying two hundred and fifty eighteen carat gold chains from a retired jeweller, Arnie Del just can't resist. Hastily, a multi-million dollar business consortium is formed - well, Mike from the Nag's Head, Trig, Boycie, Uncle Albert and a reluctant Rodney, anyway. Everything is fine until Arnie is taken ill just as the deal is about to be sealed and Del is left feeling that all that glitters.....
Cast: Cassandra (Gwyneth Strong) *Mike* (Kenneth MacDonald) *Denzil* (Paul Barber) *Arnie* (Philip McGough) *Boycie* (John Challis) *Trigger* (Roger Lloyd Pack) *Otto* (Mick Oliver) *Grayson* (Peter Rutherford) *Mario* (Frank Coda) *Woman in Crowd* (Marie Lorraine) *Seven* (Sam Howard) *Gary* (Steve Fortune)
First broadcast: Sunday January 22nd 1989 at 7.15pm
Viewing figures: 16.3 million • *Duration:* 50 minutes • *Music:* My One Temptation performed by Mica Paris, Sweet Little Mystery performed by Wet Wet Wet • *Filming locations include:* Tandoori Nights Indian restaurant in Kings Road, Hammersmith played itself in the scene where jewellery dealer Arnie fakes a heart attack.

Episode 4: The Unlucky Winner Is......
Rodney has won a holiday for three in the Mediterranean, courtesy of Del and Megaflakes drawing competition. The only snag is he's got to pretend he's fourteen years old all week. Should be a doddle - all he's got to do is keep his head down. Then the skateboarding and breakdancing competitions begin.
Cast: Cassandra (Gwyneth Strong) *Mike* (Kenneth MacDonald) *Mr Perkins* (Michael Fenton Stevens) *Carmen* (Gina Bellman) *Trudy* (Lusha Kellgren)
First broadcast: Sunday January 29th 1989 at 7.15pm

Viewing figures: 17 million • *Duration:* 50 minutes • *Music:* That Old Devil Called Love performed by Alison Moyet, Why Does Love Got To Be So Sad performed by Buckwheat Zydeco, Strange kind Of love performed by Love and Money, Love Train performed by Holly Johnson, Lucy performed by Habit, Hold Me In Your Arms performed by Rick Astley, Birdie Song performed by The Tweets , Y Viva Espagna performed by Sylvia

Episode 5: Sickness And Wealth

Excruciating stomach cramps and a constant diet of health salts might drive some people to visit a doctor, but not Del. Oh no, he knows he's only suffering from that scourge of all serious yuppies, PMA - Positive Mental Attitude! In the end he pays the doctor a visit and the news is not good...

Cast: Cassandra (Gwyneth Strong) *Boycie* (John Challis) *Mike* (Kenneth MacDonald) *Trigger* (Roger Lloyd Pack) *Marlene* (Sue Holderness) *Mickey* (Patrick Murray) *Jevon* (Steven Woodcock) *Nerys* (Andree Bernard) *Elsie Partridge* (Constance Chapman) *Dr Shaheed* (Josephine Welcome) *Dr Meadows* (Ewan Stewart) *Nurse* (Ann Bryson)

First broadcast: Sunday February 5th 1989 at 7.15pm

Viewing figures: 18.2 million • *Duration:* 50 minutes • *Music:* Where Is Your Love? performed by Gail Ann Dorsey, I Don't Want A Lover performed by Texas, Fine Time performed by Yazz, Big Area performed by Then Jericho, It's Only Love performed by Simply Red

Episode 6: Little Problems

With his diploma in computer science, new job in Cassandra's father's firm and impending marriage, Rodney's certainly on the up. Del's even promised to take care of his share of the flat deposit. Only problem is, Del's gone and got himself in a bit of bother over some hooky mobile phones with the less than understanding Driscoll brothers and unless he comes up with £2,000 sharpish, they're going to take care of him...

Cast: Cassandra (Gwyneth Strong) *Boycie* (John Challis) *Trigger* (Roger Lloyd Pack) *Mike* (Kenneth MacDonald) *Marlene* (Sue Holderness) *Mickey* (Patrick Murray) *Jevon* (Steven Woodcock) *Danny Driscoll* (Christopher Ryan) *Alan Parry* (Denis Lill) *Pamela Parry* (Wanda Ventham) *Comedian Jeff Stevenson* (Jeff Stevenson) *Registrar* (Derek Benefield)

First broadcast: Sunday February 12th 1989 at 7.15pm

Viewing figures: 18.9 million • *Duration:* 50 minutes • *Music:* I Only Want To Be With You performed by Sam Fox, Tender Hands performed by Chris de Burgh, Love Follows performed by Steven Dante, Tracie performed by Level 42, Looking For Linda performed by Hue and Cry, Bring Me Some Water performed by Melissa Etheridge, Buffalo Stance performed by Neneh Cherry, Something's Got Hold Of My Heart performed by Marc Almond and Gene Pitney, Where Is The Love performed by Mica Paris and Will Downing, Holding Back The Years performed by Simply Red

CHRISTMAS SPECIAL 1989
The Jolly Boys' Outing
Del has organised the annual Jolly Boys Outing to Margate. A fun day out is marred when their coach blows up. The lads can't get a train home because there's a strike on and most of the guest houses in Margate are chocker. The gang split up and the Trotters end up at the spooky Villa Bella and Rodney and Albert have to share a bed. Del and his brother decide to head into town where Del meets an old flame.

Cast: Cassandra (Gwyneth Strong) *Boycie* (John Challis) *Mike* (Kenneth MacDonald) *Trigger* (Roger Lloyd Pack) *Denzil* (Paul Barber) *Marlene* (Sue Holderness) *Raquel* (Tessa Peake-Jones) *Mickey* (Patrick Murray) *Jevon* (Steven Woodcock) *Sid* (Roy Heather) *Alan* (Denis Lill) *Pamela* (Wanda Ventham) *Stephen* (Daniel Hill) *Joanne* (Gail Harrison) *Trainee* (Jake Wood) *Harry* (Roy Evans) *Mrs Baker* (Katharine Page) *Helen* (Dawn Funnell) *Mrs Creswell* (Rosalind Knight) *Inga* (Bridget Erin Bates) *Ramondo* (Robin Driscoll) *Policeman* (Del Baker) *Singer* (Lee Gibson) *Drummer* (Alf Bigden) *Bass Player* (Dave Richmond) *Organist* (Ronnie Price) *Stunt arranger* (Colin Skeaping) *Betty* (Fanny Corby) *Romondo* (Robin Driscoll)

First broadcast: Monday December 25th 1989 at 4.05pm

Viewing figures: 20.1 million • *Duration:* 85 minutes • *Music:* Night Nurse performed by Gregory Isaacs, Now That We've Found Love performed by Third World, Over You performed by Roxy Music, Everybody Wants To Rule The World performed by Tears for Fears, Help performed by Bananarama, 2.4.6.8. Motorway performed by Tom Robinson Band, This Changing Light performed by Deacon Blue on album, Turn It Up performed by Simply Red, Everybody's talkin' performed by Harry Nilsson, Move On Out performed by Simply Red, Just The Way You Are performed by Lee Gibson, I May Be Wrong performed by Alf Bigden,

Ronnie Price and Dave Richmond • *Filming locations include:* The forecourt of Margate Station played itself as did Benbom Brothers Theme Park in Margate. The pub where the gang stopped for a drink was the Roman Galley, Thanet Way, Canterbury. The market scenes were filmed at Ramsgate greyhound stadium.

CHRISTMAS SPECIAL 1990
Rodney Come Home

Rodney has gone up in the world and has landed a job at Cassandra's Dad's printing firm. Albert has taken over Rodney's old job as Del's look-out and is helping Del sell some dodgy talking dolls. Rodney and Cassandra aren't getting on well and Del decides to help heal the rift but only suceeds in making it worse. Things are looking good for Del though, as Raquel has moved into the flat.

Cast: Cassandra (Gwyneth Strong) *Raquel* (Tessa Peake-Jones) *Mickey* (Patrick Murray) *Alan* (Denis Lill) *Michelle* (Paula Anna Bland) *Frank* (Philip Blaine) *Chris* (Tony Marshall) *Woman in club* (Jean Harington) *Neighbour* (Linda James) *TV announcer* (Patrick Lunt)

First broadcast: Tuesday 25th December 1990 at 5.10pm

Viewing figures: 18 million • *Duration:* 75 minutes • *Music:* Reckless Man, Born To Be King performed by Magnum, Let Me Be performed by Feargal Sharkey, True performed by Spandau Ballet, Fascinating Rhythm performed by Bassomatic, Don't Be A Fool performed by Loose Ends, This Is The Right Time performed by Lisa Stanfield, Rebel Yell performed by Billy Idol, Did I Happen To Mention and Your Lovely Face performed by Julia Fordham, Somebody Who Loves You performed by Joan Armatrading • *Filming locations include:* The nightclub was the Parkside Nightclub, Bath Road, Bristol. Scenes at Alan Parry's printing firm were shot at Gemini Graphics and Print Ltd, York Street, Bristol. The shopping precinct where Del tries to sell his dodgy dolls was the Broadwalk Shopping Centre in Knowle.

SERIES SEVEN
Episode 1: The Sky's The Limit

Boycie's new satellite dish has been stolen and he asks Del to try to buy it back from whoever has nicked it. It doesn't take Del long to find it and he thinks he's in line for a few quid from Boycie. What he doesn't realise is that the satellite dish on his balcony isn't Boycie's one at all and that it is the main cause of the chaos at Gatwick Airport which has resulted in Cassandra's flight being diverted and Rodney's romantic plans ruined.

Cast: Raquel (Tessa Peake-Jones) *Alan* (Denis Lill) *Boycie* (John Challis) *Mike* (Kenneth MacDonald) *Trigger* (Roger Lloyd Pack) *Marlene* (Sue Holderness) *Bronco* (Ron Aldridge) *Henry* (Gordon Warnecke) *Stewardess* (Lucy Hanoca) *Newsreader* (Richard Whitmore) *Baby Tyler* (Elliot Russell)

First broadcast: Sunday December 30th 1990 at 7.15pm

Viewing figures: 15 million • *Duration:* 50 minutes • *Music:* Float On performed by The Floaters, Opposites Attract and Straight Up performed by Paula Abdual, Reckless Man performed by Magnum • *Filming locations include:* Airport scenes were shot at Stansted Airport.

Episode 2: The Chance Of A Lunchtime

Del dreams of shifting a thousand 'National Anthem' musical doorbells. Raquel's audition sets her dreaming of stardom. While she gets the chance to join the world of cravats and codpieces, Rodders loses his job in true plonker style. But Raquel might have to wait that bit longer for fame - just when Del was thinking that the best thing in life is a door bell that plays 'Long Live Swaziland' his greatest dream comes true.

Cast: Raquel (Tessa Peake-Jones) *Cassandra* (Gwyneth Strong) *Alan* (Denis Lill) *Boycie* (John Challis) *Mike* (Kenneth MacDonald) *Trigger* (Roger Lloyd Pack) *Marlene* (Sue Holderness) *Man in the Pub* (Ian Barritt) *Trudy* (Helen Blizard) *Jules* (Paul Opacic) *Adrian* (Ian Redford) *Baby Tyler* (Elliott Russell)

First broadcast: Sunday January 6th 1991 at 7.15pm

Viewing figures: 16.6 million • *Duration:* 50 minutes • *Music:* All Around The World performed by Lisa Stansfield, Promised Land performed by Style Council, Do The Strand performed by Roxy Music, Love And Affection performed by Joan Armatrading, Old friends performed by Guitar Moods, Where Are You Baby performed by Betty Boo, Eyes Without A Face performed by Billy Idol, Masquerade performed by Swing Out Sister • *Filming locations include:* The restaurant used for Raquel's meeting with a theatre producer was actually Henry Africa's Hothouse, Whiteladies Road, Bristol. The floating restaurant where Rodney and Cassandra went for dinner was called Shoots and was moored at Cannons Road and is now located at Hotwell Road, Bristol.

Episode 3: Stage Fright

With Raquel pregnant, Del's plan to achieve millionaire status must move up a gear. So the chance to supply the cabaret at the Starlight Rooms for an old 'friend' Eric to the tune of six hundred quid is too good to miss. With Raquel dusting off her vocal chords in the kitchen and Trig's mate Tony the singer dustman, waiting in the wings, everything's sorted. Until Del discovers who the real owner of the club is and the extent of Tony's vocal range.

Cast: *Raquel* (Tessa Peake-Jones) *Boycie* (John Challis) *Mike* (Kenneth MacDonald) *Trigger* (Roger Lloyd Pack) *First woman* (Lyn Langridge) *Eric* (Trevor Byfield) *Eugene* (Roger Blake) *Tony Angelino* (Philip Pope) *First broadcast:* Sunday January 13th 1991 at 7.15pm

Viewing figures: 16.6 million • *Duration:* 50 minutes • *Music:* Peace Through The World performed by Maxi Priest, Love Is The Drug performed by Roxy Music, Kick It In performed by Simple Minds, Looking Out For Linda performed by Hue and Cry, and, of course, Delilah and I'll Never Fall In Love Again sung by Philip Pope as Tony Angelino, Do You Know The Way To San José sung by Tessa Peake-Jones as Raquel and their duet Crying. • *Filming locations include:* Scenes at the Down At The Riverside Club were shot at a club called The Studio which was demolished in early 1998. Raquel's audition took place at the Courage Social Club at Willway Road, Bedminster, Bristol.

Episode 4: The Class Of '62

A class of '62 reunion in the Nag's Head signals Roy Slater's return to Civvy Street after years in the "nick". But why has this crooked ex-copper decided to come back to Peckham where he is universally loathed? Just as Trig, Del, Boycie and Denzil begin to believe that he really has changed for the better, Del discovers the real reason for his return...

Cast: *Raquel* (Tessa Peake-Jones) *Boycie* (John Challis) *Trigger* (Roger Lloyd Pack) *Mike* (Kenneth MacDonald) *Denzil* (Paul Barber) *Roy Slater* (Jim Broadbent)

First broadcast: Sunday January 20th 1991 at 7.15pm

Viewing figures: 16.2 million • *Duration:* 50 minutes • *Music:* Never Enough performed by The Cure, People performed by Soul II Soul, Mighty Quinn performed by Manfred Mann, All Around The World performed by Lisa Stansfield, Valentine's Day performed by Betty Boo

Episode 5: He Ain't Heavy, He's my Uncle

Albert is pumping iron and looking like a born again Teddy Boy, while Rodders' drinking bouts leave him looking like one of the living dead. Del attempts to pamper the pregnant Raquel by buying a bargain banger from Boycie and takes on the unemployable Rodney as Director of Commercial Development. As Rodney gets to his first project: washing the car, Albert gets mugged on his way home from the over sixties club.

Cast: Raquel (Tessa Peake-Jones) *Boycie* (John Challis) *Trigger* (Roger Lloyd Pack) *Marlene* (Sue Holderness) *Mike* (Kenneth MacDonald) *Dora* (Joan Geary) *Knock Knock* (Howard Goorney) *Mechanic* (Herb Johnson) *Ollie* (Tony London) *Cassandra* (Gwyneth Strong)

First broadcast: Sunday January 27th 1991 at 7.15pm

Viewing figures: 17.2 million • *Duration:* 50 minutes • *Music:* Uncle Albert performed by Paul and Linda McCartney • *Filming locations include:* The scenes of Del and Rodney looking for Albert were shot on Tower Bridge, HMS Belfast, Portobello Green, Acklam Road East, Malton Road and Portobello Road Market.

Episode 6: Three Men, A Woman, And A Baby

Del's about to become a father but even that can't cheer up Rodney the vegetarian. The polar cap is melting, the rain forest is dying, the sea is being poisoned, and he hasn't had a "bit for months". Not even one of Del's new ponytail wigs could enhance his image in Cassandra's eyes...

Cast: Raquel (Tessa Peake-Jones) *Cassandra* (Gwyneth Strong) *Trigger* (Roger Lloyd Pack) *Mike* (Kenneth MacDonald) *Midwife* (Ken Drury) *Sister* (Constance Lamb)

First broadcast: Sunday February 3rd 1991 at 7.15pm

Viewing Figures: 18.9 million • *Duration:* 50 minutes • *Music:* Movies performed by Hothouse Flowers, You Don't Have To Say You Love Me performed by Dusty Springfield, Street Life performed by Roxy Music, Nothing Compares To You performed by Sinead O'Connor, Concerto in D Major by Vivaldi • *Filming locations include:* The hospital was the West Middlesex Hospital, Hillingdon.

CHRISTMAS SPECIALS 1991

Miami Twice: Part one: The American Dream

It's time for Damien's christening and the chance for his Godparents Rodney and Cassandra to get together. Their marriage is still having problems and they are only seeing each other at weekends. Then Rodney gets an unexpected windfall and Del kindly uses the money to book two non-refundable tickets to Miami for Rodney and Cassandra, the trouble is she can't go. Step forward a volunteer to take her place - Del Boy.

Cast: Raquel (Tessa Peake-Jones) *Cassandra* (Gwyneth Strong) *Alan* (Denis Lill) *Pam* (Wanda Ventham) *Mickey* (Patrick Murray) *Vicar* (Treva Etienne) *Trigger* (Roger Lloyd Pack) *Boycie* (John Challis) *Marlene* (Sue Holderness) *Mike* (Kenneth MacDonald) *Denzil* (Paul Barber) *Sid* (Roy Heather) *Baby Tyler* (Danny Rix) Baby *Damien* (Grant Stevens)

First broadcast: Tuesday December 24th 1991 at 7.30 pm

Viewing figures: 17.7 million • *Duration:* 50 minutes • *Music:* Every Heartbeat performed by Amy Grant, Hot Summer Salsa performed by Jive Bunny and the Mastermixers, Englishman In New York, White Wedding performed by Billy Idol, Cold, Cold Heart performed by Midge Ure, Let There Be Love performed by Simple Minds • *Filming locations include:* The interior of the church was St John's Church, Ladbroke Grove and the exterior was St John's Church, Kentish Town.

Miami Twice: Part two: Oh To Be In England

Over in Florida, Del can't quite get his head around the idea that they drive on the other side of the road and nearly kills Rodney and himself in the dilapidated camper van they've hired. They then run into trouble when the local Mafia see Del and realise he's a dead-ringer for their boss, Don Occhetti, who is in big trouble with the law. They see the answer to all their prayers in Del but the trouble is he'll have to be shot in order to help them.

Cast: Raquel (Tessa Peake-Jones) *Cassandra* (Gwyneth Strong) *Boycie* (John Challis) *Marlene* (Sue Holderness) *Trigger* (Roger Lloyd Pack) *Mike* (Kenneth MacDonald) *Alan* (Denis Lill) *Mickey* (Patrick Murray) *Denzil* (Paul Barber) *Sid* (Roy Heather) *Baby Damien* (Grant Stevens) Vicar (Treva Etienne)

First broadcast: Wednesday December 25th 1991 at 3.10pm

Viewing figures: 14.9 million • *Duration:* 95 minutes • *Music:* Rockin' All Over The World performed by Status Quo, Summer In The City performed by The Gutter Brothers, Baby Baby performed by Amy Grant, Hyperreal performed by The Shamen, Killer performed by Seal, Rush Rush performed by Paula Abdul, Saltwalter performed by Julian Lennon, Born Free performed by Vic Reeves

CHRISTMAS SPECIAL 1992
Mother Nature's Son

When Del finds out just how much bottles of mineral water sell for he decides to 'discover' his own spring on Grandad's old allotment. It's not long before business is booming in Peckham Spring Water and the Trotters have money rolling in. But how long will it be before anyone realises that it's only really tap water? Not long when there's a chemical leak in the local reservoir.

Cast: *Raquel* (Tessa Peake-Jones) *Cassandra* (Gwyneth Strong) *Denzil* (Paul Barber) *Boycie* (John Challis) *Myles* (Robert Glenister) *Marlene* (Sue Holderness) *Mike* (Kenneth MacDonald) *Trigger* (Roger Lloyd Pack) *Alan Parry* (Denis Lill) *Chris* (Tony Marshall) *Mickey* (Patrick Murray) *Pam Parry* (Wanda Ventham) *Damien* (Robert Liddement) *Newscaster* (Richard Whitmore) *Diver* (Luke Brannigan) *Stunt arranger* (Michael Potter)

First broadcast: Friday December 25th 1992 at 6.55pm

Viewing figures: 20.1 million • **Duration:** 65 minutes • **Music:** Incidental music by Graham Jarvis, Merry Christmas Everybody performed by Slade, Crocodile Rock performed by Elton John, Who's Gonna Ride Your Wild Horses performed by U2, Could It Be Magic performed by Take That, Santa Claus Is Coming To Town performed by Bjorn Again, Money performed by The Beatles • **Filming locations include:** The exterior of the Nag's Head was the White Admiral Pub, Lower Bevendean, Brighton; allotment scenes were shot off Natal Road, Lower Bevendean, Brighton.

CHRISTMAS SPECIAL 1993
Fatal Extraction

Del has gone back to his old ways of drinking, gambling and staying out late. Raquel leaves him, taking Damien with her and on the rebound Del fixes up a date with Beverley, his dentist's receptionist. He soon realises his mistake and stands her up at the last minute. When he's back with Raquel, he becomes convinced that Beverley is following him...

Cast: *Raquel* (Tessa Peake-Jones) *Cassandra* (Gwyneth Strong) *Boycie* (John Challis) *Trigger* (Roger Lloyd Pack) *Mike* (Kenneth MacDonald) *Denzil* (Paul Barber) *Sid* (Roy Heather) *Mickey* (Patrick Murray) *Damien* (Jamie Smith) *Beverley* (Mel Martin) *The Dentist* (Andrew Charleson) *Lady on the bus* (Kitty Scopes) *Arthur* (Derek Martin) *Mick* (Nick Maloney) *Vi* (Lyn Langridge) *Policeman* (Linford Brown) *Texo* (Bryan Brittain) *Casino waitress* (Lorraine Parsloe)

First broadcast: Saturday December 25th 1993 at 6.05 pm
Viewing figures: 19.6 million • *Duration:* 85 minutes • *Music:* Incidental music by Graham Jarvis, Hands Up performed by Right Said Fred, Step Into Christmas performed by Elton John, Hope In A Hopeless World performed by Paul Young, One Voice performed by Barry Manilow, Whisper A Prayer performed by Mica Paris, It's Alright performed by East 17, Twist and Shout performed by Chaka Demus and Pliers, Babe performed by Take That, Bye Bye Blackbird performed by Nick Maloney, I Wish It Could Be Christmas Everyday performed by Roy Wood with Wizzard, Stay (Faraway, So Close) performed by U2

CHRISTMAS TRILOGY 1996
Episode 1: Heroes and Villains
Del's home improvement grant is rejected and Rodney is on a sex programme that would leave Roger Rabbit knackered in attempts for Cassandra to conceive. But there's always the fancy dress party to cheer them up and while dressed as the caped crusaders the pair inadvertently become street vigilantes and find that for once being on the right side of the law has positive advantages.

Cast: Raquel (Tessa Peake-Jones) *Cassandra* (Gwyneth Strong) *Boycie* (John Challis) *Trigger* (Roger Lloyd Pack) *Mike* (Kenneth MacDonald) *Marlene* (Sue Holderness) *Denzil* (Paul Barber) *Sid* (Roy Heather) *Councillor Murray* (Angela Bruce) *Old Damien* (Douglas Hodge) *Damien* (Jamie Smith) *Kenny* (Steve Weston) *Gary* (Scott Marshall) *Scott* (Dan Clark) *Kevin* (Fuman Dar) *Dawn* (Sheree Murphy) *Old Lady* (Bay White) *Mayor* (Robin Meredith) *Photographer* (Richard Hicks) *Market Lads* (Lee Barritt and Leonard Kirby)

First broadcast: Wednesday December 25th 1996 at 9.00pm
Viewing figures: 21.3 million • *Duration:* 60 minutes • *Music:* Incidental music by Graham Jarvis, Sight For Sore Eyes performed by M People, I Got You Babe performed by UB40 with Chrissie Hynde, Knocking On Heaven's Door performed by The Children Of Dunblane, Coming Home Now performed by Boyzone, 2 Become 1 performed by The Spice Girls

Episode 2: Modern Men
Del's been reading the new man's guide to the twenty-first century but Raquel hasn't noticed any big improvement. Meanwhile the Trotters' finances hit an all-time low and Dr Singh is after Del's blood. Rodney and

Cassandra face heartache when she loses the baby she's carrying. Rodney won't talk about how he feels and it falls to Del to get him to open up.

Cast: Raquel (Tessa Peake-Jones) *Cassandra* (Gwyneth Strong) *Trigger* (Roger Lloyd Pack) *Mike* (Kenneth MacDonald) *Boycie* (John Challis) *Marlene* (Sue Holderness) *Denzil* (Paul Barber) *Sid* (Roy Heather) *Dr Singh* (Bhasker Patel) *Damien* (Jamie Smith) *Mickey* (Patrick Murray) *Man in hospital* (Phil Cornwell) *Sister* (Beverley Hills) *Doctor* (James Oliver) Nurse (Corrine Britton) *Receptionist* (Lorraine Ashley)

First broadcast: Friday December 27th 1996 at 8.00pm

Viewing figures: 21.3 million • *Duration:* 60 minutes • *Music:* Incidental music by Graham Jarvis, Roll With It performed by Oasis, Light Of My Life performed by Louise, Love Me For A Reason performed by Boyzone, Country House performed by Blur

Episode 3: Time On Our Hands

Raquel is nervous about her parents coming to dinner and Albert doesn't help matters by mixing up the coffee and the gravy granules. The following day Raquel's Dad James spots an old watch in amongst the junk in Del's garage which he thinks might be worth a few bob. He's absolutely right and the antique timepiece goes for more money than even Del has dreamed of. This time he really is a millionaire.

Cast: Raquel (Tessa Peake-Jones) *Cassandra* (Gwyneth Strong) *Mike* (Kenneth MacDonald) *Trigger* (Roger Lloyd Pack) *Boycie* (John Challis) *Marlene* (Sue Holderness) *Denzil* (Paul Barber) *Mickey* (Patrick Murray) *Damien* (Jamie Smith) *James* (Michael Jayston) *Audrey* (Ann Lynn) *Auctioneer* (Seymour Matthews) *Tony* (Jotham Annan)

First broadcast: Sunday December 29th 1996 at 8.00pm

Viewing figures: 24.3 million • *Duration:* 60 minutes • *Music:* Incidental music by Graham Jarvis, Take Me In To Your Heart Again performed by Vince Hill, Under The Moon Of Love and I Wonder Why performed by Showaddywaddy, Our House performed by Crosby, Stills, Nash and Young

COMIC RELIEF SPECIAL

In this episode for Comic Relief, Rodney complains to Del about his money issues after realising he and Cassandra will not be able to go to Greece once all their bills are paid. Uncle Albert decides to make them both realise how lucky they are compared to many others in the world...

First broadcast: Friday March 14th 1997 • *Viewing figures:* 10.6 million

CHRISTMAS SPECIAL 2001
If They Could See Us Now

The Trotters enjoy their newly acquired millions in style, and it's just as well, as with the Trotter brothers in charge of stocks and shares investments, it could never really last and they find themselves back on their uppers... Back in Peckham, Del sees a new game show as the answer to all their prayers...

Cast: *Raquel* (Tessa Peake-Jones) *Cassandra* (Gwyneth Strong) *Boycie* (John Challis) *Marlene* (Sue Holderness) *Trigger* (Roger Lloyd Pack) *Denzil* (Paul Barber) *Uncle Albert* (Buster Merryfield) *Mickey* (Patrick Murray) *Sid* (Roy Heather) *Damien* (Benjamin Smith) *Justin* (Kim Wall) *Marion* (Joan Hodges) *Roland* (Colum Convey) *Tony* (Daniel Hope) *Sexy Girl* (Sonia Doubell) *Maitre'D* (Philip Delancy) *Concierge* (Dominque Combe) *Clerk of Court* (Paul Strike) *The Producer* (Richard Braine) *Game show contestant* (Jessica Willcocks) *Game show contestant* (Conrad Nelson) *Matrons* (Clare Duffy, Laura Greene, Jenny Reeves) *Funeral goers* (Gillian Coles, Carol Gentle, Adrian Harris) *Restaurant goers* (Mark Paul Jones, Claire Reynolds) *Passer-by* (Ken Netsall) *Contestants* (John Brown, David Garry, Nicky Inwood) *Stand-in* (Rupert Regis) *Gameshow audience* (Shirley Netsall) *Nags Head punter* (Adrian James) and *Jonathan Ross* as himself

First broadcast: Tuesday December 25th 2001 at 9.05pm

Viewing figures: 21.34 million • **Duration:** 71 minutes • **Music:** Incidental music by Graham Jarvis, Livin La Vida Loca performed by Ricky Martin, Gold performed by Spandau Ballet, Red Sails at Sunset, Toccata and Fugue in D minor performed by Bach, Something Stupid performed by Robbie Williams and Nicole Kidman, Mozart Symphony in D Major, Never Had a Dream Come True performed by S Club 7, Can't Get You Out of My Head performed by Kylie Minogue, Can't Get Enough Of Your Love Babe performed by Barry White, Mack The Knife performed by Robbie Williams (DVD replacement for Barry White), A Song For The Lovers performed by Richard Ashcroft (DVD replacement for Barry White), Mambo Number 5

CHRISTMAS SPECIAL 2002
Strangers On The Shore
Del and Rodney say goodbye to the recently passed Uncle Albert and decide to attend a reunion in France in his honour. But on their return to Peckham they discover that cheap booze isn't the only thing they've brought back…

Cast: Raquel (Tessa Peake-Jones) *Cassandra* (Gwyneth Strong) *Boycie* (John Challis) *Marlene* (Sue Holderness) *Trigger* (Roger Lloyd Pack) *Denzil* (Paul Barber) *Mickey* (Patrick Murray) *Sid* (Roy Heather) *Damien* (Benjamin Smith) *George* (James Ellis) *Mr Mahmoon* (Nasser Memarzia) *Radio 5 sports presenter* (Alan Green) *French Mayor* (Martin Friend) *Secretaries* (Fabienne Alousque, Claudia Blondeau) *News presenter* (Charles Rhodes Davies) *Uncle Albert lookalikes* (Tony Scarlo, Richard Kirk, John Denton, Michael Cole, David Clarke) *Interpreter* (David Olufemi) *Neighbour* (Tamara Hinchco) *Gary* (Nabil Elouahabi) *Belgian TV reporter* (Connie Pollard)

First broadcast: Wednesday December 25th 2002 at 9.40pm

Viewing figures: 17.40 million • *Duration:* 73 minutes • *Music:* Incidental music by Graham Jarvis, Dancing in the Moonlight performed by Toploader, Flowers In The Window performed by Travis

CHRISTMAS SPECIAL 2003
Sleepless In Peckham
Just as the bankrupt Trotters face ruin, Uncle Albert's will saves the day. Meanwhile as Cassandra is about to give birth, Rodney discovers an old photograph that finally reveals the truth about his parentage.

Cast: Raquel (Tessa Peake-Jones) *Cassandra* (Gwyneth Strong) *Boycie* (John Challis) *Marlene* (Sue Holderness) *Trigger* (Roger Lloyd Pack) *Denzil* (Paul Barber) *Sid* (Roy Heather) *Mickey* (Patrick Murray) *Cartwright the solicitor* (Peter Blythe) *Matrons* (Jenny Reeves, Clare Duffy) *Man in hospital* (Jay Kilby) *Nurse* (Louise Mantle) *Secretary* (Pauline Whittaker) *Double Trouble vocalist* (Alan Nichol) *Double Trouble guitarist* (Norman Langton) *Lordy Geordie* (Dave Merrett and Tony Plant)

First broadcast: Thursday December 25th 2003 at 9.20pm

Viewing figures: 16.37 million • *Duration:* 73 minutes • *Music:* Incidental music by Graham Jarvis, Shoulda Woulda Coulda performed by Beverley Knight, Uptown Girl by Westlife, I Want It That Way by Backstreet Boys, Eternal Flame performed by Atomic Kitten, Chain Reaction performed by Steps, Dancing in the Moonlight by Toploader, Sing by Travis

PHOTO CREDITS

Jacket: *Radio Times* • Internal pages: *Radio Times* • www.scopefeatures.com; **Plate section 1:** Page 1) The Sun/NI Syndication; Brian Moody/www.scopefeatures.com Page 2) *Radio Times*; Mirrorpix; Victor Watts/Rex Features Page 3) *Radio Times* Page 4) *Radio Times*; Chris Craymer/www.scopefeatures.com Page 5) Ipswich Evening Star; Brian Moody/www.scopefeatures.com Pages 6-7) Courtesy of Paul Barber; Mirrorpix. **Plate section 2:** Page 1) *Radio Times* • Page 2) *Radio Times* • Page 3) *Radio Times* • Page 4) © Alan Davidson / www.alandavidson.net Page 5) *Radio Times*; Alex Lentati/Evening Standard/Rex Features • Page 6) Monte Carlo picture: Noble/Draper • Page 7) The Green Green Grass pictures © Shazam Productions • Page 8: www.splashnews.com • Other pictures courtesy of The *Only Fools and Horses* Appreciation Society.

THANKS

Thanks to *Radio Times* for permission to quote from its articles and to the BBC Written Archives for permission to quote from its BBC Broadcasting Research Viewing Panel Report.

Only Fools and Horses (Theme Song)

Stick a pony in me pocket
I'll fetch the suitcase from the van
Coz if you want the best'uns
And you don't ask questions
Then, brother, I'm your man

Where it all comes from
Is a mystery
It's like the changing of the seasons
And the tides of the sea
But here's the one what's driving me berserk
Why do only fools and horses work
La la lala – la la la la la (etc)

Hooky Street (Closing Credits)

We've got some half-priced cracked-ice
And miles and miles of carpet tiles
TVs, deep-freeze and David Bowie LPs
Pool games, gold chains, wossnames
And at a push
Some Trevor Francis track-suits
From a mush in Shepherds Bush, Bush, Bush, Bush

No income-tax, no VAT
No money back, no guarantee
Black or white, rich or broke
We'll cut prices at a stroke

God bless Hooky Street
Viva Hooky Street
Long live Hooky Street
C'est Magnifique Hooky Street
Magnifique Hooky Street, Hooky Street (etc)

Words and music by John Sullivan

Index